AF576682

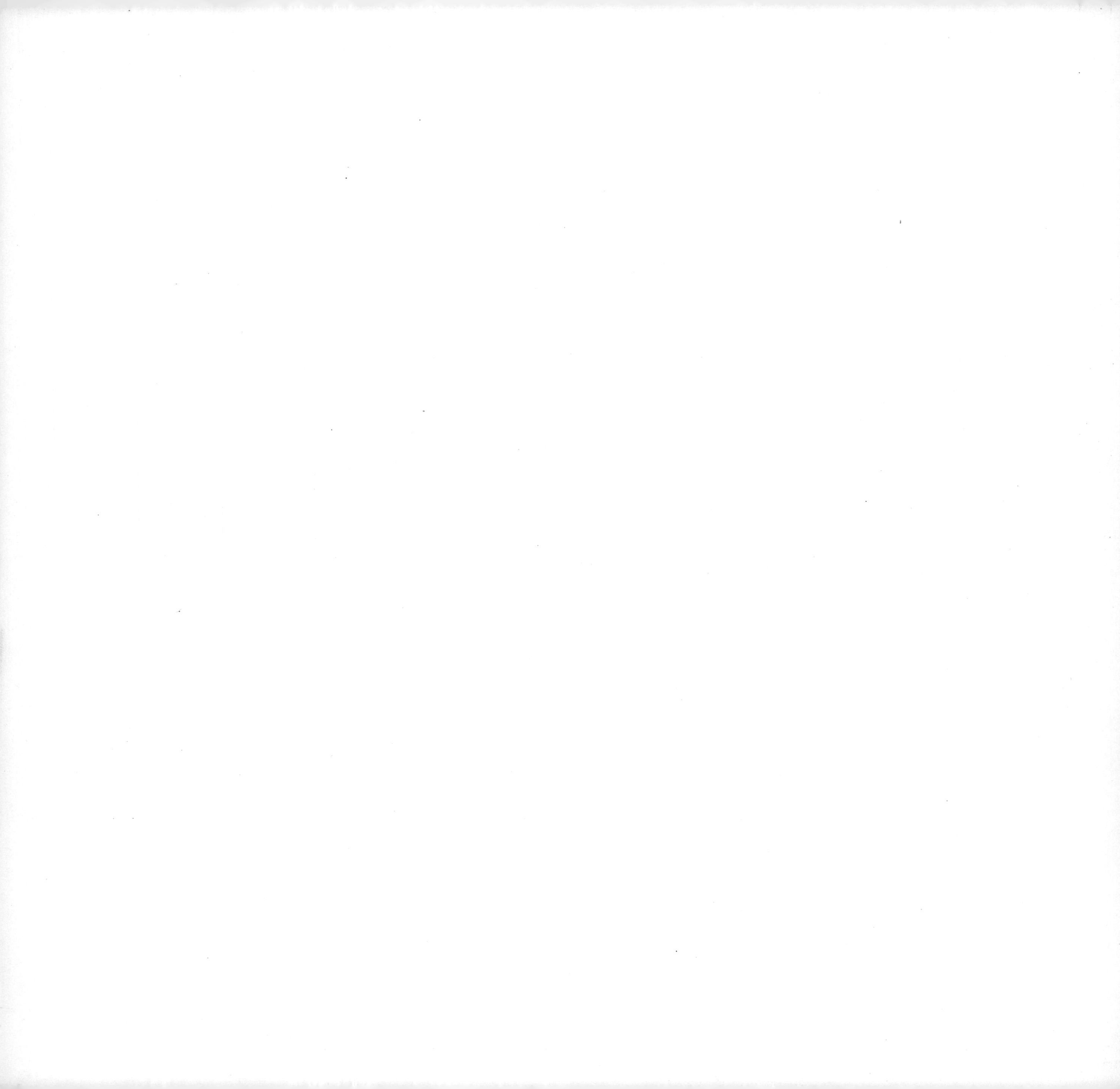

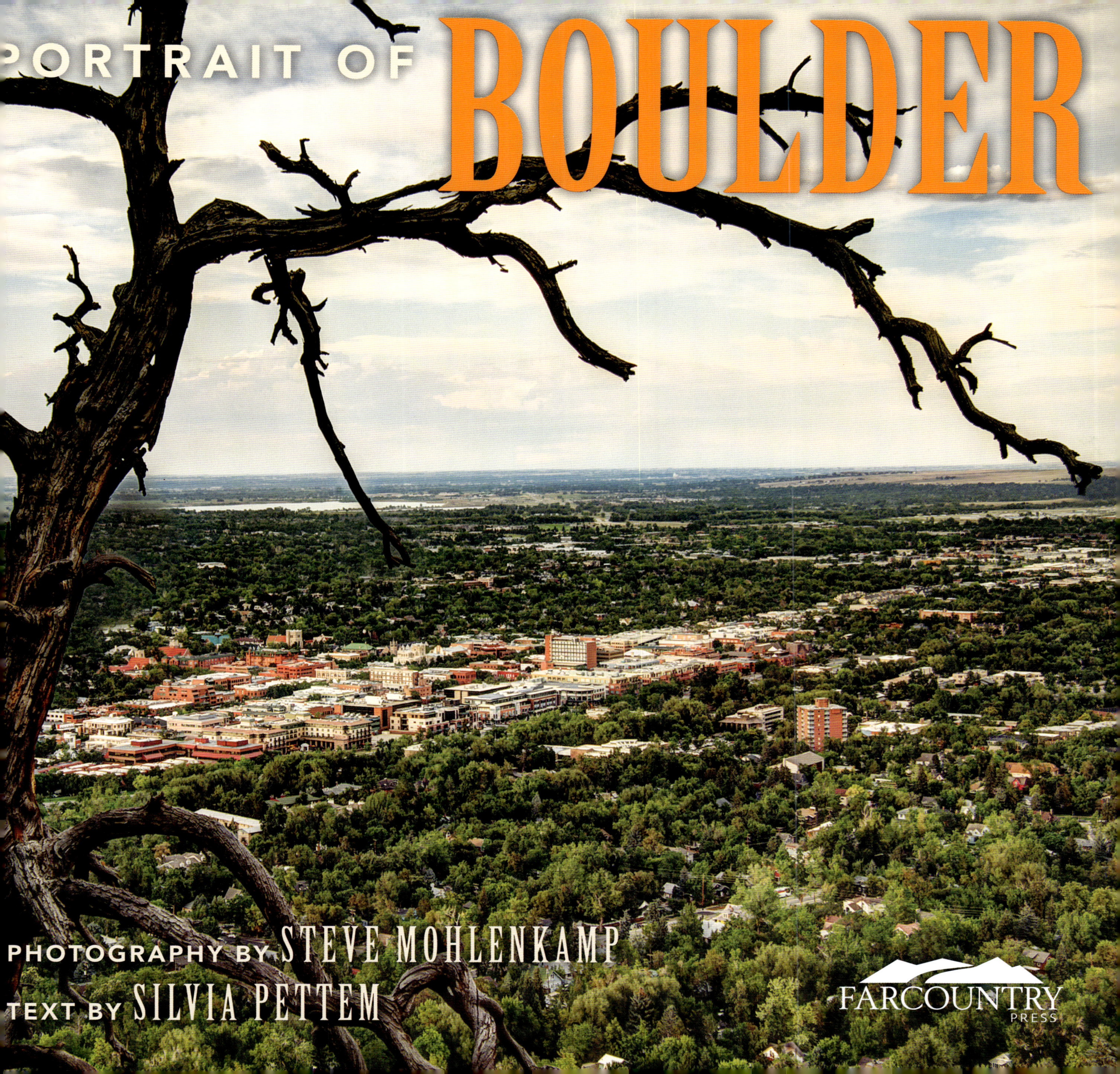
PORTRAIT OF
BOULDER
PHOTOGRAPHY BY STEVE MOHLENKAMP
TEXT BY SILVIA PETTEM
FARCOUNTRY
PRESS

FRONT COVER: Early morning light bathes Boulder's Flatirons in a hue of orange as red sumac displays its last vibrant colors before a long winter.

BACK COVER: With a colorful past and perhaps an even more colorful outside, the Boulder Theater hosts musical performances and shows year-round.

FRONT FLAP, TOP: A manhole cover with Boulder stamped on it will stand the test of time.

FRONT FLAP, BOTTOM: A parachutist enjoys solitude in the sky.

TITLE PAGE: The city of Boulder and Boulder County stretch into the horizon as viewed from Flagstaff Mountain.

RIGHT: The Lions Club built the Central Park band shell in 1938. The Art Deco structure was designed by architect Glen H. Huntington, with site design by Saco R. DeBoer.

This book is dedicated to my three wonderful kids, their two wonderful children, and theirs and theirs in generations yet to come downstream. I leave for them as a family legacy, this, my spirit of the West.

- Steve Mohlenkamp

ISBN 10: 1-56037-540-X
ISBN 13: 978-1-56037-540-1

For more information about our books, write Farcountry Press, P.O. Box 5630, Helena, MT 59604; call (800) 821-3874; or visit www.farcountrypress.com.

Created, produced, and designed in the United States.
Printed in China.

17 16 15 14 13 1 2 3 4 5 6

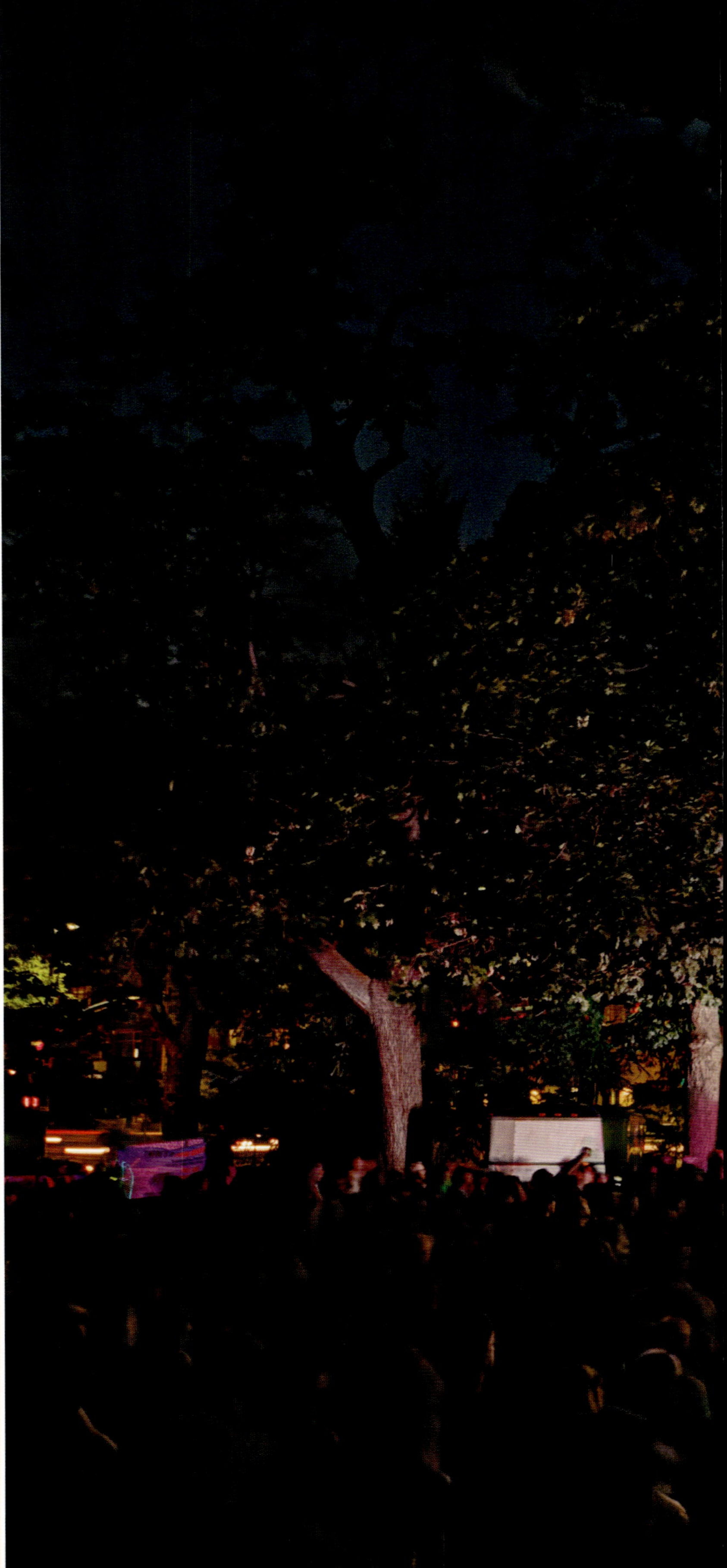

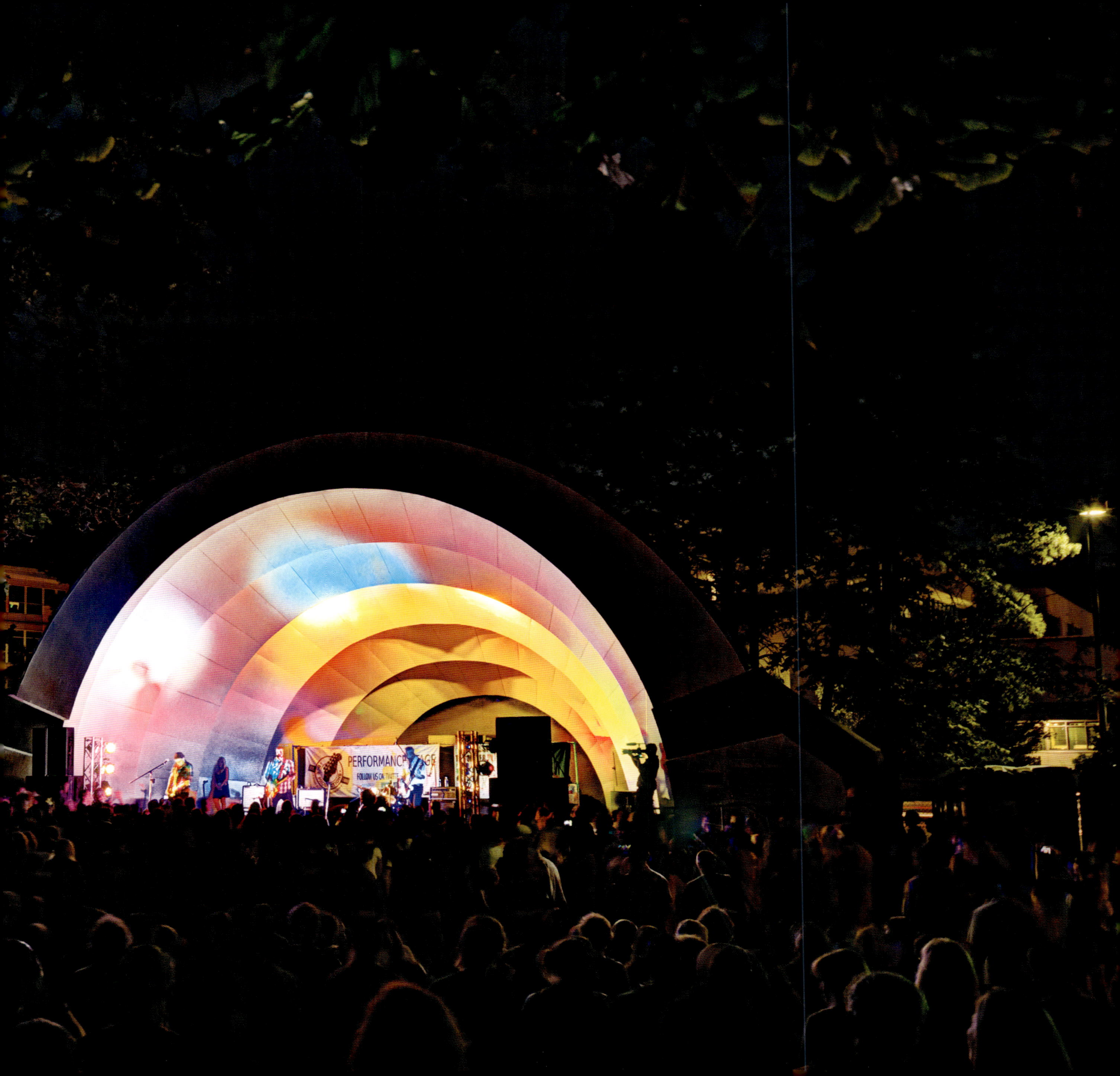

FOREWORD
BY SILVIA PETTEM

"The mountains look right for gold, and the valleys look rich for grazing," prospector Thomas Aikins was quoted as saying in the fall of 1858. After weeks of traversing the seemingly endless plains, he paused at Fort St. Vrain and aimed his field glasses at the Rocky Mountains. The mystique of Boulder had begun.

Aikins and his men soon pitched their tents in the shadows of the sandstone slabs that towered over the future site of Boulder. The men had neighbors—the Arapahos. According to federal decree, all the land belonged to the Indians. But the prospectors were successful in discovering gold in the mountains, and the lure of gold was strong. On February 10, 1859, Aikins and his men formed the Boulder City Town Company, recording their hopes that their settlement would soon become an important town.

Eventually, others would find silver, tungsten, and fluorspar, as well. Some of Boulder's early inhabitants, however, turned to farming—the occupation they knew best. Before long, the early settlers sent for their families. In 1860, Boulder residents built the very first schoolhouse in what would become Colorado.

With a solid economy built on mining and agriculture, tax money began to pour into Boulder, turning the hastily built supply town of log and false-fronted frame buildings into a permanent city of brick and stone. Next came plans for higher education. With matching funds from the Colorado Territorial Legislature, the University of Colorado opened its doors in September 1877—one year after Colorado was granted statehood.

Boulder also became a railroad hub, boosting the economy and bringing in tourists. Among the first to arrive were the health-seekers, with hopes for cures in the dry, moderate climate. In 1895, the Boulder Colorado Sanitarium invited guests to enjoy "refreshment of the mind, body, and spirit" and to eat "health foods," invented by founder and cereal magnate John Harvey Kellogg.

Schoolteachers from Texas also enjoyed Boulder's cool summer evenings. In 1898, they opened a cultural and educational retreat, initially called the Texas-Colorado Chautauqua—part of a nationwide movement that hosted a circuit of speakers and entertainers. Today, only three Chautauquas remain in the country. In Boulder, the association's auditorium, dining hall, academic hall, and cottages are still in use, and the Colorado Chautauqua has been designated a National Historic Landmark.

Meanwhile, as Aikins had done decades earlier, the city's residents turned their eyes to their mountain backdrop. In 1898, Boulder applied for and received two land patents, first for the west side of Flagstaff Mountain and then for the east—the city's earliest acquisitions of open space.

A few years later, funds raised by public subscription built the Hotel Boulderado, in part, to attract the convention trade. The locals also invested in an opera house, while the Boulder Chamber of Commerce proudly promoted the city as the "Athens of the West." Despite all the hype, Boulder's population in 1910 was barely more than 9,000.

By the time of the 1950 census, the number of residents had crept up to 19,999. Then the population exploded, as the county's economic base changed to science and technology. The National Bureau of Standards (now the National Institute of Standards and Technology) relocated from Washington, D.C., and opened in 1954. Ten years later, construction began on the National Center for Atmospheric Research.

As Boulder residents watched their city's population double, and then double again in the mid-1960s, they no longer encouraged growth but became determined to limit it. New purchases of open space became a way of preserving the city's identity and slowing urban sprawl.

An influx of hippies in the late 1960s gave way to an era of social upheaval in the 1970s. Buddhist teacher Trungpa Rinpoche founded the Naropa Institute, now Naropa University, where "beat" poet Allen Ginsberg started the Jack Kerouac School of Disembodied Poetics. Tourists were seeking *Mork and Mindy* (opening shots to the television program were filmed in Boulder), while "new age"

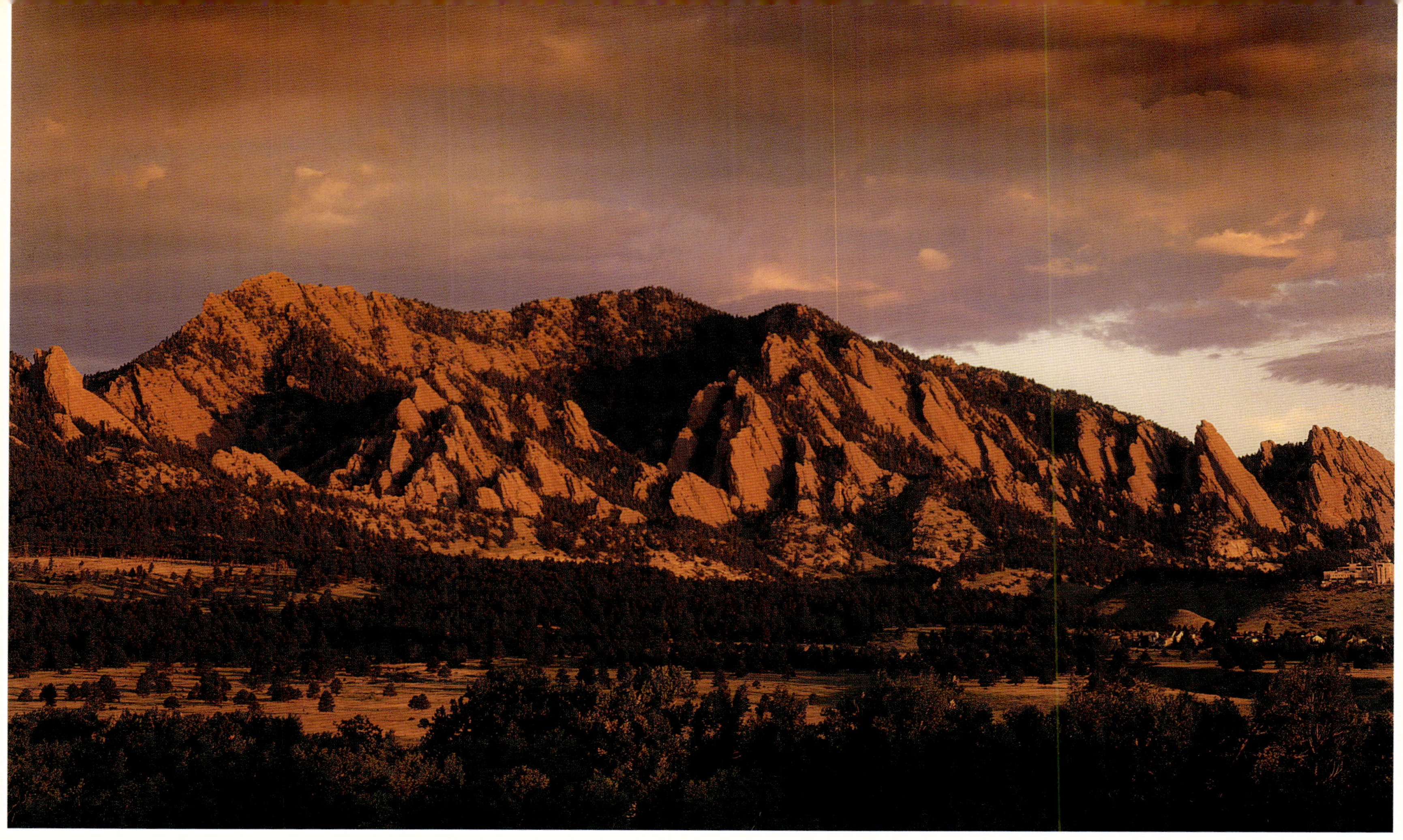

ABOVE: A rising sun colors Boulder's landscape in a wash of reddish tones.

groups, avid cyclists, and 20,000 University of Colorado students made Boulder their home. The city gained a reputation as a "laid-back" community, where out-of-work doctoral candidates took jobs as taxi drivers.

In 1972, after the demolition of the century-old Central School, historic preservationists came out of the woodwork. Five years later, the city turned four blocks of Pearl Street—the city's main thoroughfare—into a vibrant pedestrian mall that revitalized the historic downtown. Before long, entrepreneurs brought in gourmet restaurants, art galleries, and boutiques, complete with sidewalk cafés and street performers. The city also held on to its founding values—a continued emphasis on health, education, and culture. While striding into the twenty-first century, Boulder has retained its natural beauty and sense of place.

Boulder's population has grown to 100,000. It is the largest city in Boulder County—741 square miles that range from an elevation of approximately 5,000 feet on the eastern plains, to 14,259 feet near its northwestern boundary on the Continental Divide. Recreational opportunities include rock climbing in internationally known Eldorado Canyon, hiking in the Indian Peaks Wilderness, and much more.

The city's defining feature—its mountain backdrop—has remained the same. In Boulder, nearly everyone knows someone who has said, "I came over the hill from Denver, looked down at Boulder, and knew I was home."

Silvia Pettem is a Boulder-based historical researcher, newspaper columnist, and author of more than a dozen books, including *Boulder: Evolution of a City* and *Separate Lives: The Story of Mary Rippon*. For more information and to contact Pettem, please go to www.silviapettem.com.

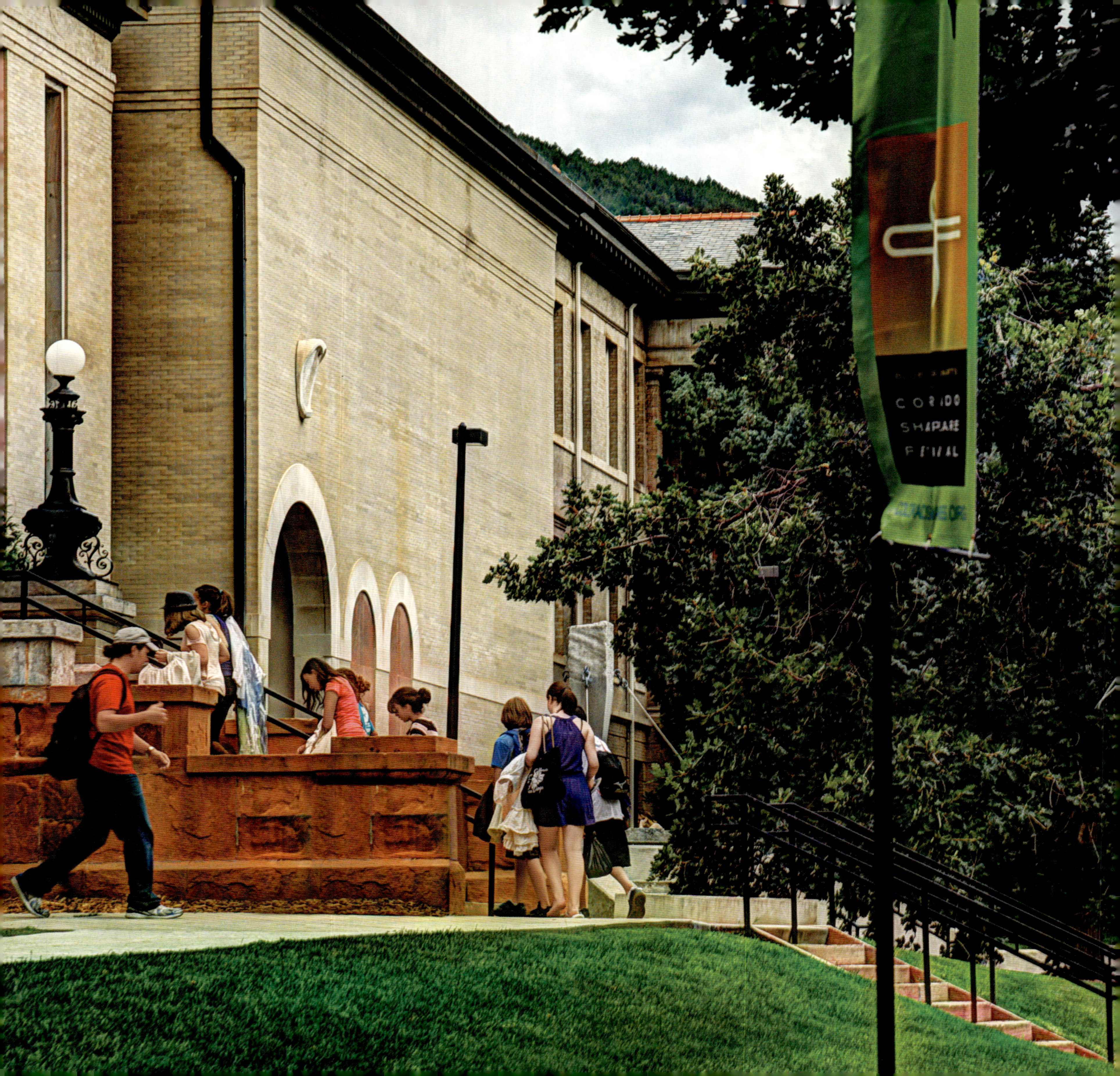

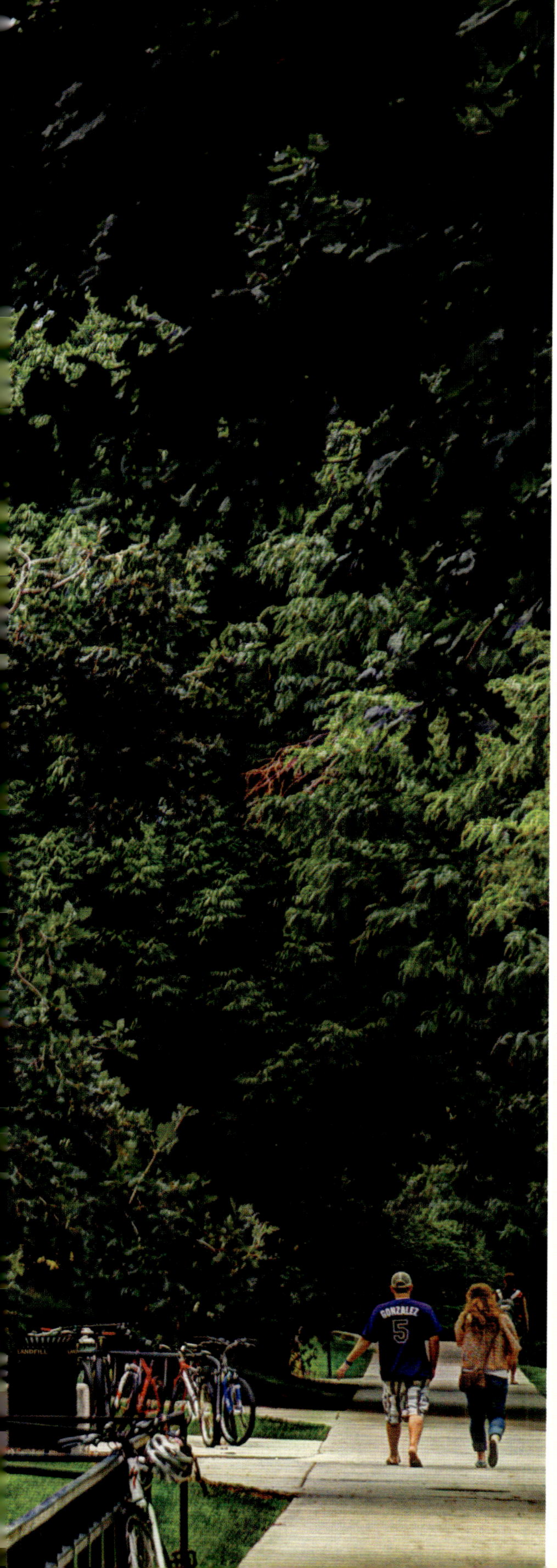

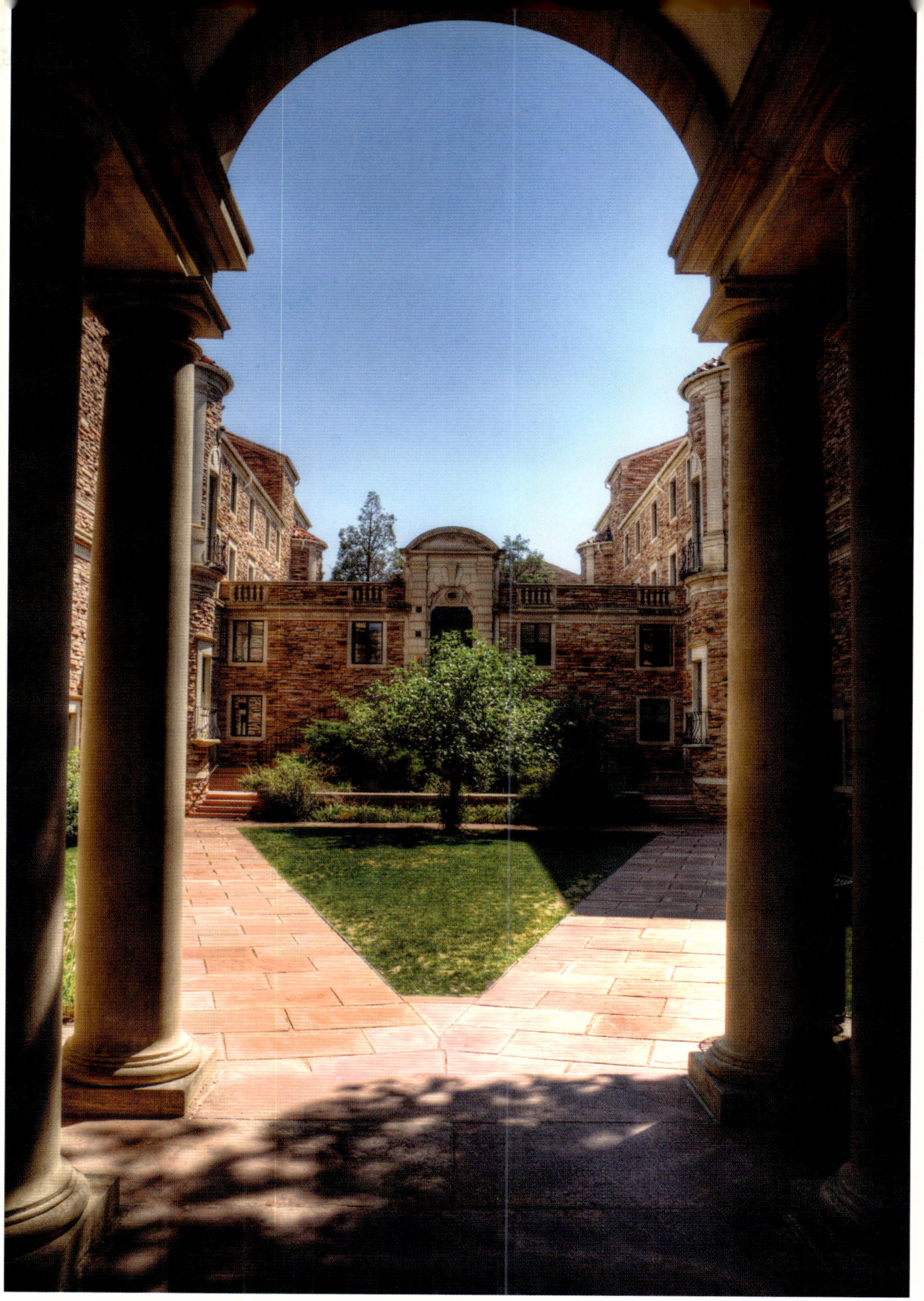

ABOVE: Sewall Hall, built in 1936 as a women's dormitory, was named for Joseph A. Sewall, the University of Colorado's first president. The building is an outstanding example of architect Charles Klauder's Tuscan Vernacular Revival style.

LEFT: University of Colorado students gather on the steps of the University Theatre on a glorious summer day. When the university opened in 1877, there was a total of forty-four students; now the student population of the Boulder campus tops 30,000.

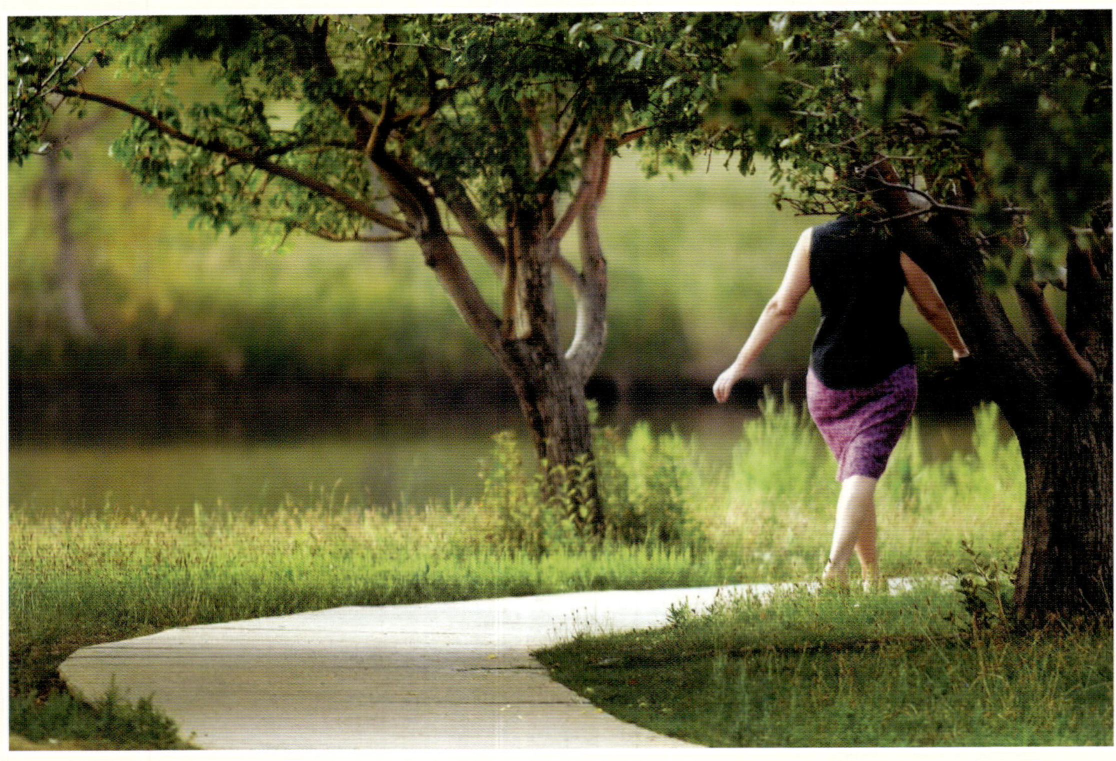

ABOVE: Boulder prides itself on being pedestrian-friendly. The seven-mile Boulder Creek Path welcomes walkers, runners, bicyclists, and dogs on leashes.

RIGHT: A cool stream rushes through the Indian Peaks Wilderness, which hugs the Continental Divide and abuts the southern boundary of Rocky Mountain National Park. The area's subalpine vegetation is in sharp contrast to the grasslands of the county's eastern plains.

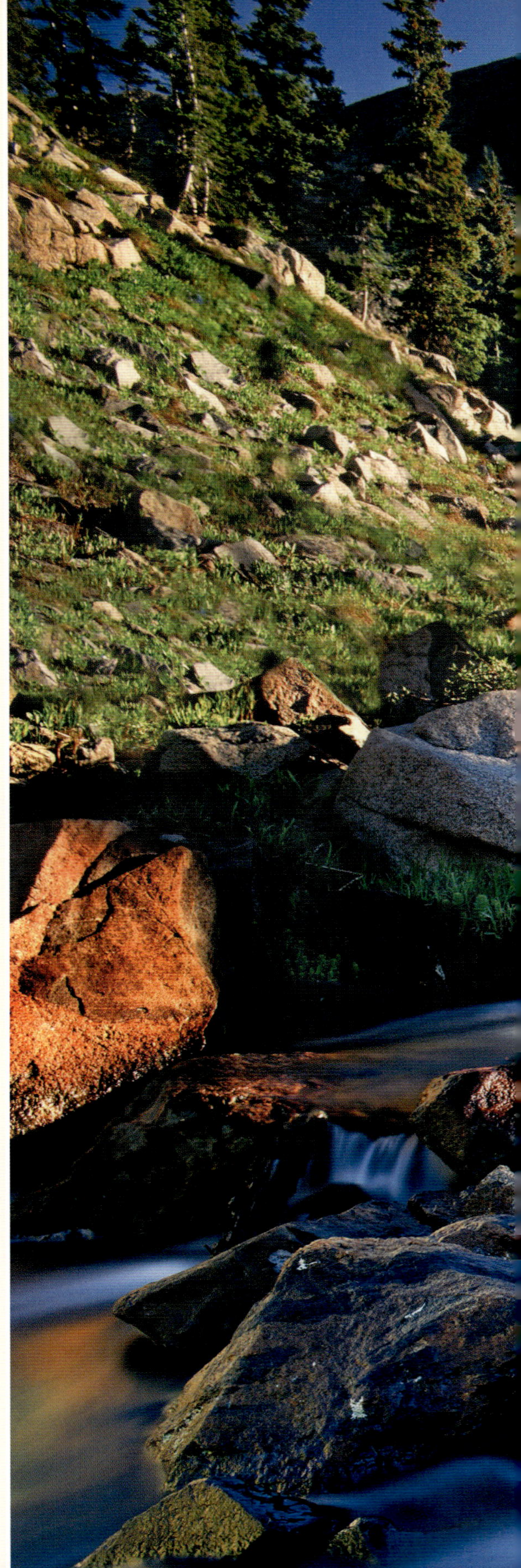

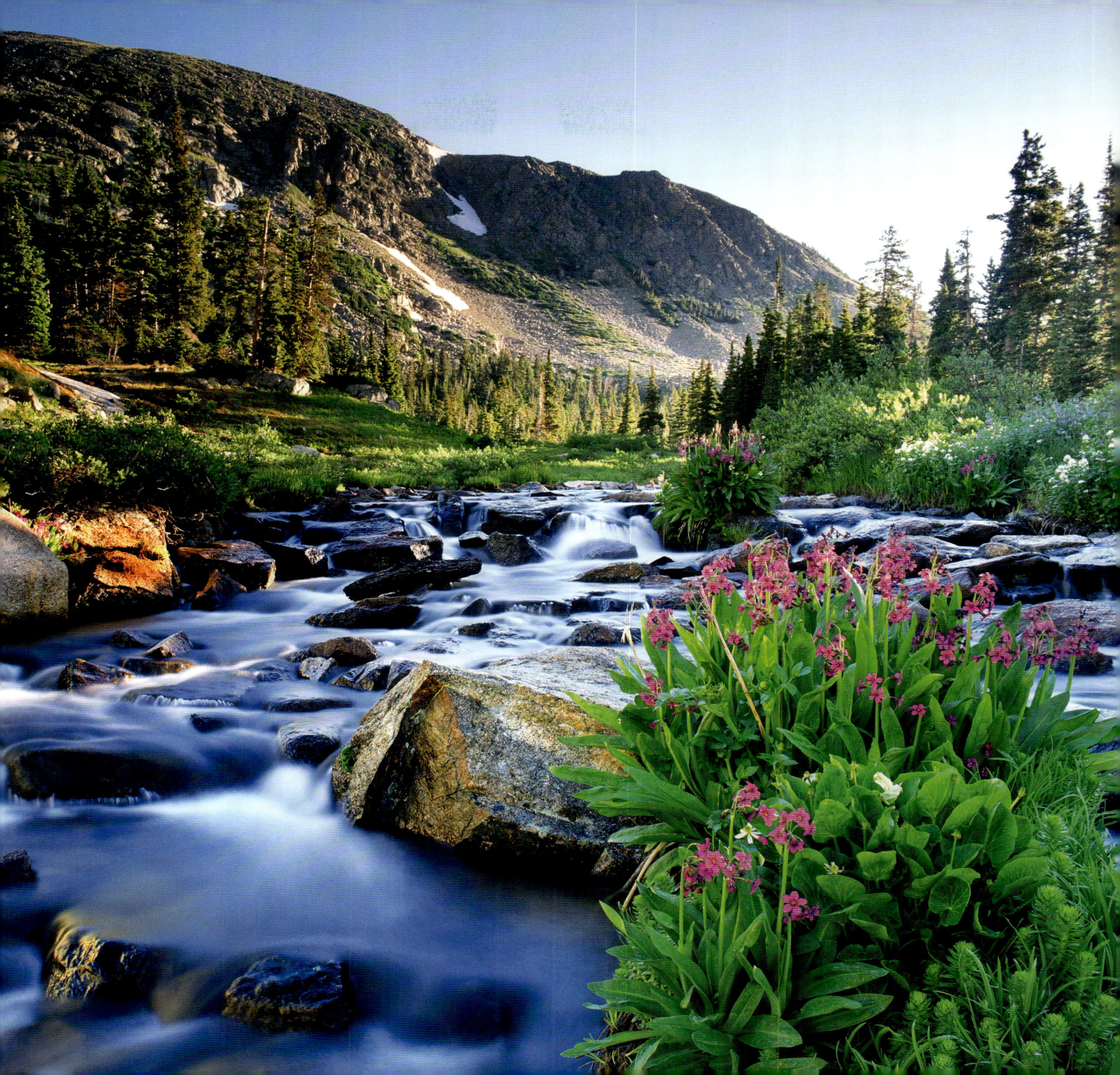

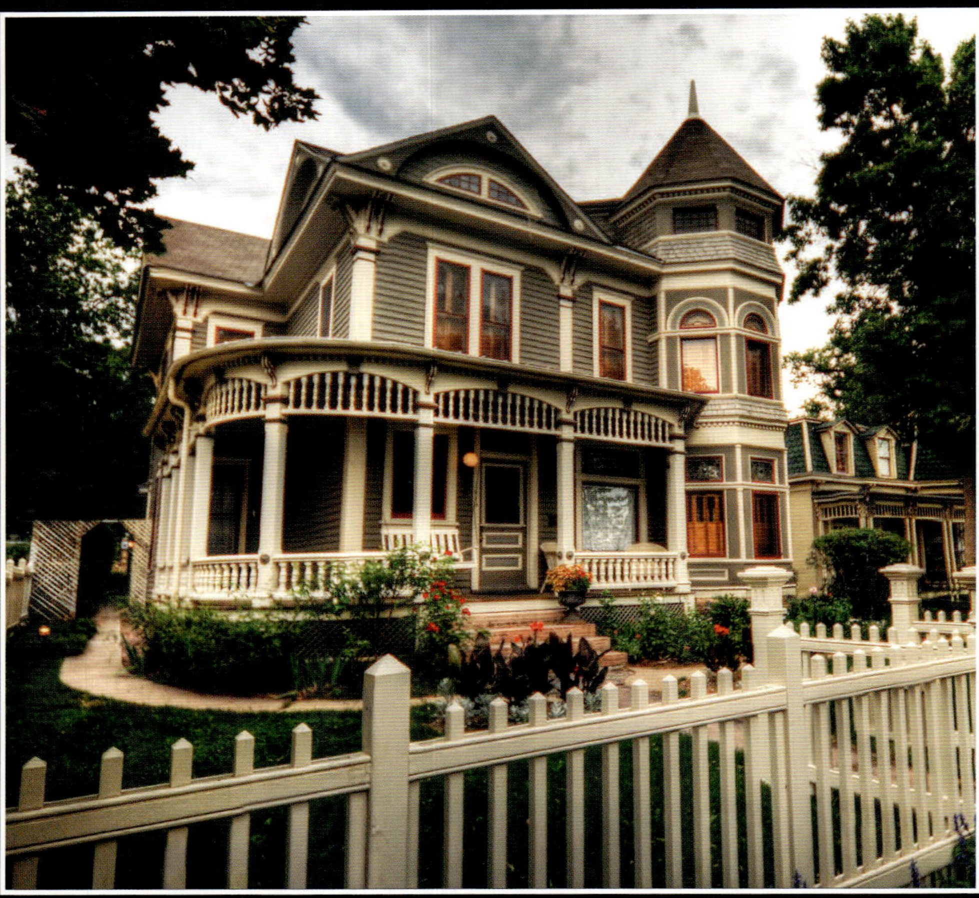

ABOVE: Adorned with a white picket fence, this Queen Anne–style house was built in 1883 by lumber company owner Ira T. McAllister. In the late 1970s and early 1980s the house was filmed in the opening shots of the television comedy *Mork and Mindy*.

RIGHT: The Dushanbe Teahouse features intricate details inside and outside. All the art (as well as the entire building) was constructed in one of Boulder's sister cities—Dushanbe, Tajikistan—then it was taken apart, crated, and shipped to Boulder where the building and its art were reassembled.

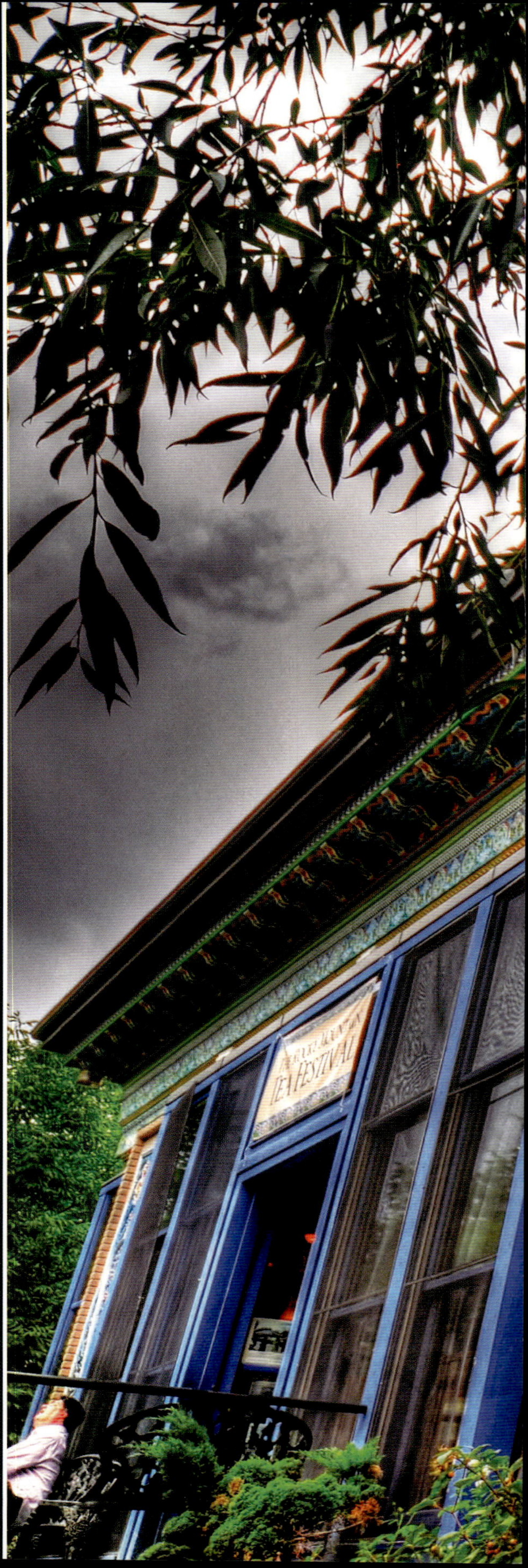

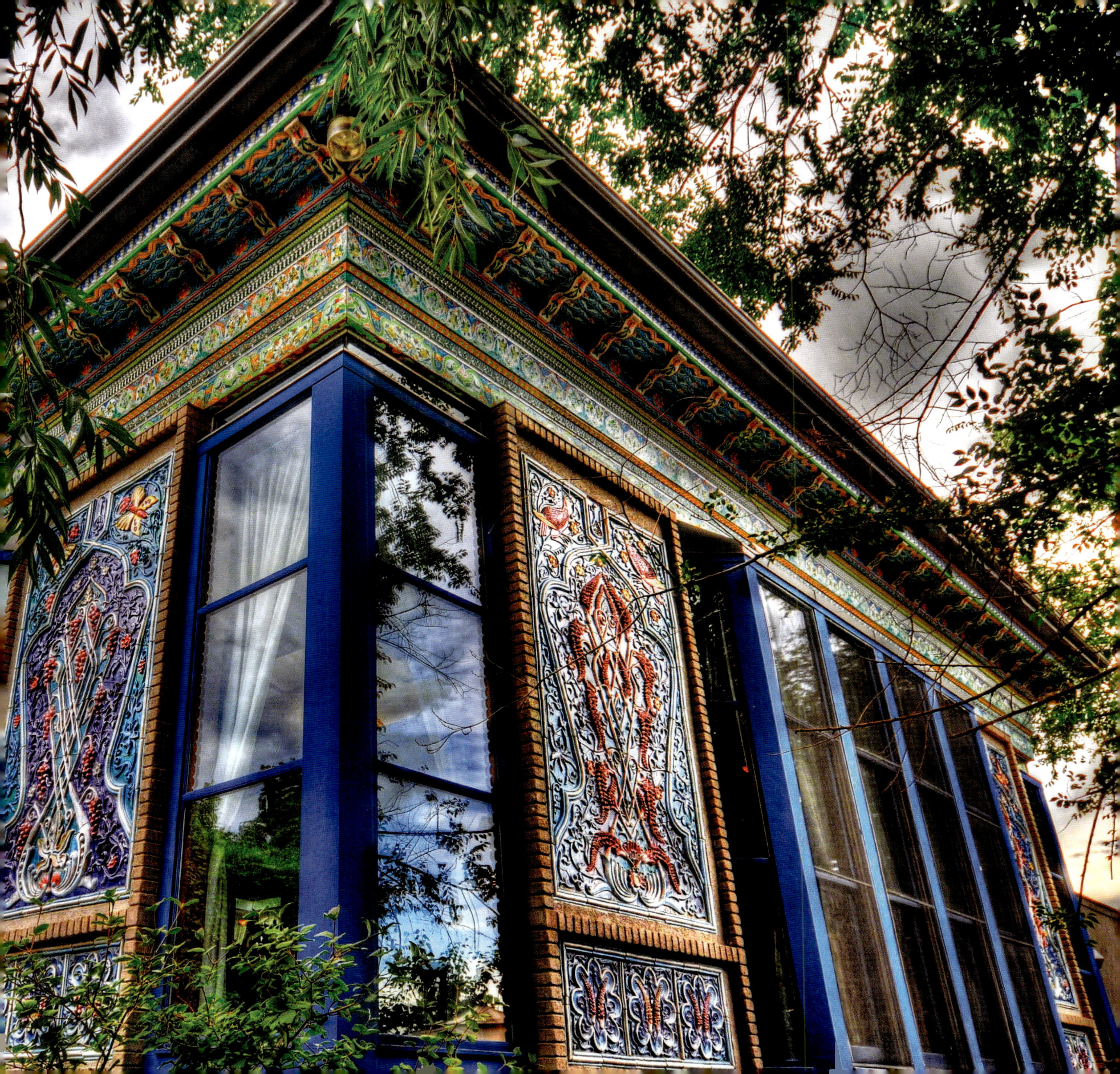

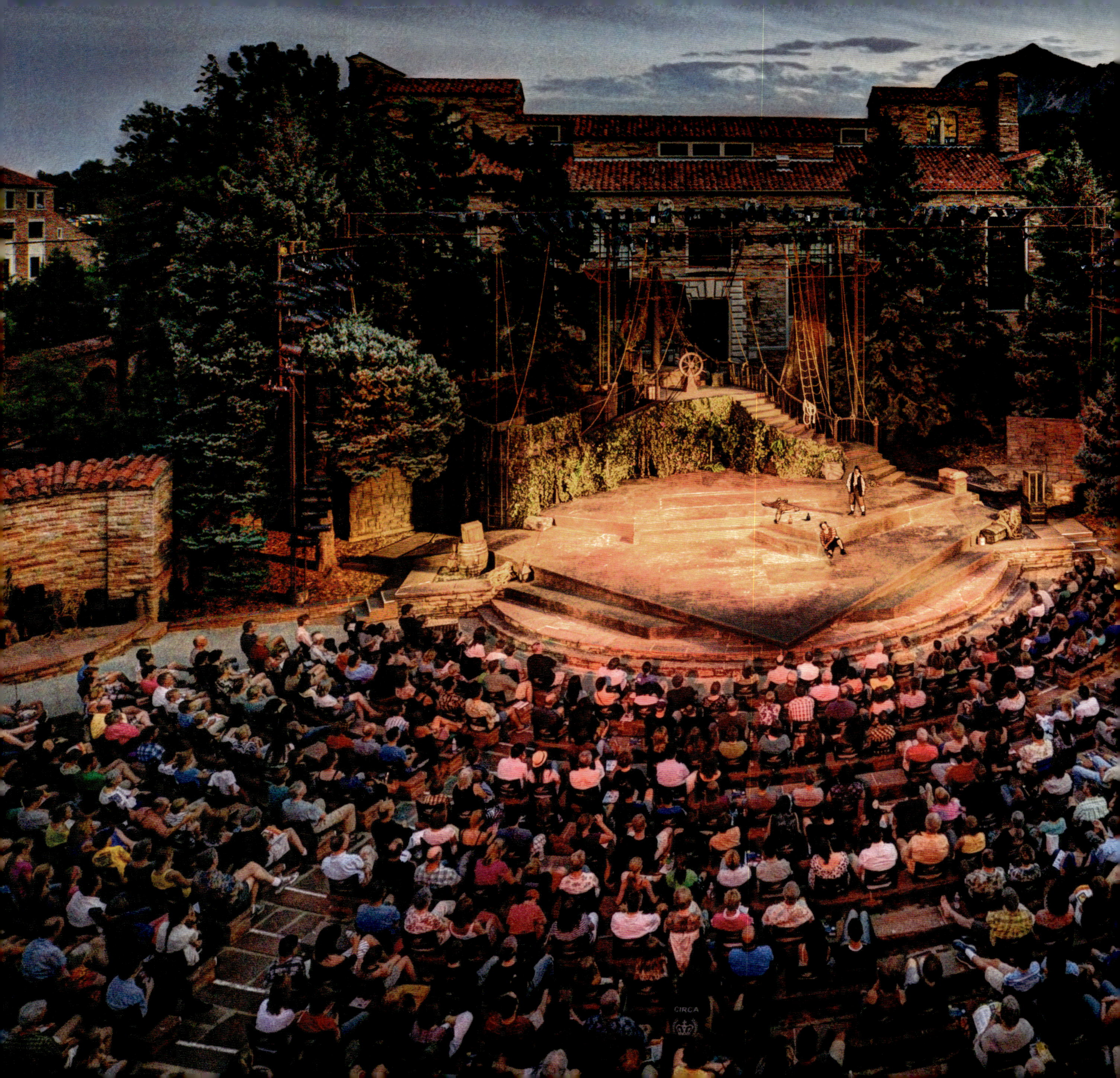

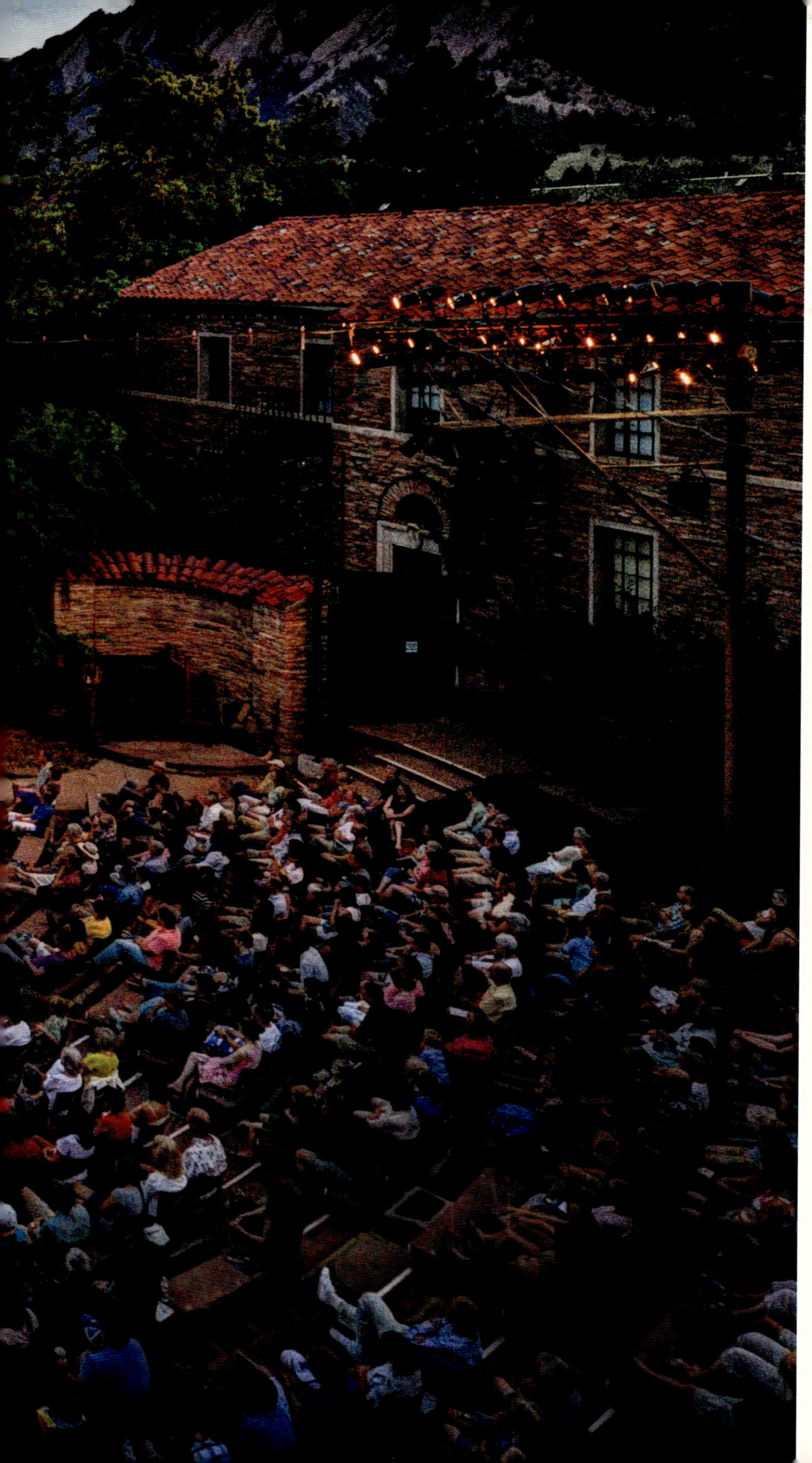

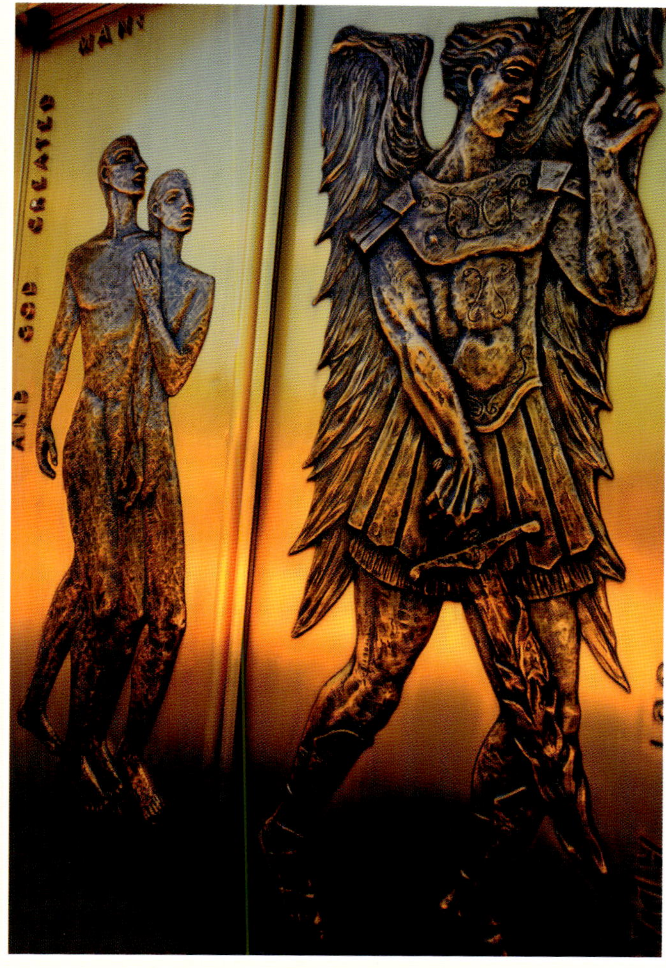

ABOVE: Bas-relief figures with the inscription "and God created man," cover one of three metal doors at the Sacred Heart of Jesus Church. The other doors continue the dialog with "and he cast out Adam," "and Moses went up to God," "and Jesus too was baptized," followed by "he is risen, he is not dead."

LEFT: Spectators watch the Colorado Shakespeare Festival, a tradition on the University of Colorado campus since the festival's founding in 1958. The performances are held in the Mary Rippon Outdoor Theatre, named for CU-Boulder's first woman professor.

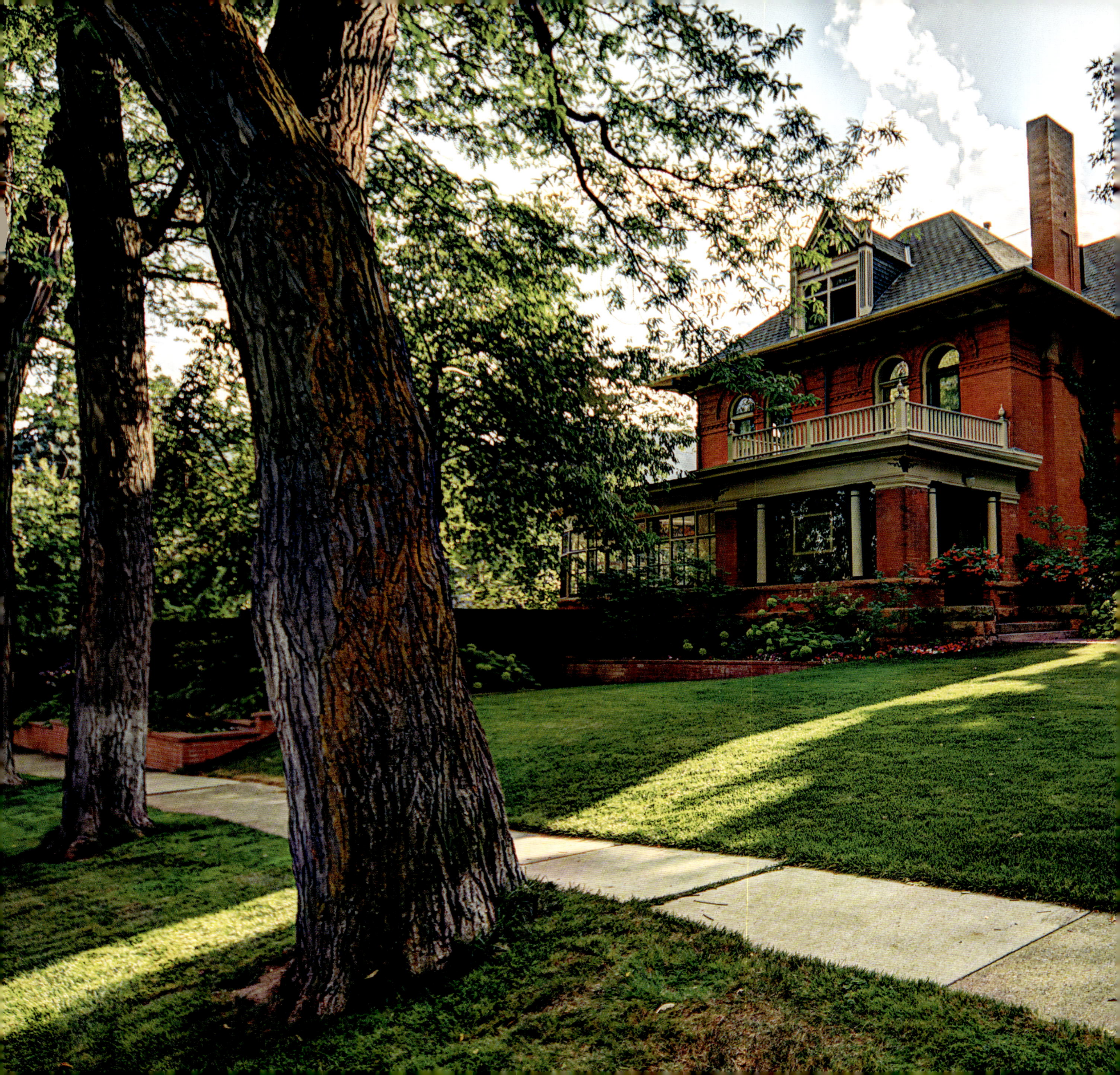

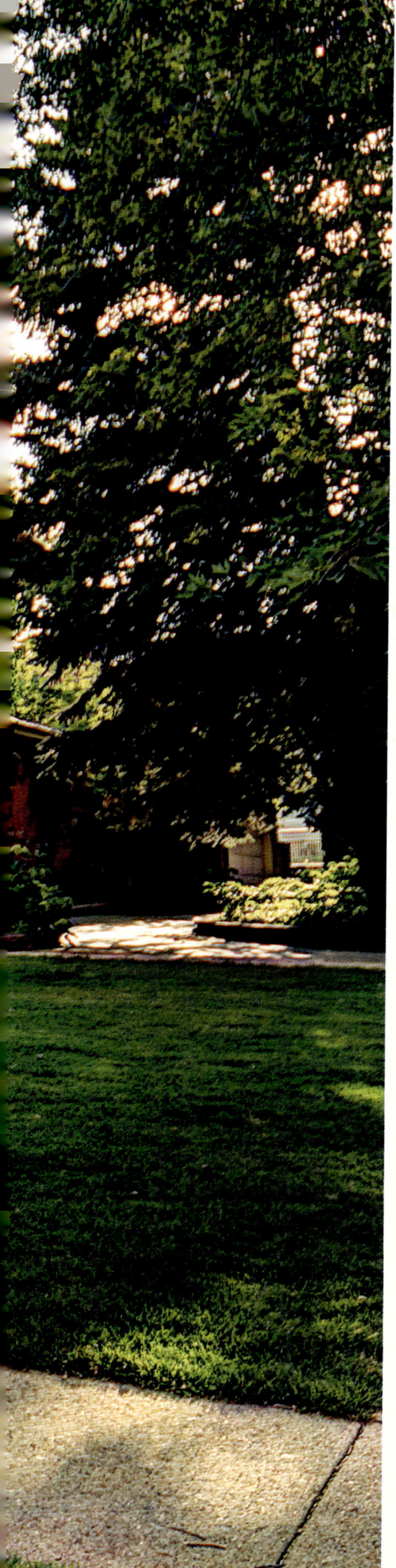

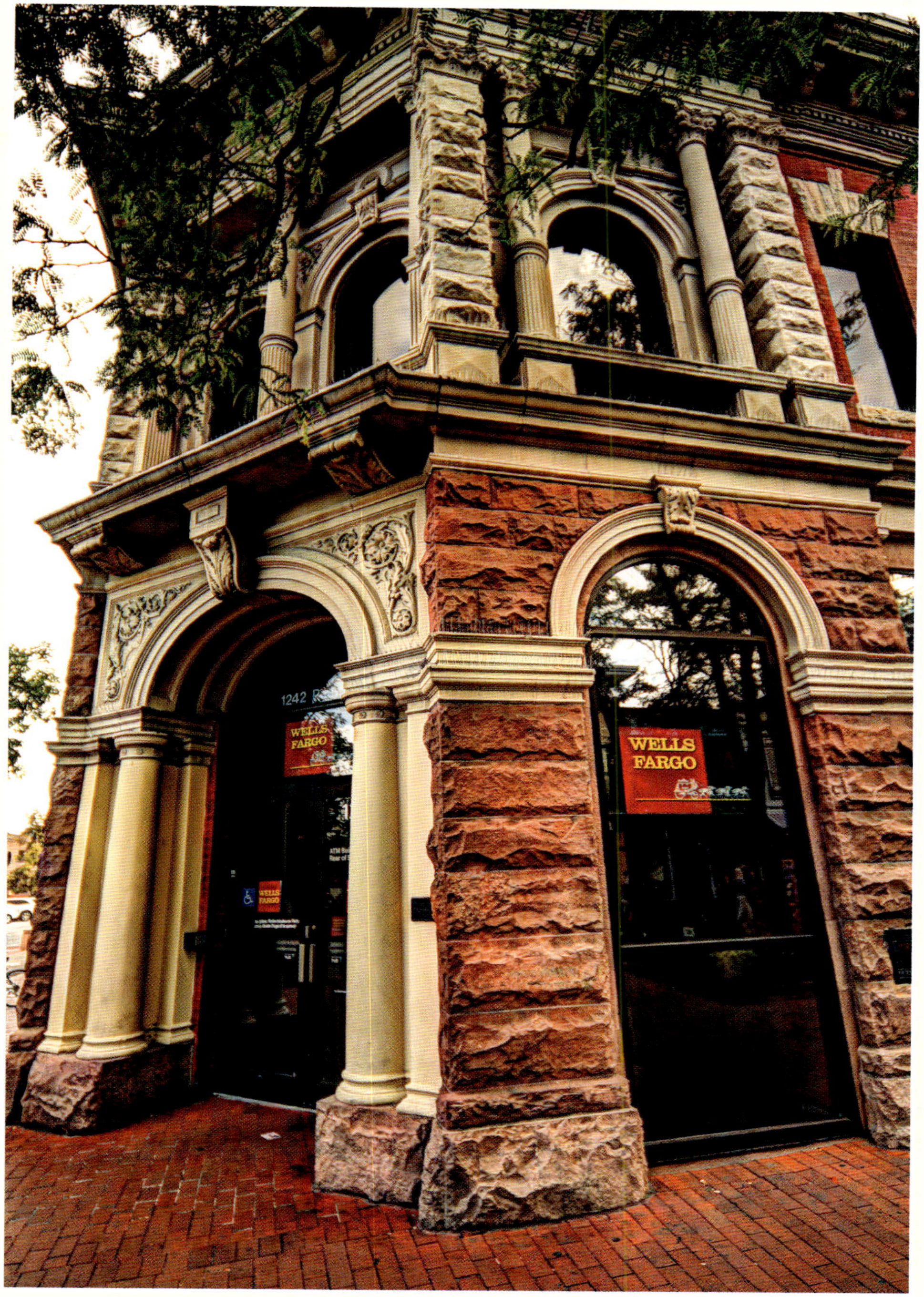

ABOVE: The Wells Fargo Bank, located on the Pearl Street Mall, was constructed in 1900 as the National State Bank building. Its red and white sandstones were quarried in Boulder County.

LEFT: Many of Boulder's most stately homes are located on Mapleton Hill—well out of the floodplain. This Edwardian Vernacular–style home was built in 1895 by an early Boulder physician, Dr. Horace O. Dodge.

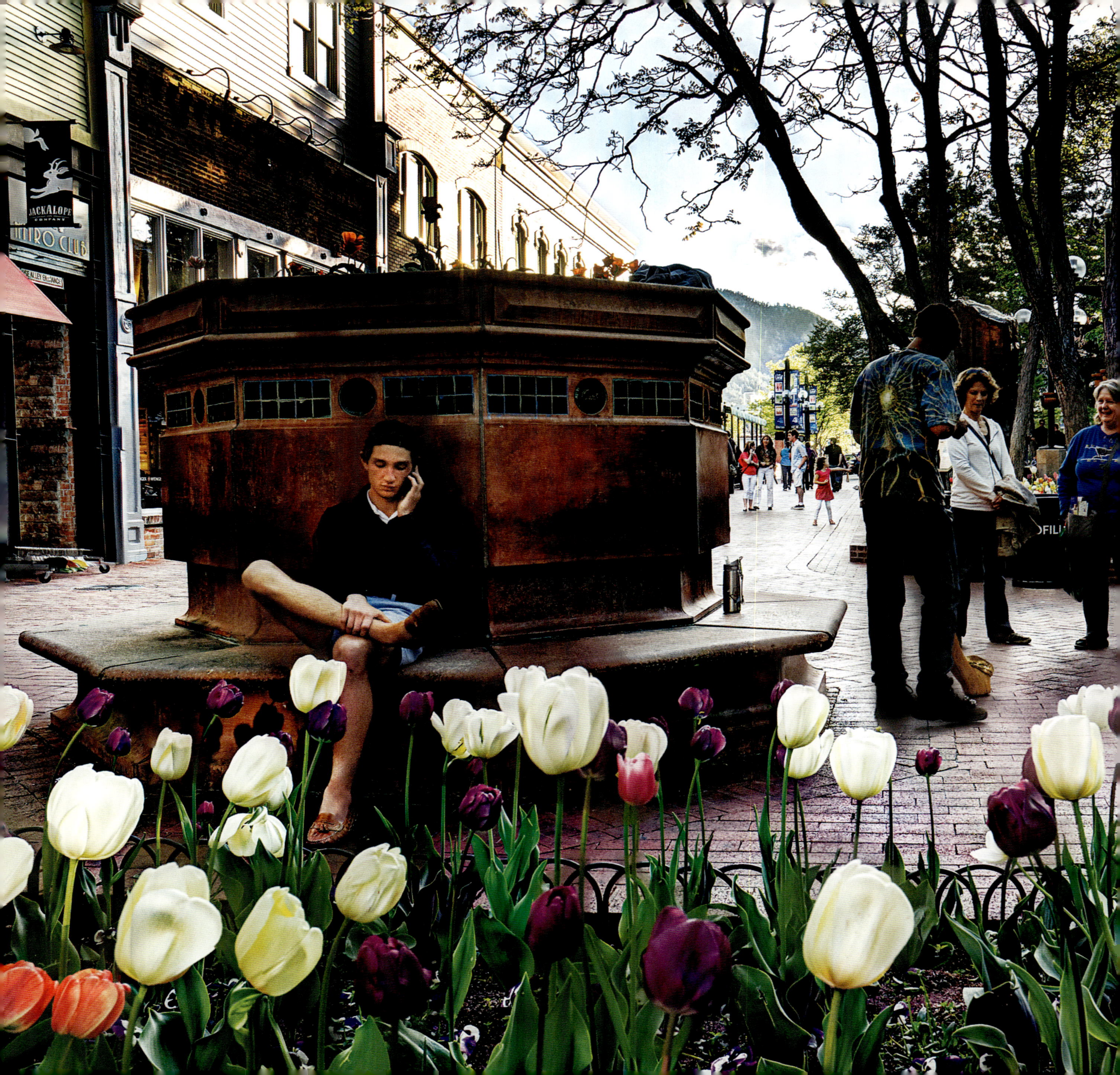
JACKALOPE
COMPANY

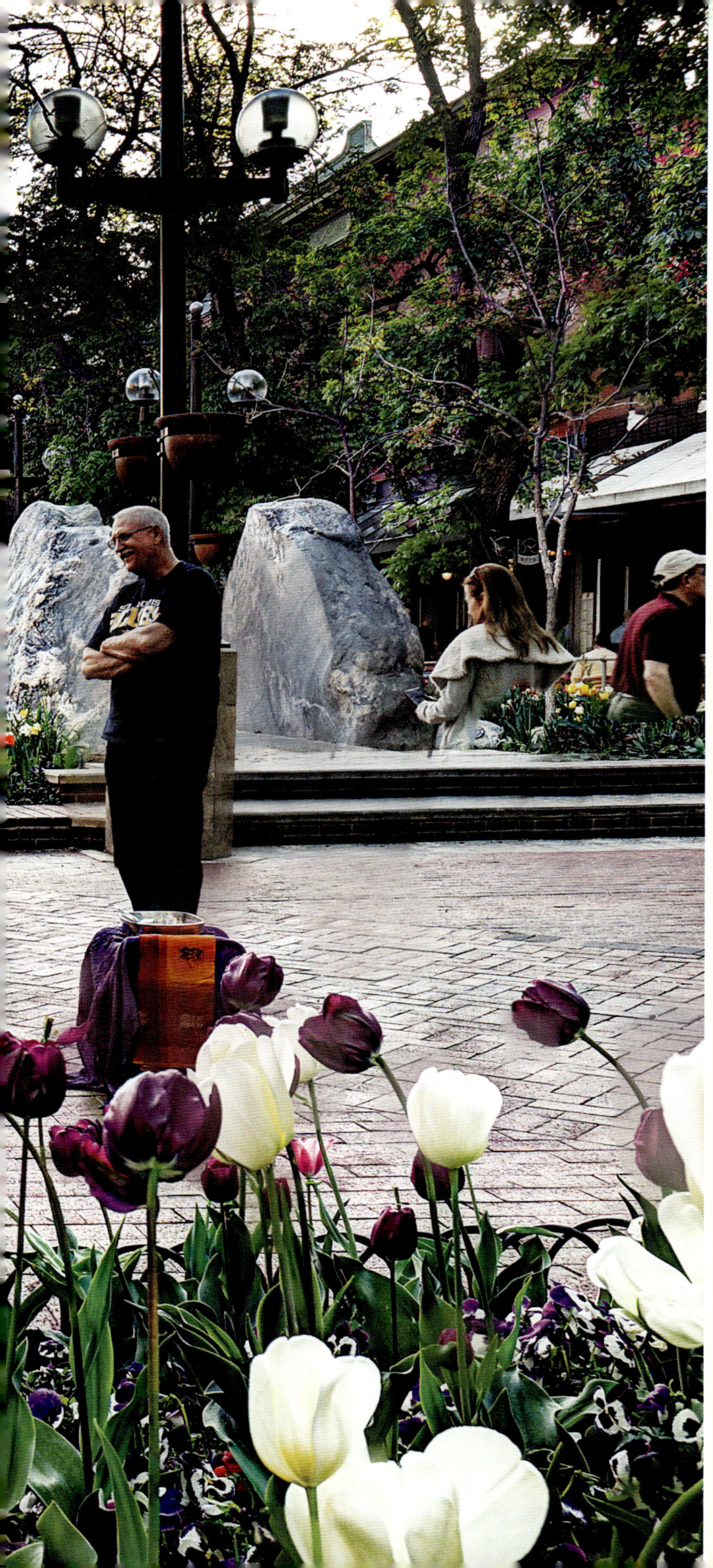

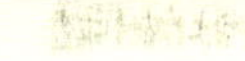

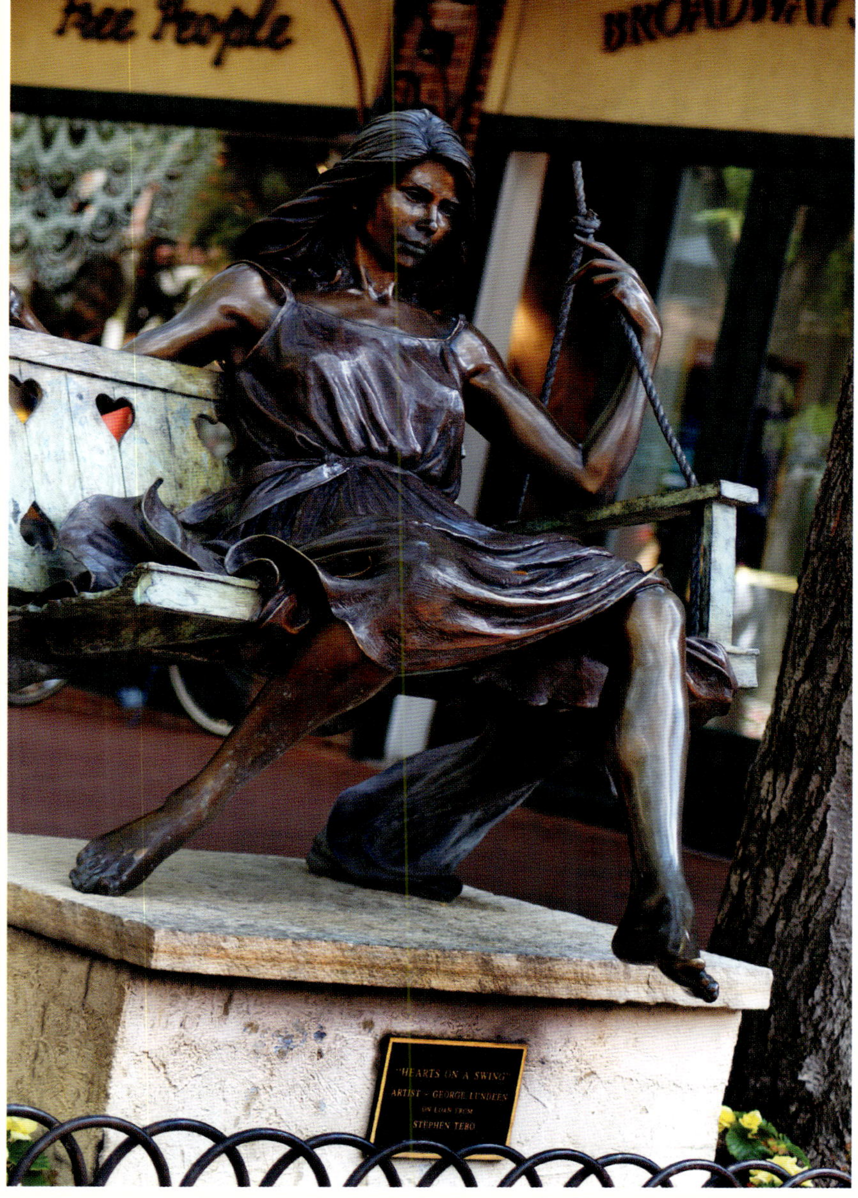

ABOVE: *Hearts on a Swing,* is the name of this bronze sculpture on the Pearl Street Mall. The sculpture, created by Loveland artist George Lundeen, was first displayed in 1987.

LEFT: The Pearl Street Mall is a popular gathering spot—especially in May when these gorgeous tulips are in bloom. The mall opened in August 1977, when the city of Boulder reconfigured Pearl Street, between 11th and 15th Streets, from vehicular to pedestrian-only traffic.

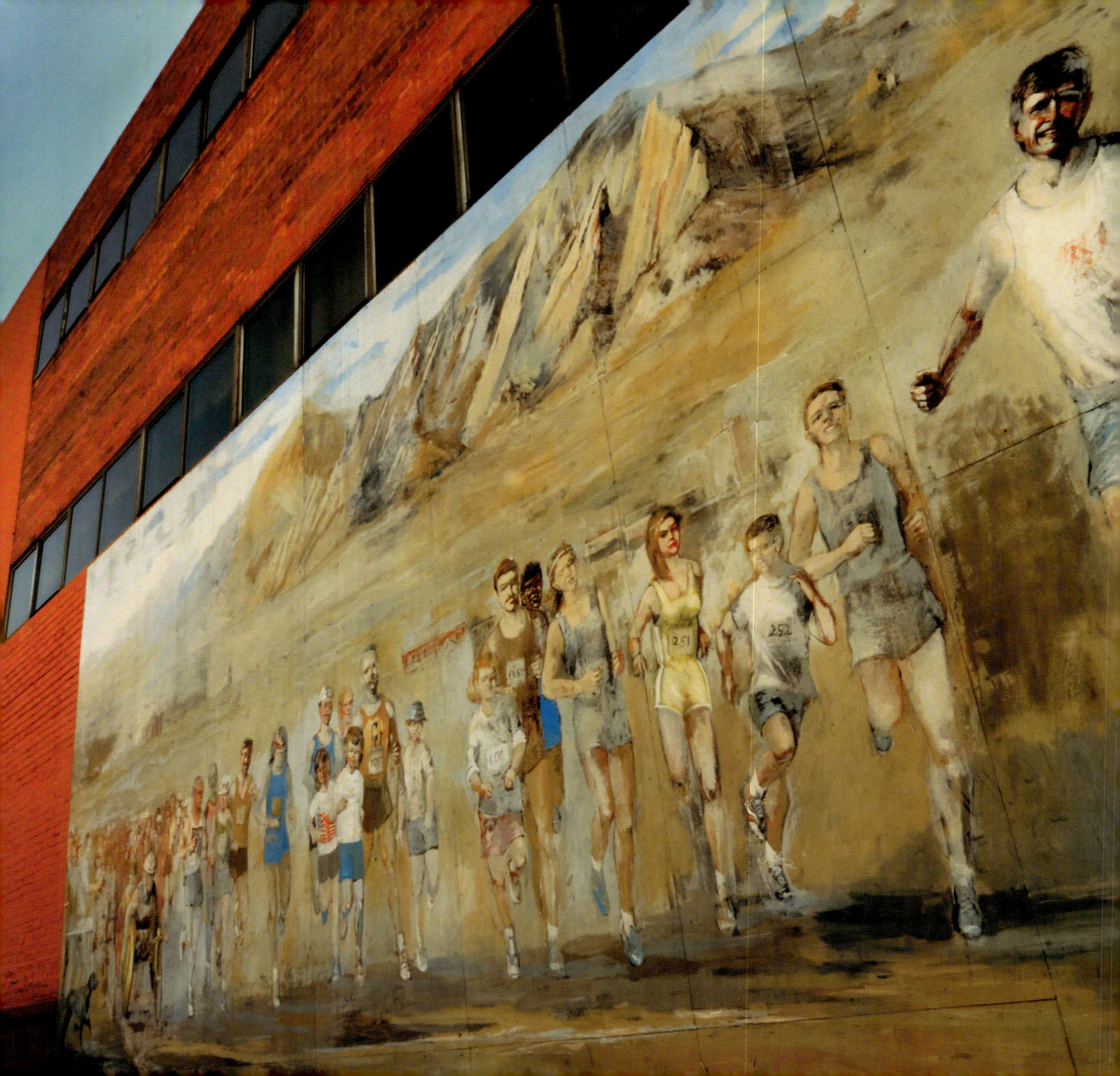
251
252

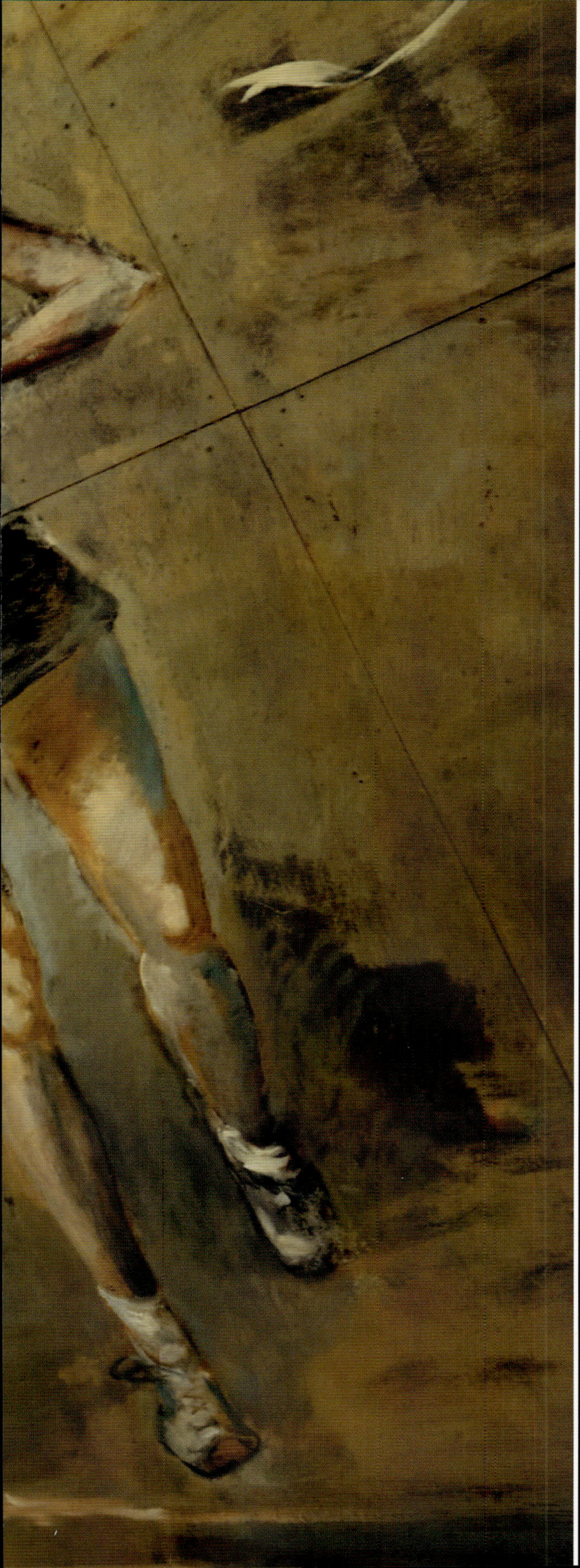

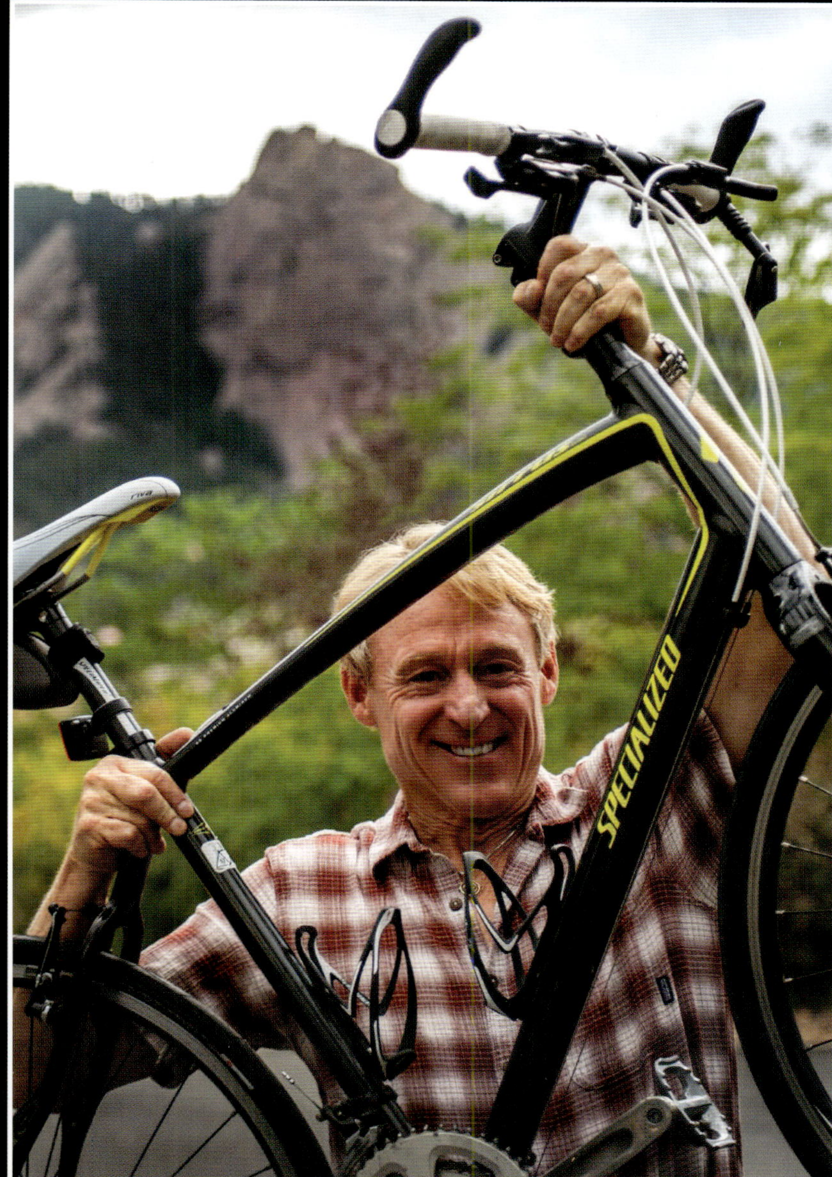

ABOVE: Mo Siegel founded Celestial Seasonings and also started the Red Zinger Bicycle Classic, naming it after one of his popular herbal teas. The race ran for five years, expanding in scope and prestige each summer, before transforming into the Coors Classic in 1980. With its debut in 2011, the USA Pro Cycling Challenge has revived Colorado's standing in the international bike-racing scene.

LEFT: Former long-distance runner and Olympic gold-medal winner Frank Shorter co-founded the 10-kilometer Bolder Boulder road race. This mural shows Shorter leading the pack.

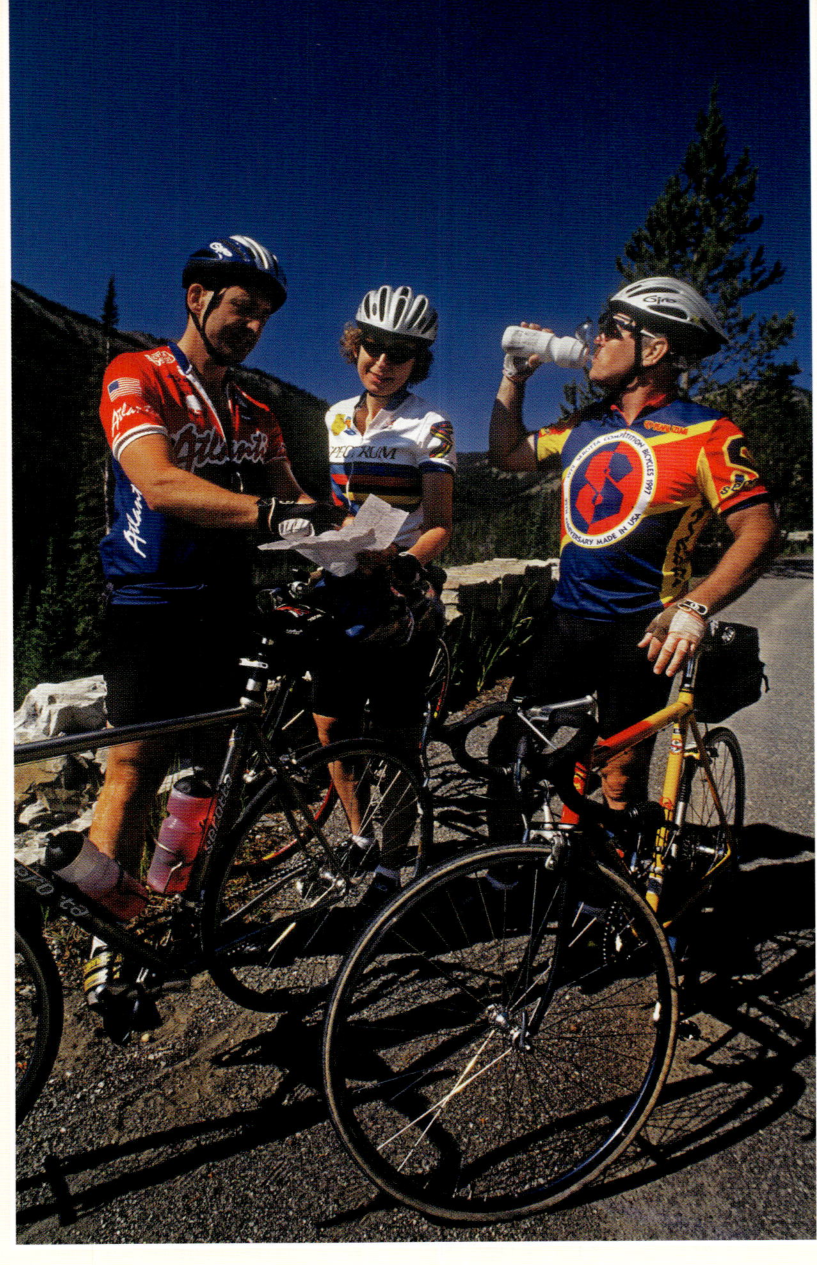

ABOVE: Boulder bikers plan a day's outing on the Peak to Peak Highway, a popular north–south route through the mountains of western Boulder County.

RIGHT: Standing in front of a rainbow of colors, Jeff Meeker, president of Fair Winds Hot Air Balloon Flights, shows off one of his balloons. The early morning flights typically last for ninety minutes.

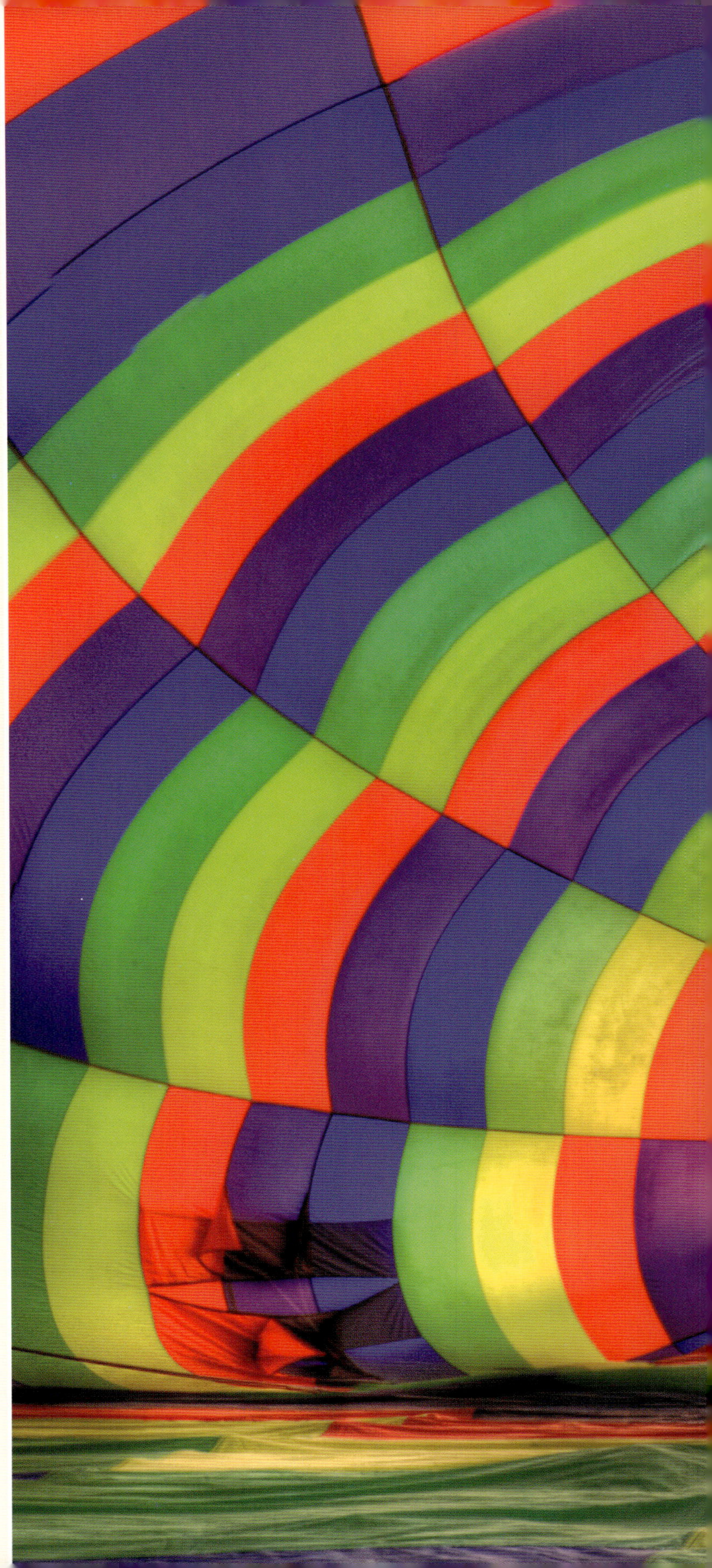

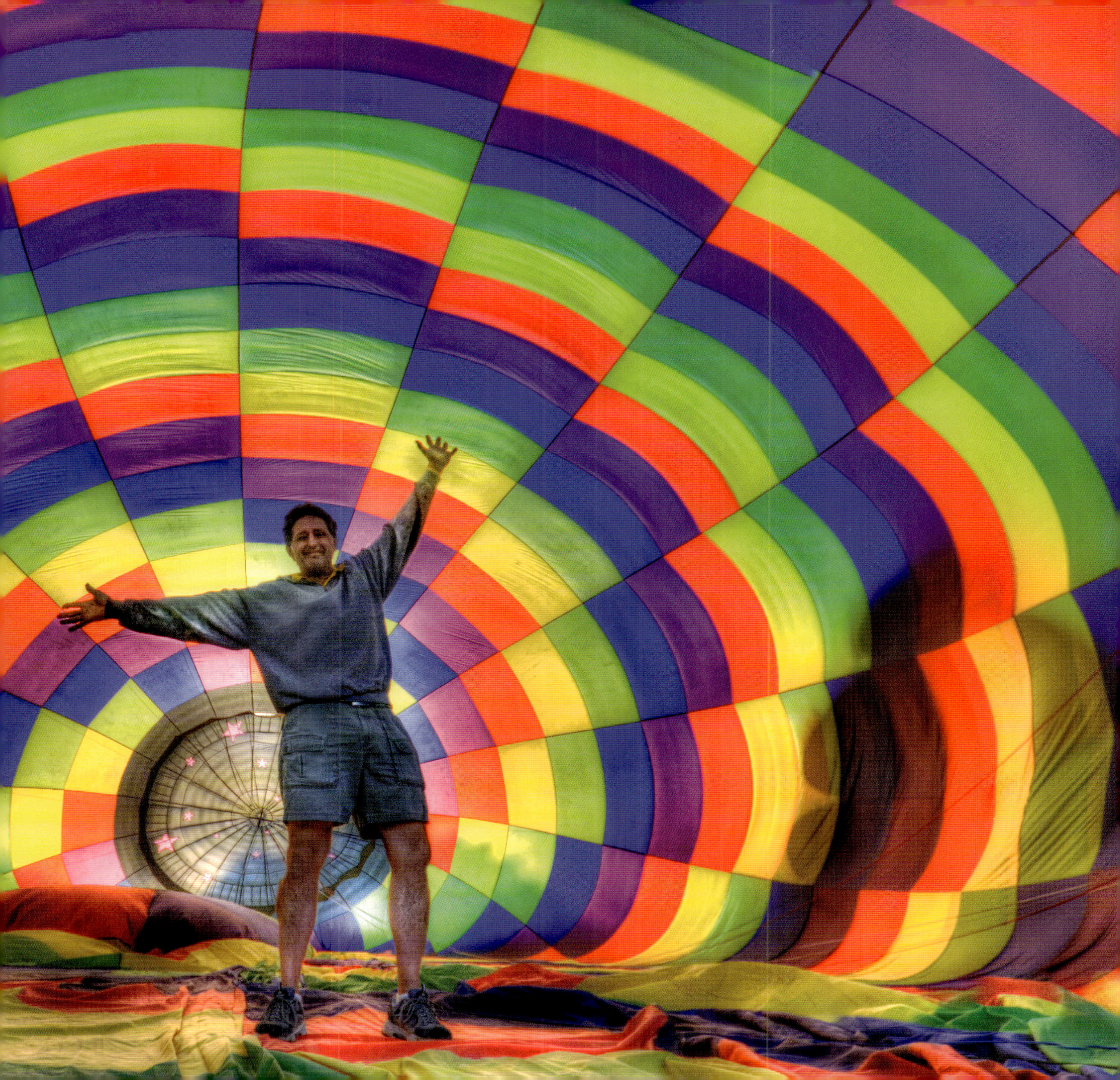

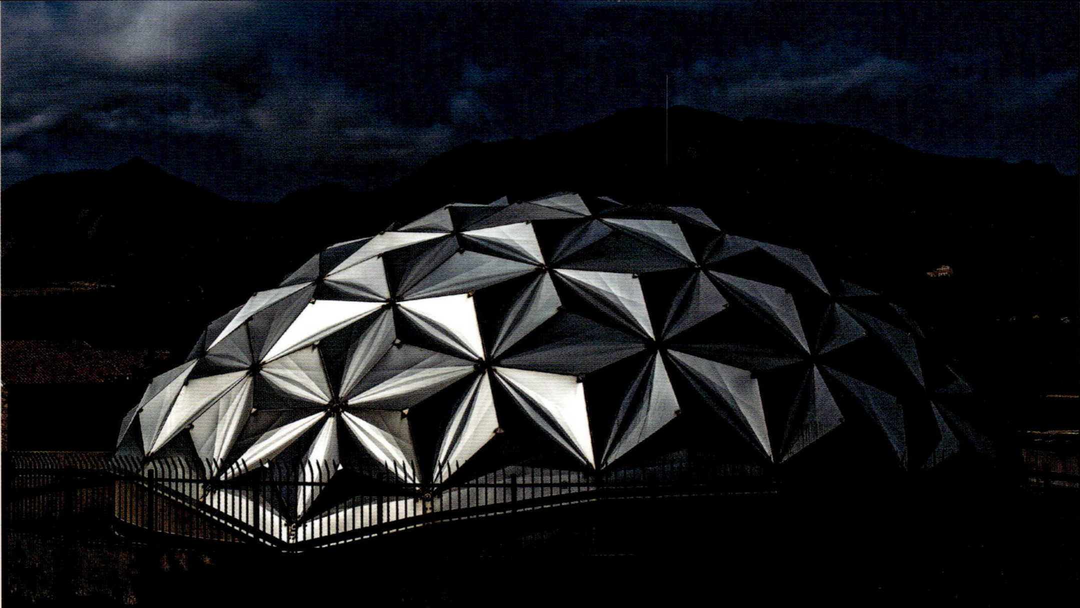

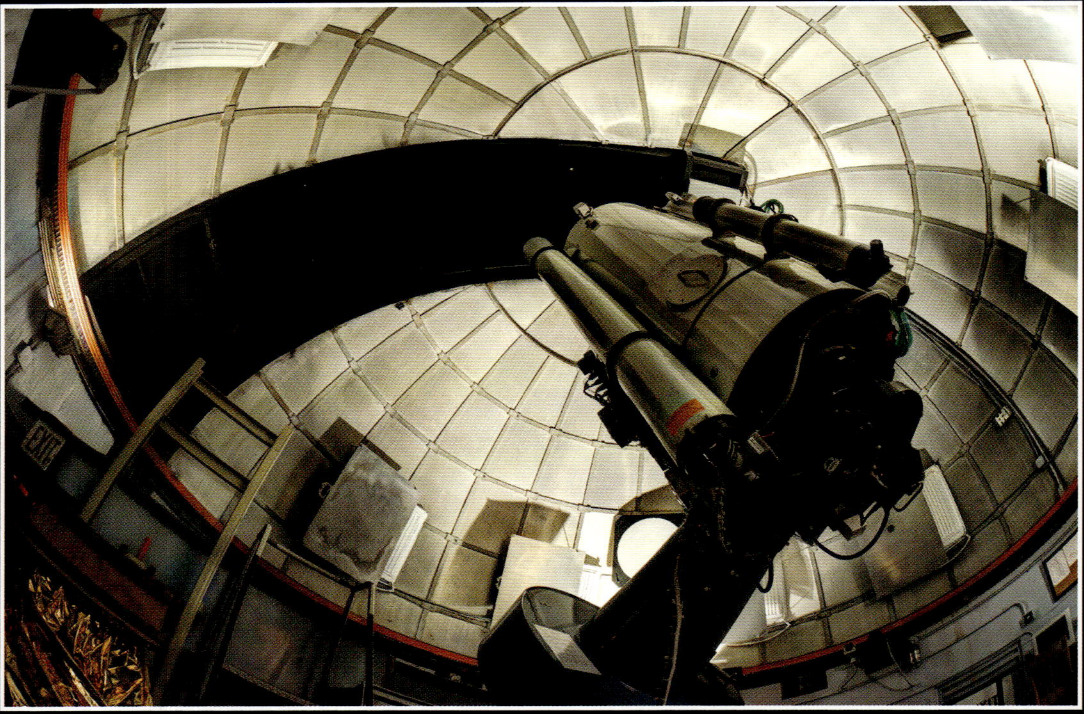

ABOVE, TOP: Standing out against Boulder's evening sky, the Fiske Planetarium and Science Center is part of CU-Boulder's Department of Astrophysical and Planetary Sciences. The complex offers a wide variety of star shows and astronomy lectures.

ABOVE, BOTTOM: On Friday evenings during the University of Colorado's spring, summer, and fall semesters, members of the public are invited to the Sommers Bausch Observatory. Using sixteen- and eighteen-inch telescopes, the public can view the moon, planets, and stars.

FACING PAGE: The Fiske Planetarium's star projector, known affectionately as "Fritz," has taught a generation how to find the North Star and constellations, as well as to trace the motions of the planets in the heavens.

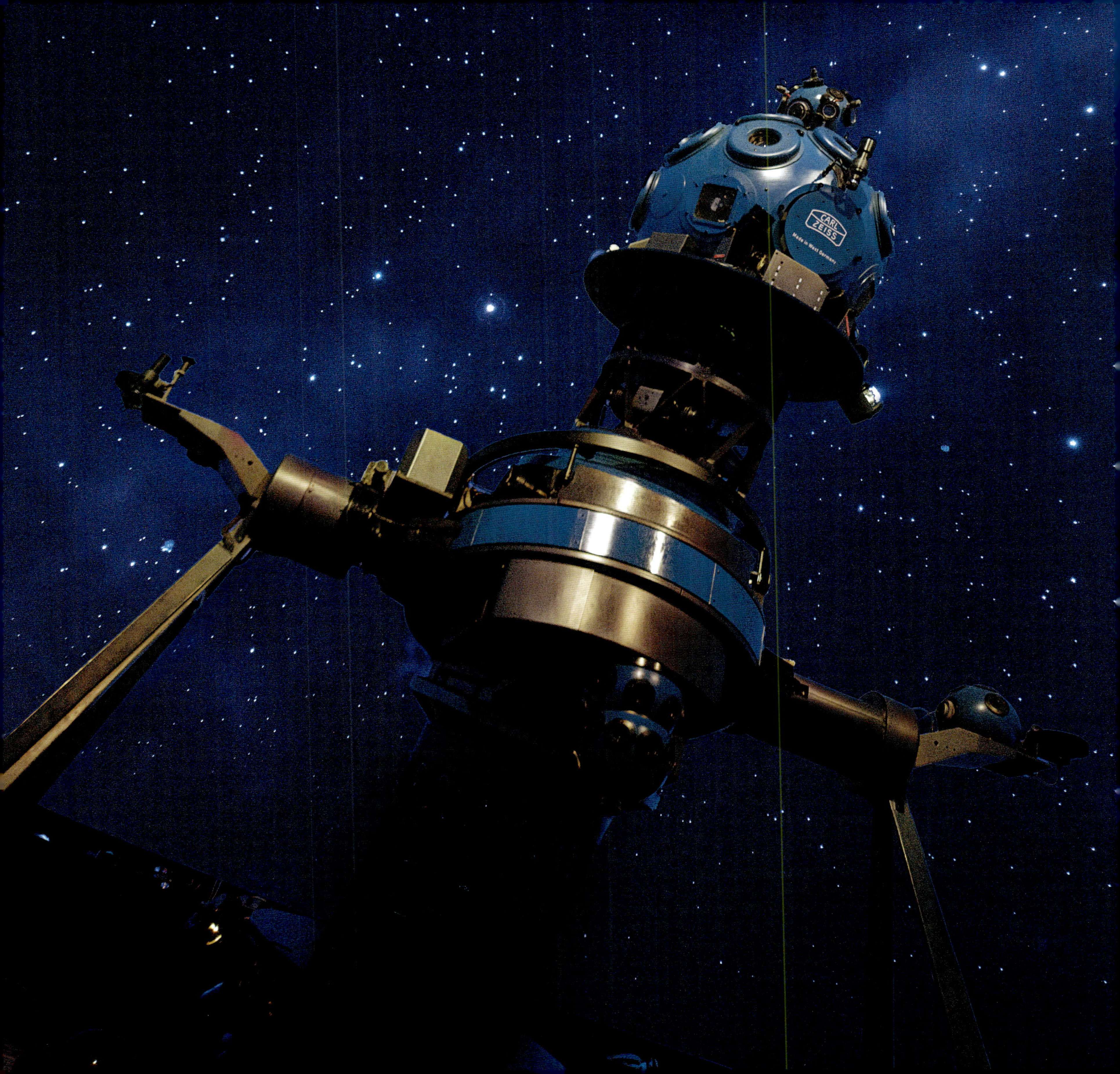
CARL
ZEISS
Made in West Germany

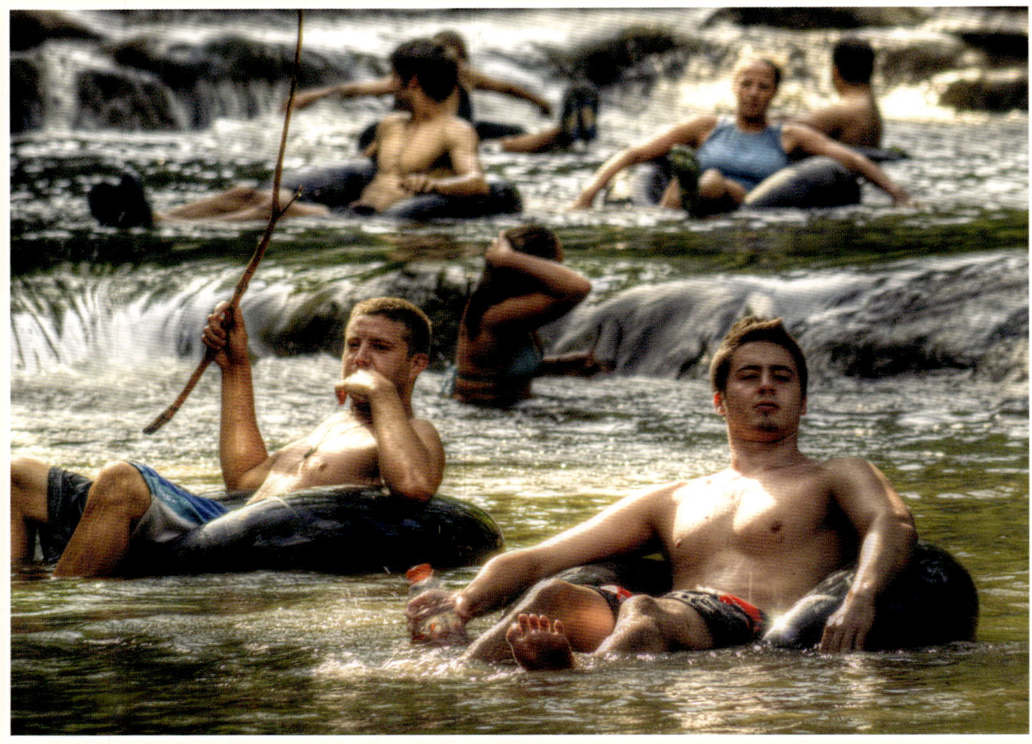

ABOVE: Tubing in Boulder Creek is one way to cool off on a hot day.

RIGHT: Eben G. Fine Park (named for a former secretary of the Boulder Chamber of Commerce) is the starting point for many tubers. Fifteen minutes after plunging into Boulder Creek, inner-tube riders can climb out in Central Park or continue downstream.

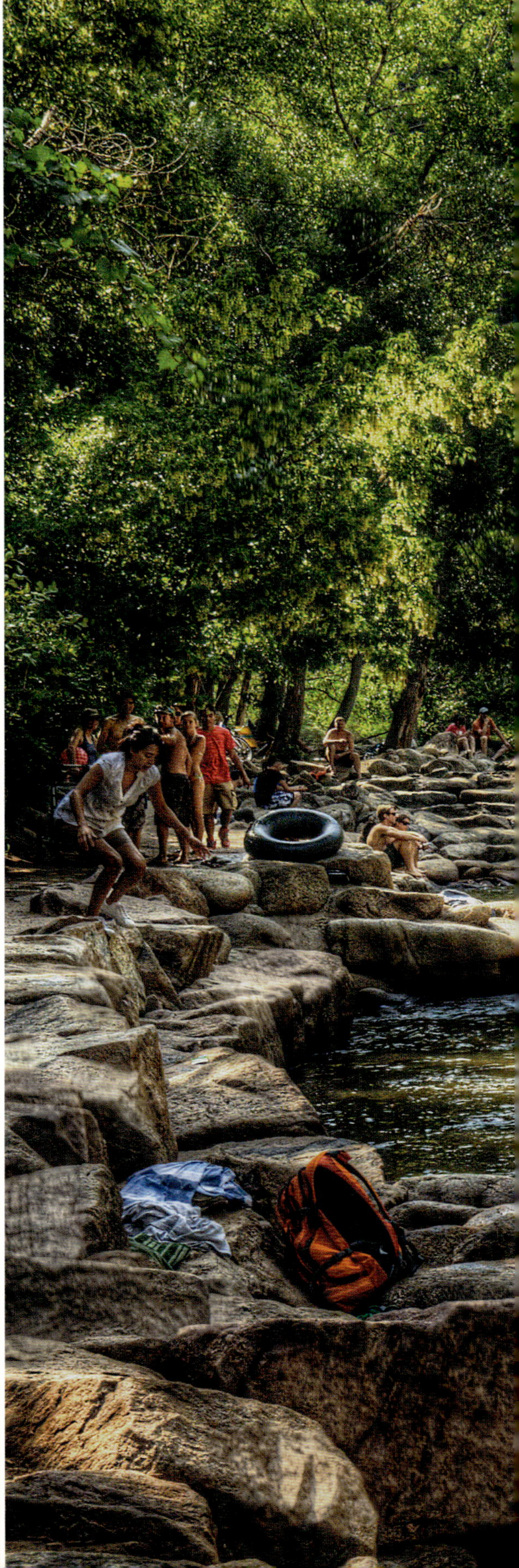

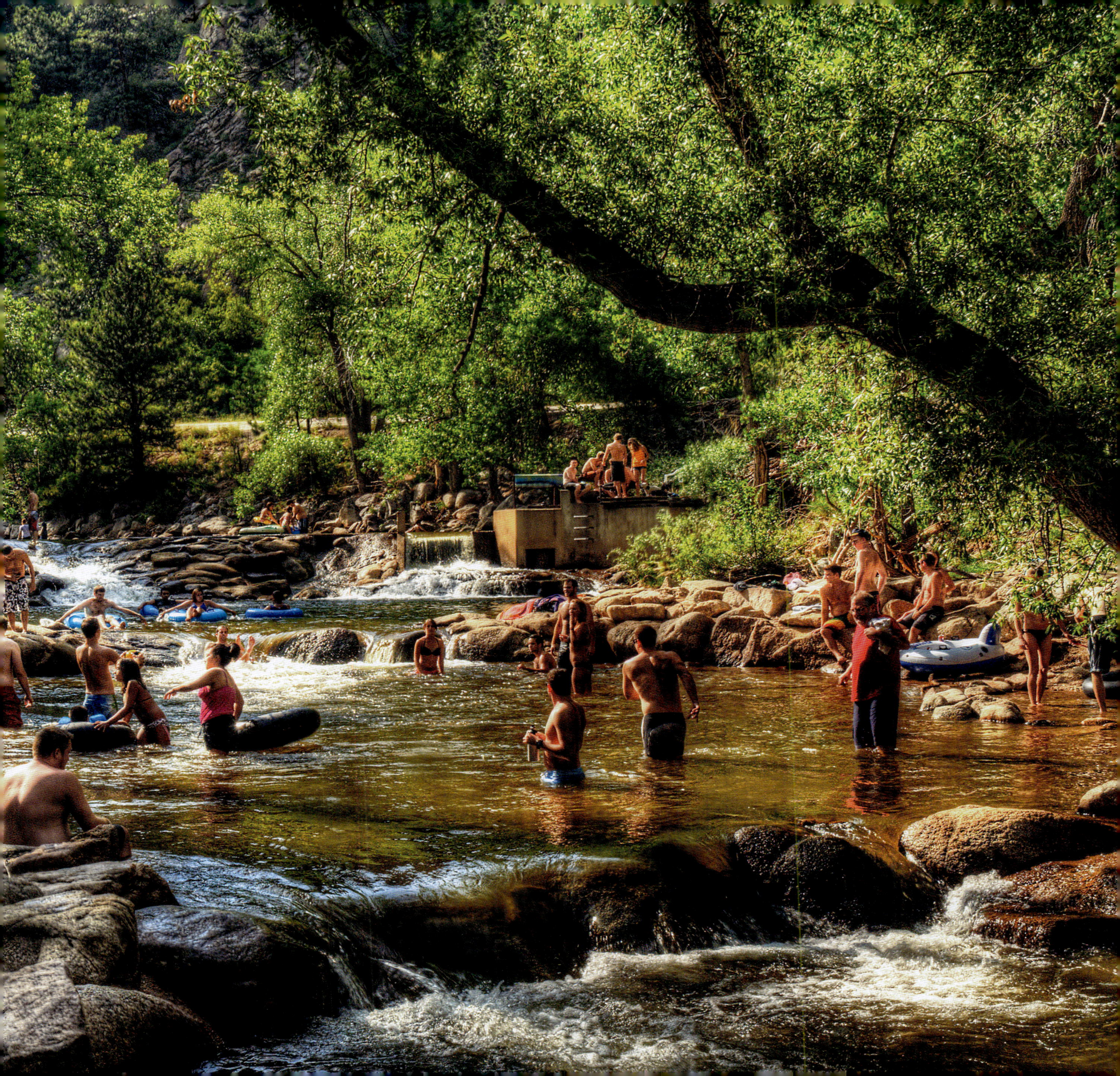

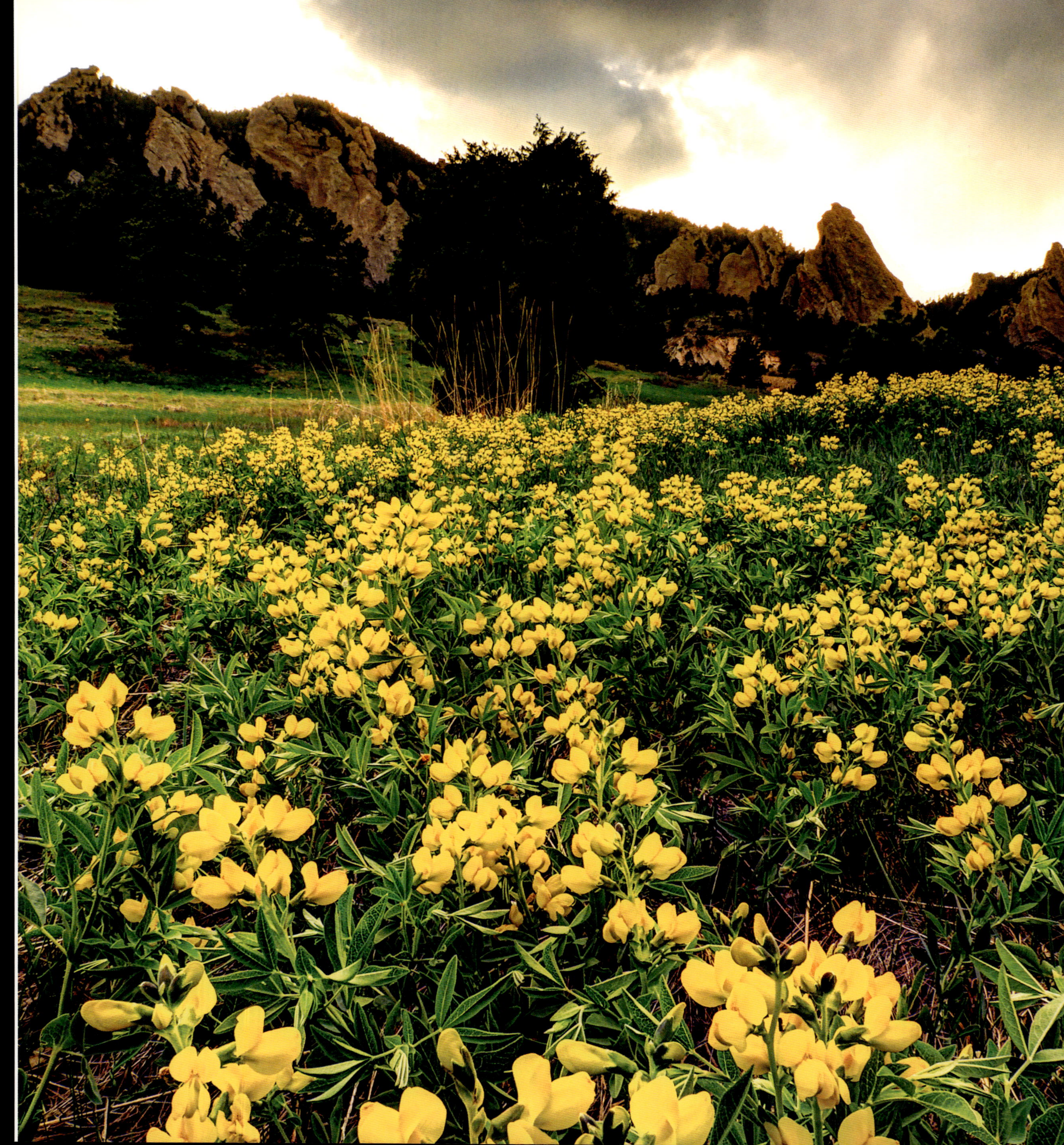

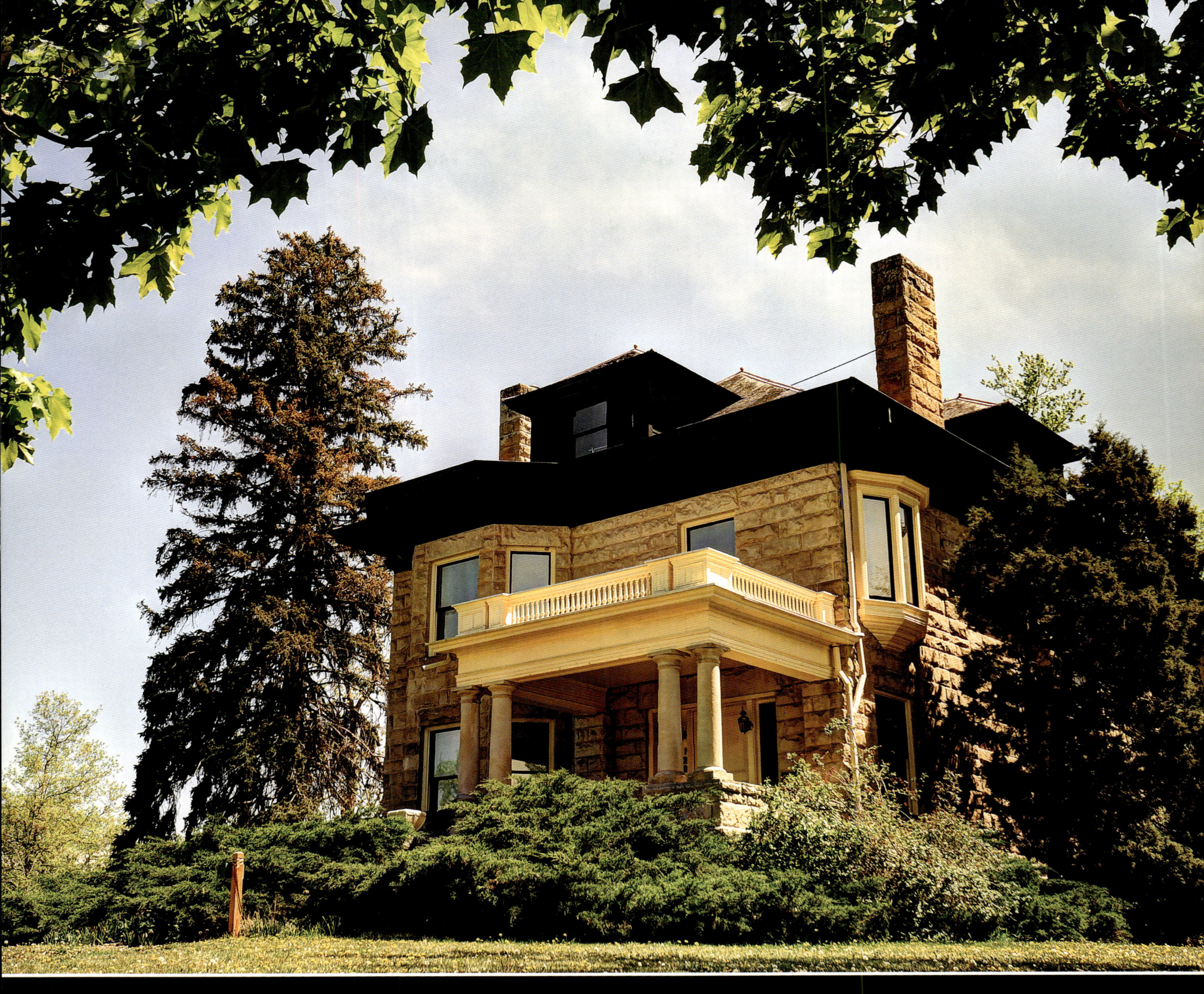

ABOVE: New York stockbroker John Harbeck built this stone house as a summer residence in 1899. The building was landmarked by the city of Boulder in 1979 and is now the home of the Boulder History Museum.

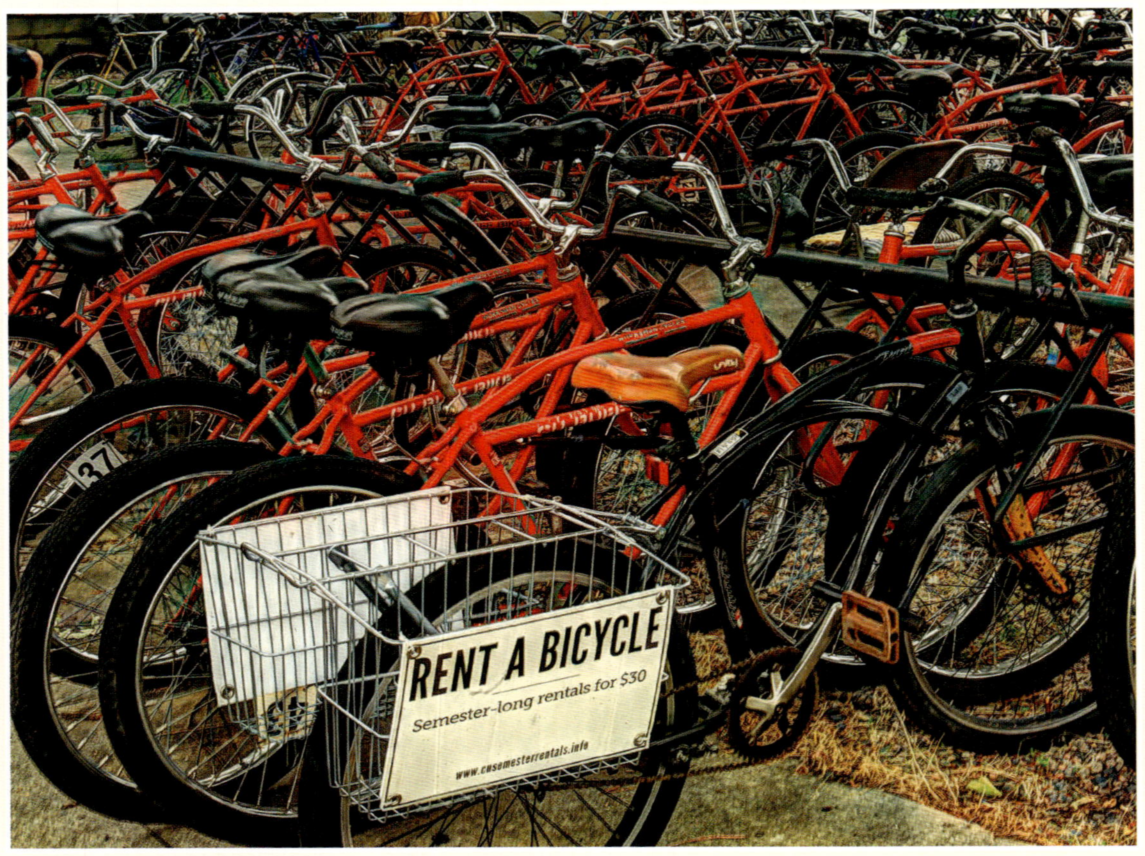

ABOVE: The Environmental Center at the University of Colorado-Boulder offers bicycles for semester rental to its students, faculty, and staff.

RIGHT: Diners enjoy a sunny summer day at the Community Plaza Shopping Center. Featuring a serpentine-roofed canopy, the shopping center opened in 1960 and was one of more than 200 structures designed by Boulder architect Hobart D. Wagener.

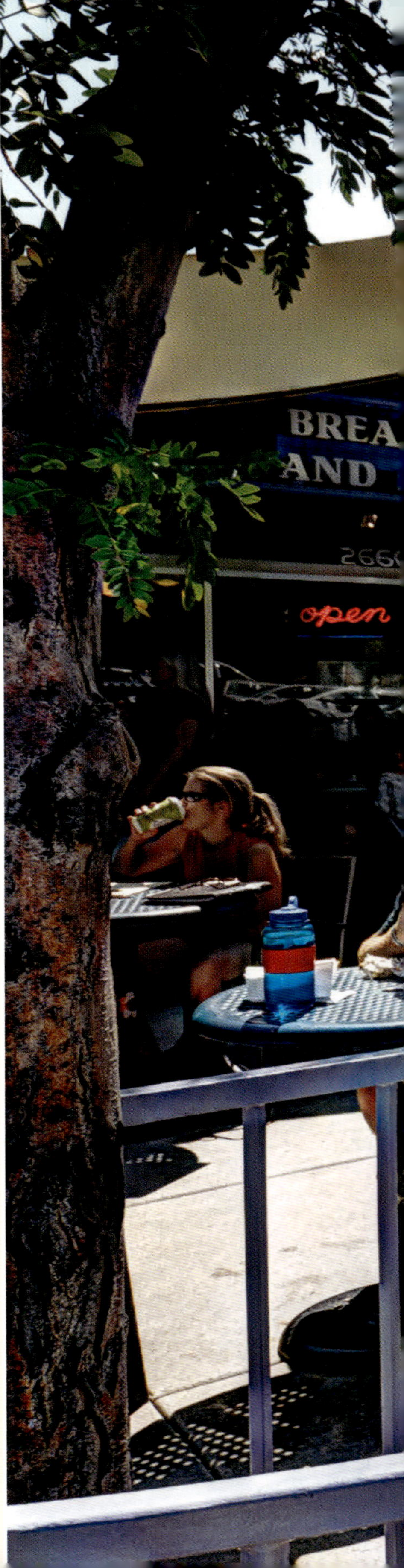

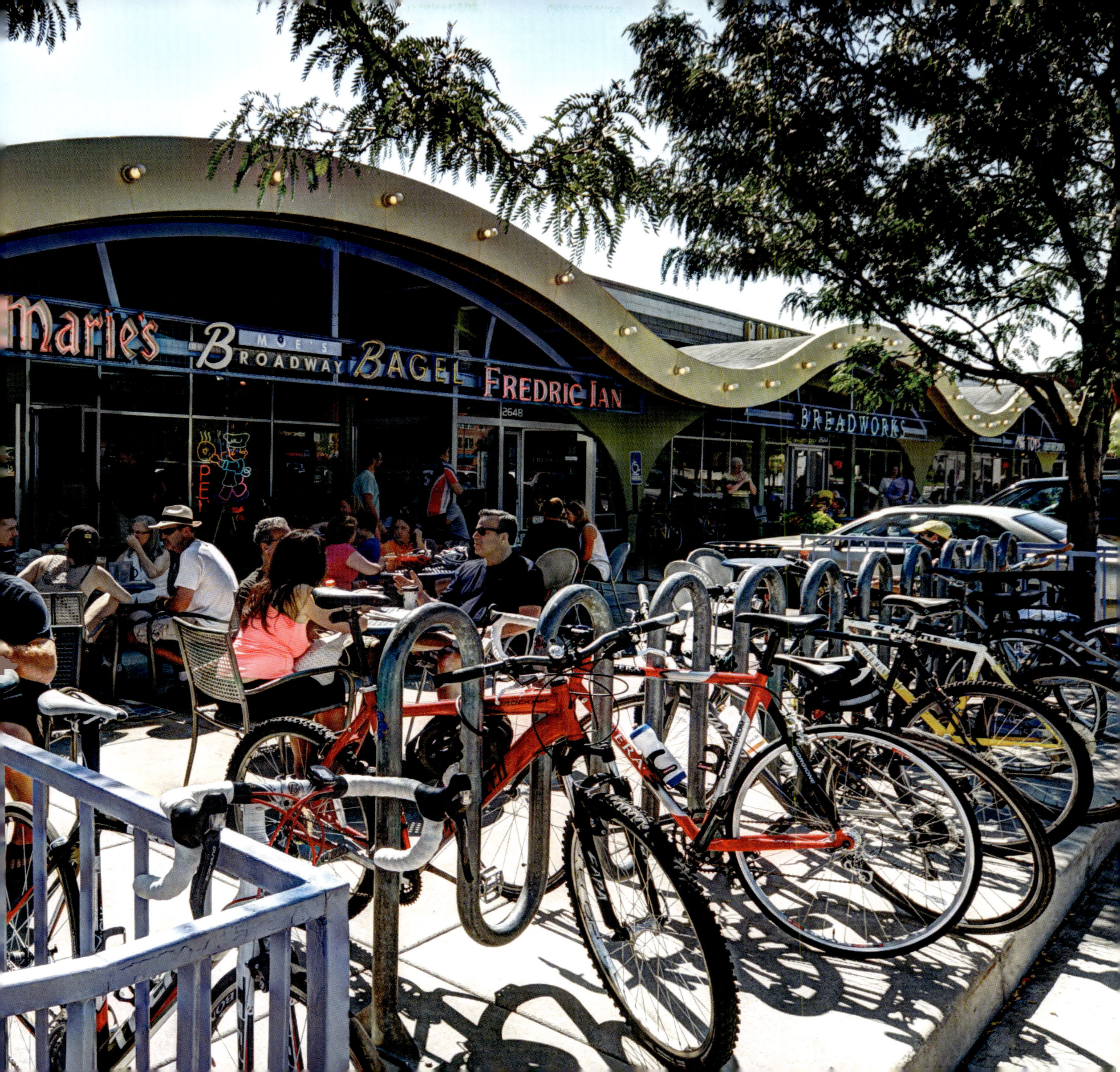
marie's
MOE'S
BROADWAY BAGEL
FREDRIC IAN
2648
BREADWORKS

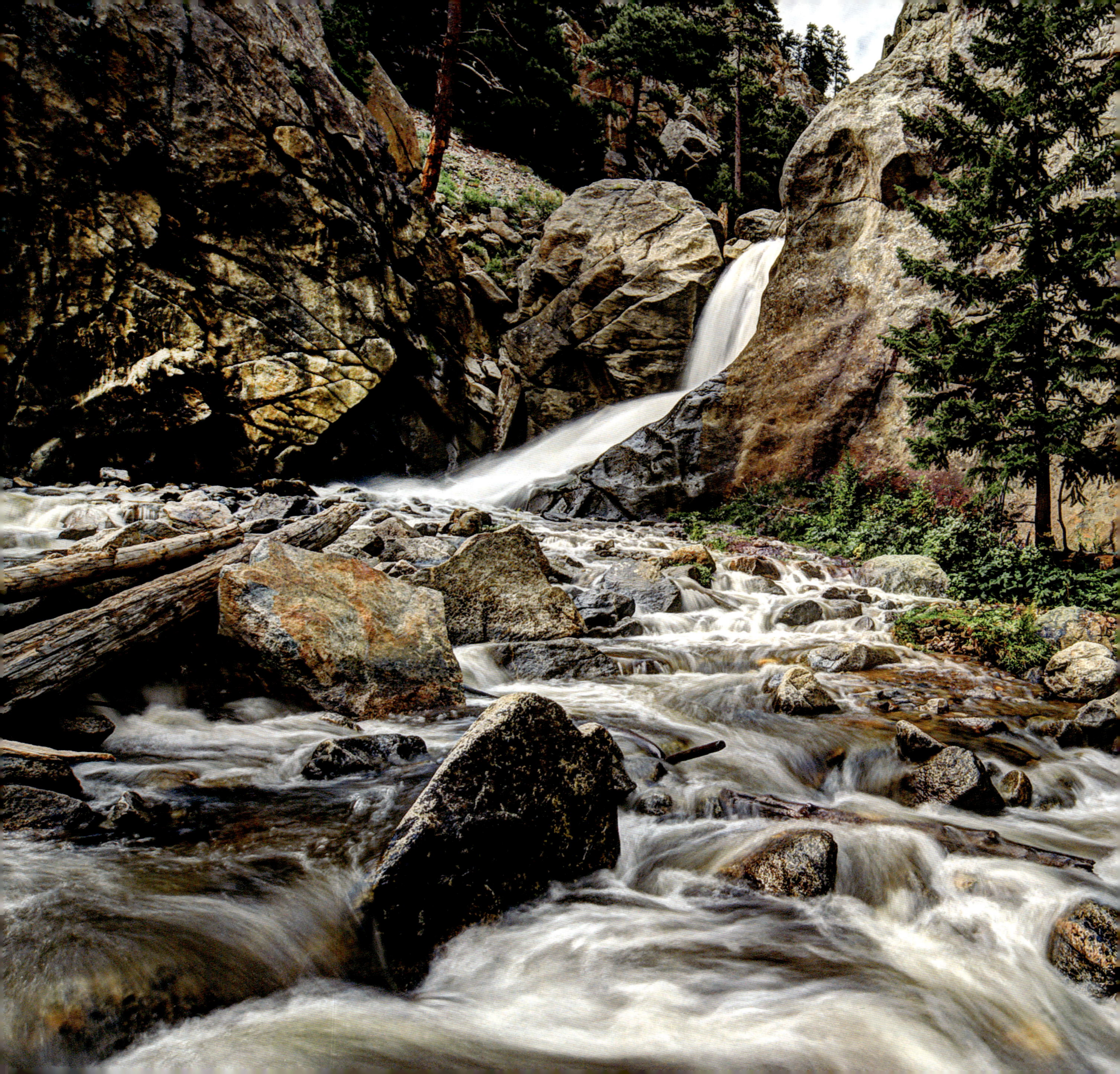

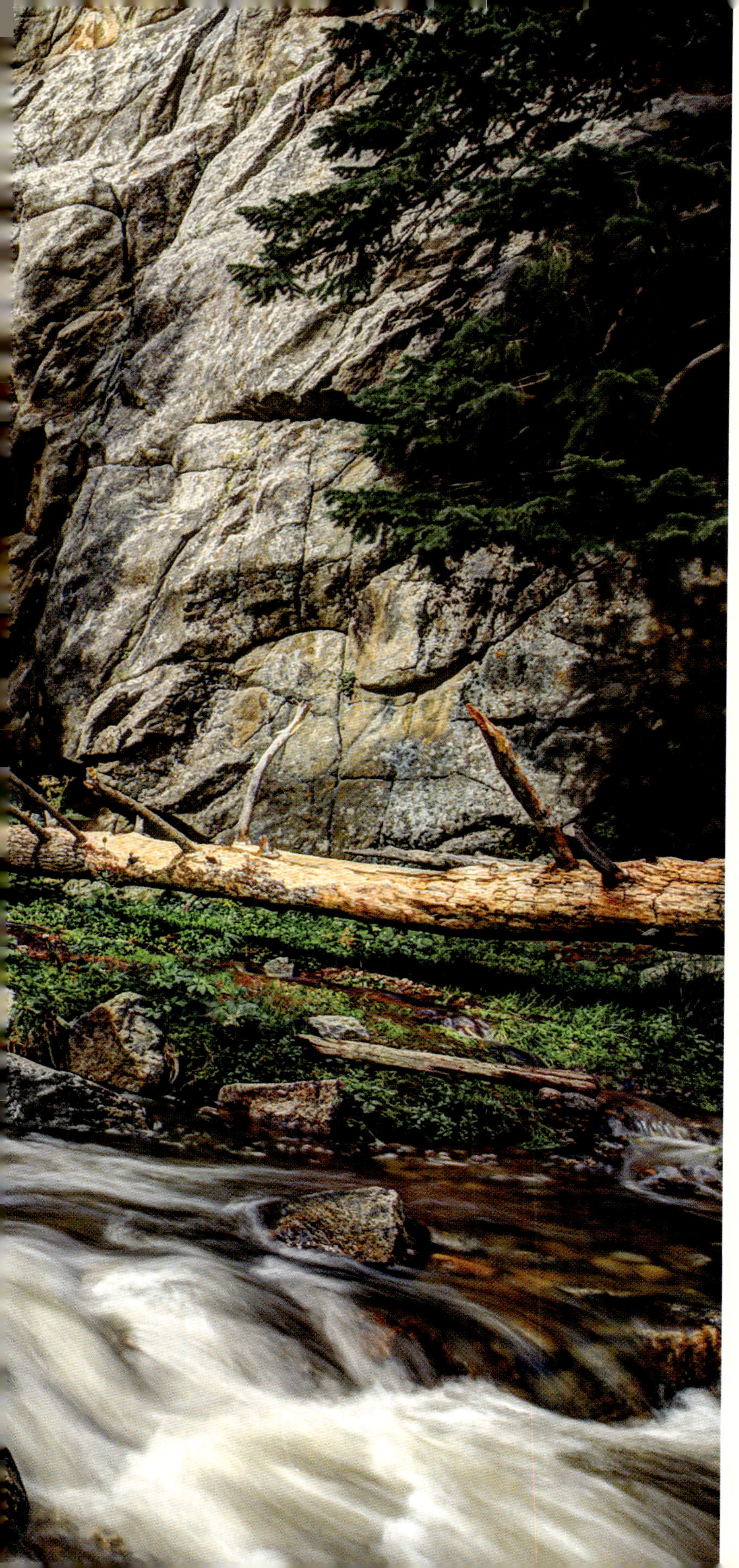

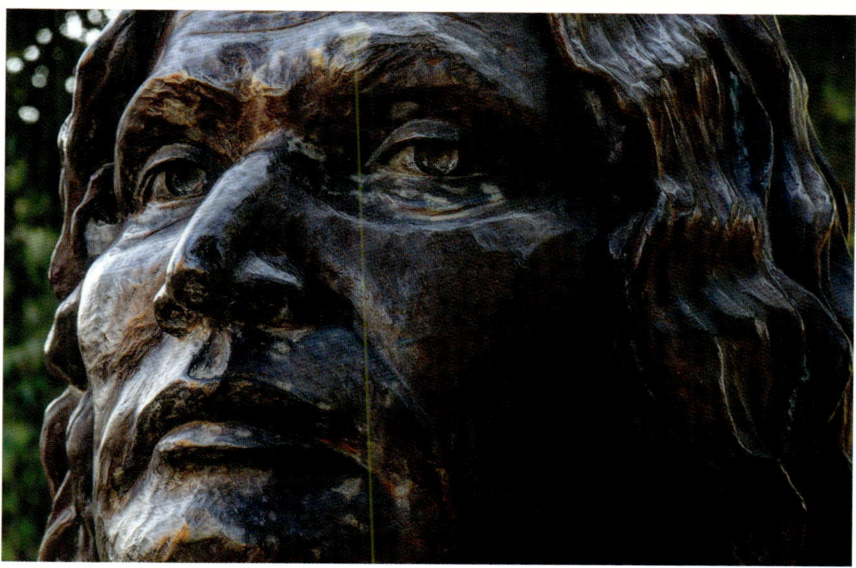

ABOVE: A bronze bust of Chief Niwot, on the Boulder County Courthouse lawn, commemorates the Arapaho people who lived on the plains of Colorado. Niwot means "Left Hand," and both names mark several geographical locations in Boulder County.

LEFT: Crashing to the canyon floor below, Boulder Falls, approximately nine miles west of Boulder in Boulder Canyon, has been a destination point for residents and tourists for more than a century.

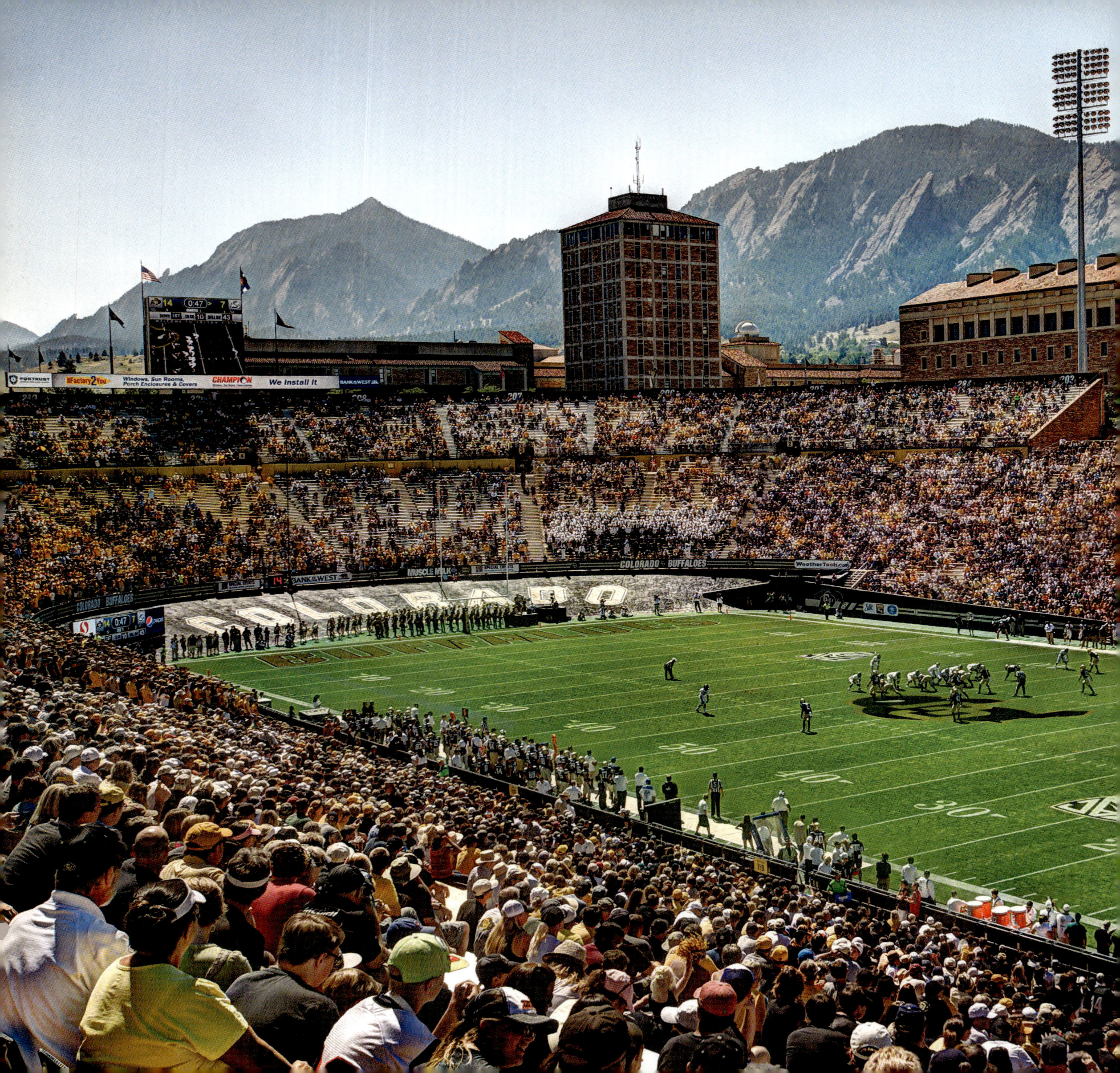
FORTRUST
Factory2You
Windows, Sun Rooms, Porch Enclosures & Covers
CHAMPION
We Install It
BANK of the WEST
MUSCLE MILK
COLORADO BUFFALOES
WeatherTech.com
COLORADO

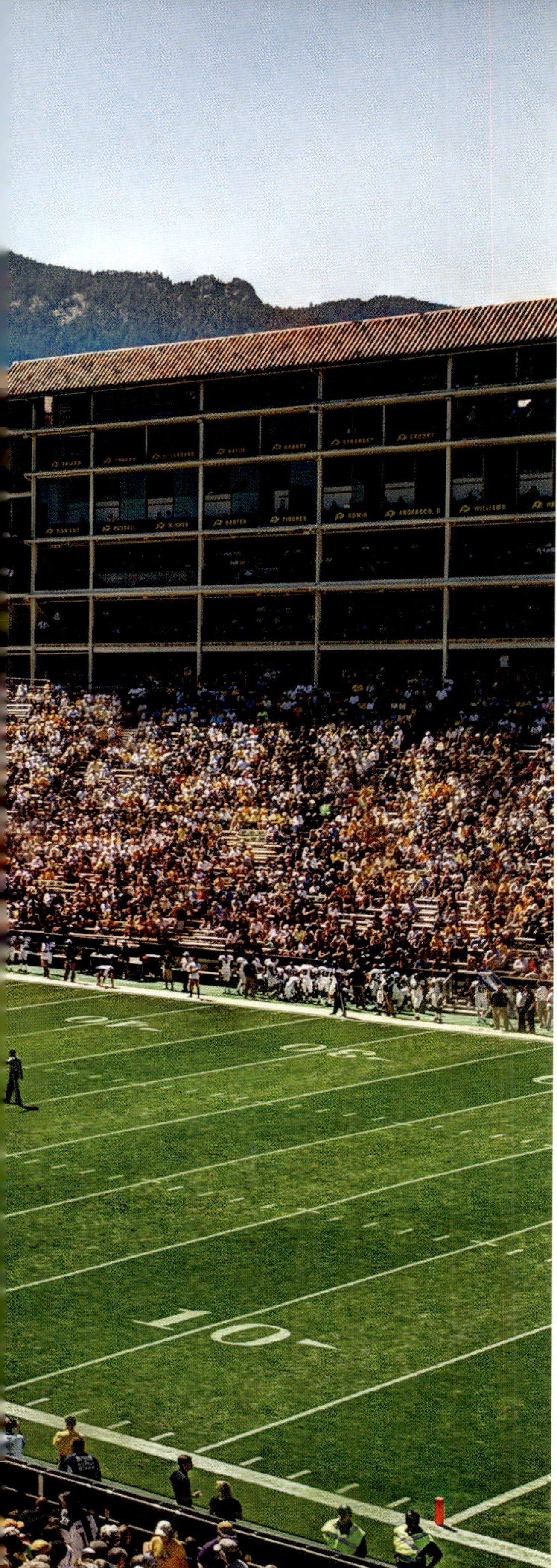

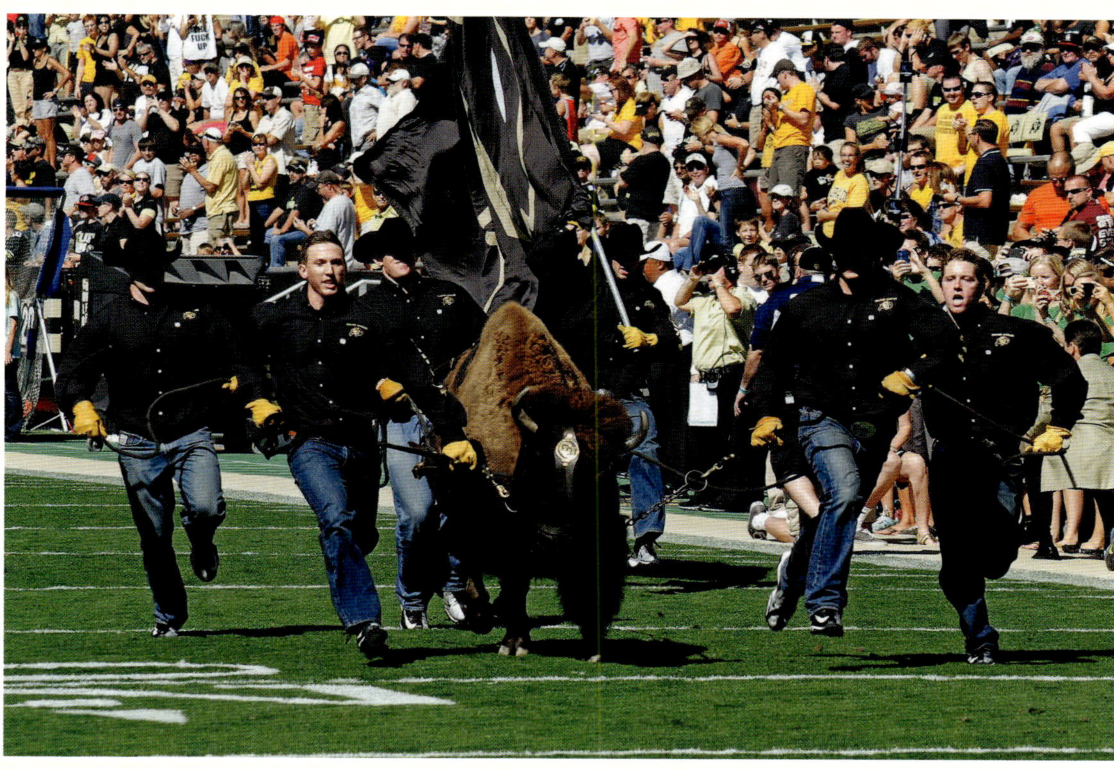

ABOVE: Ever since 1934, a buffalo has been the University of Colorado's mascot. Here, Ralphie V (the fifth, and latest, in a succession of live buffaloes) leads CU's football team onto the field.

LEFT: Spectators fill Folsom Field on a sunny day. The field was named after Fred Folsom, who was one of the university's better-known football coaches.

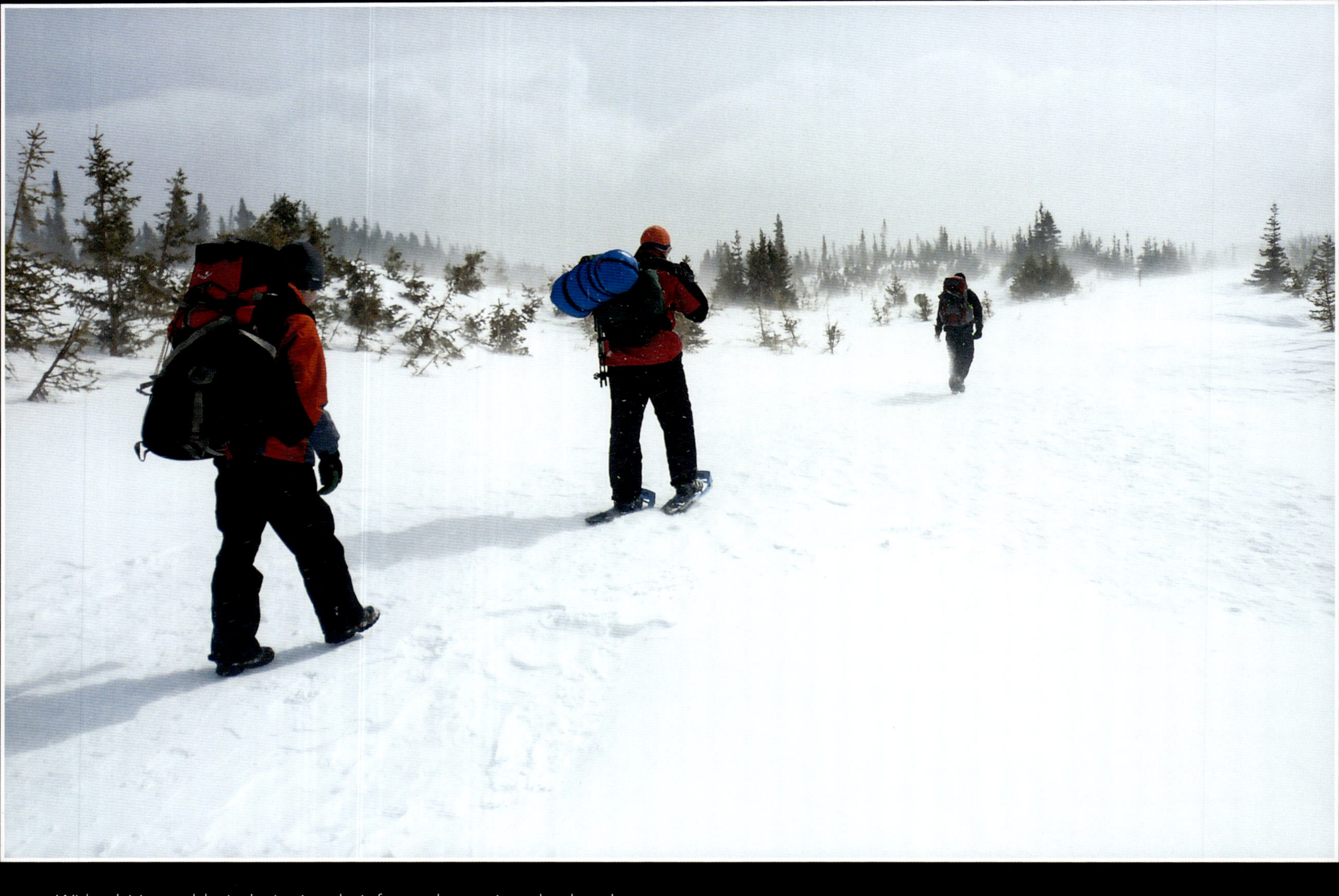

ABOVE: With a biting cold wind stinging their faces, these winter backpackers traverse a snow-crusted landscape near Brainard Lake in western Boulder County. The Brainard Lake Recreation Area, west of Ward, is also popular with cross-country skiers.

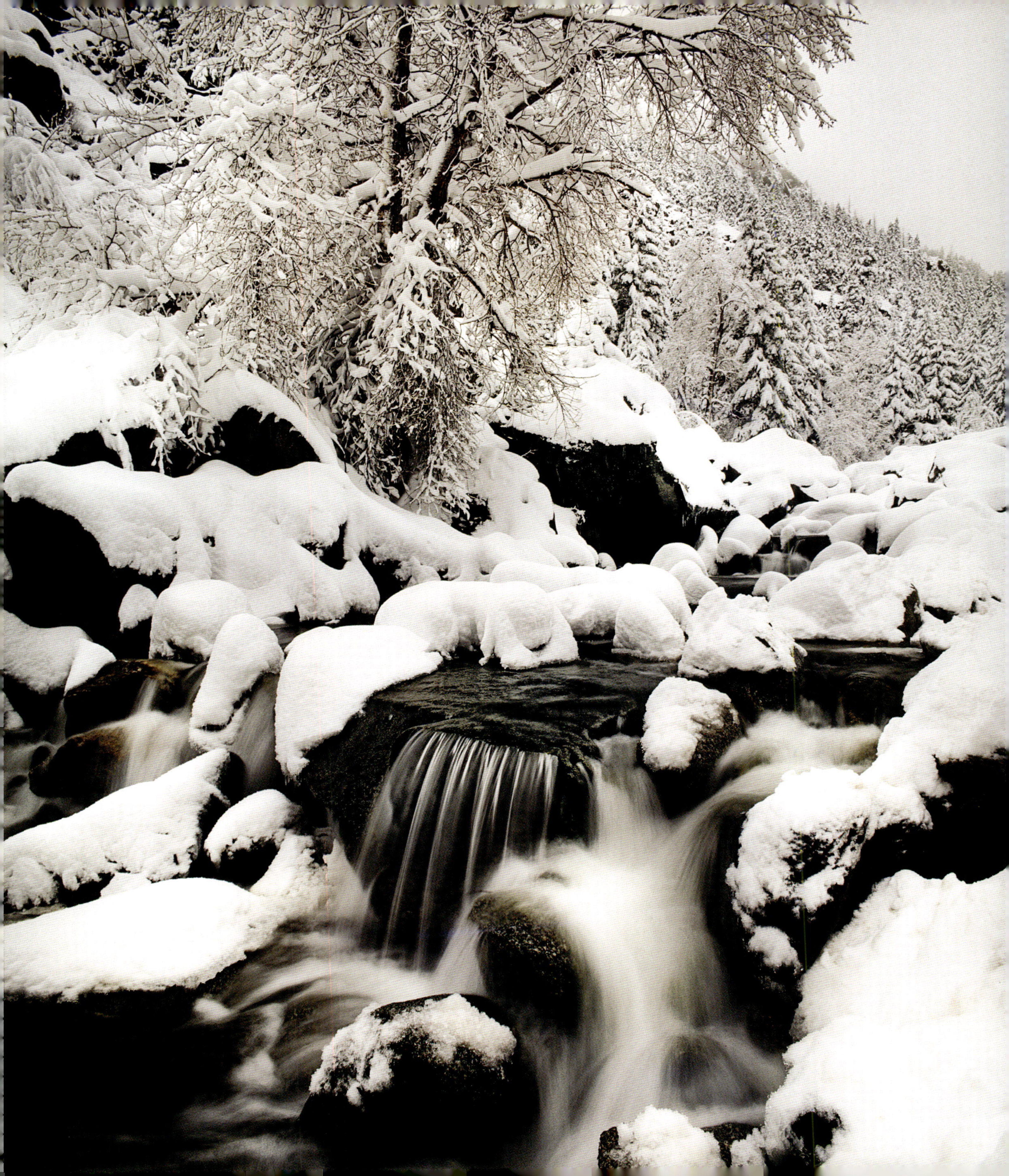

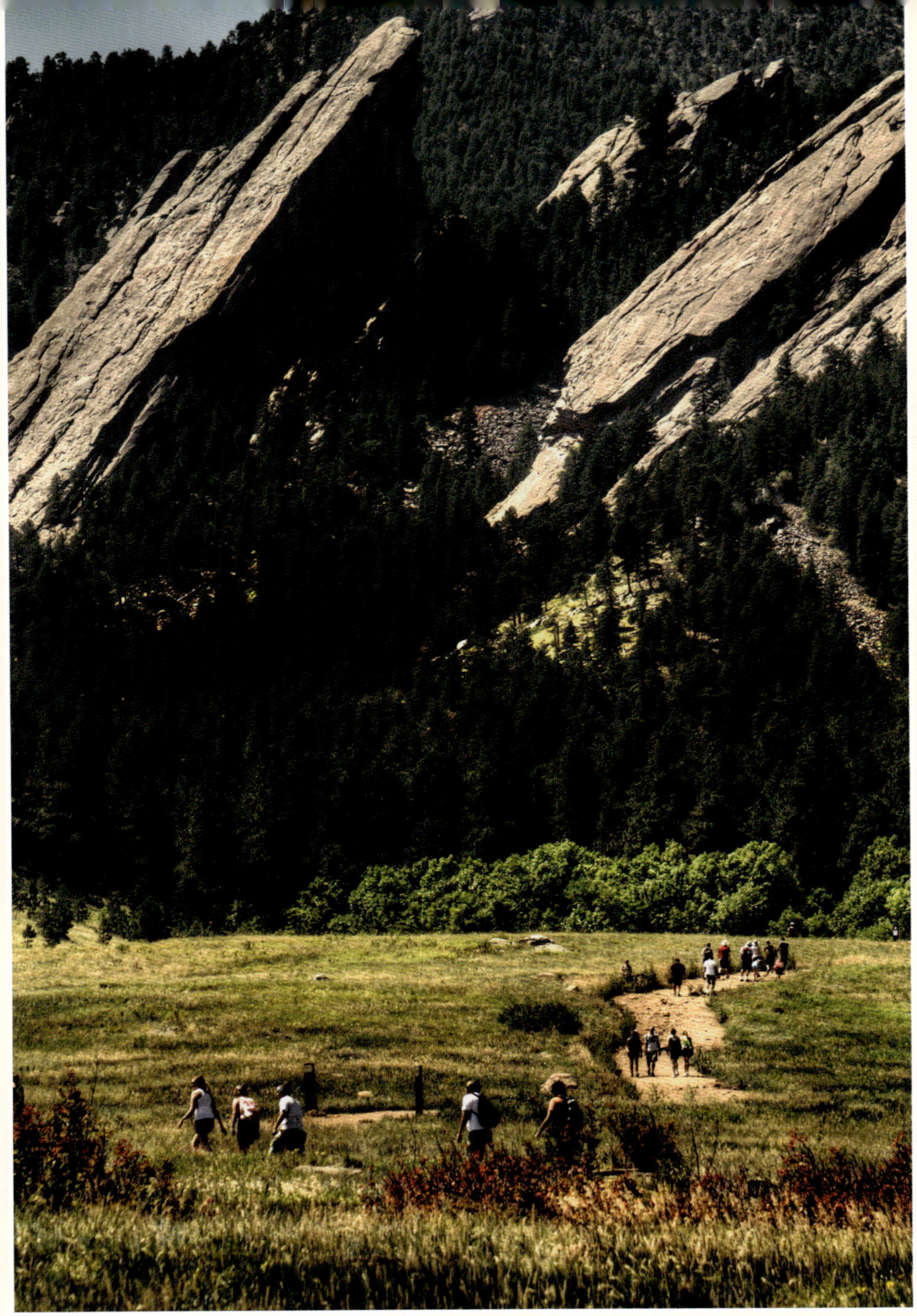

ABOVE: Hiking is a popular activity for Boulder residents and visitors alike. Boulder's mountain backdrop is defined by the Flatirons, the name given to the distinctive sandstone slabs that tower over these hikers near Chautauqua Park. The first use of the word showed up in a geological publication in the early 1900s as a reference to the shape of an iron (for pressing clothes) in an upright position.

RIGHT: Chautauqua, a nationwide association of cultural and educational resorts, opened its Boulder location in 1898. The picturesque Flatirons loom above the Chautauqua Dining Hall, built the same year and still in business as a restaurant.

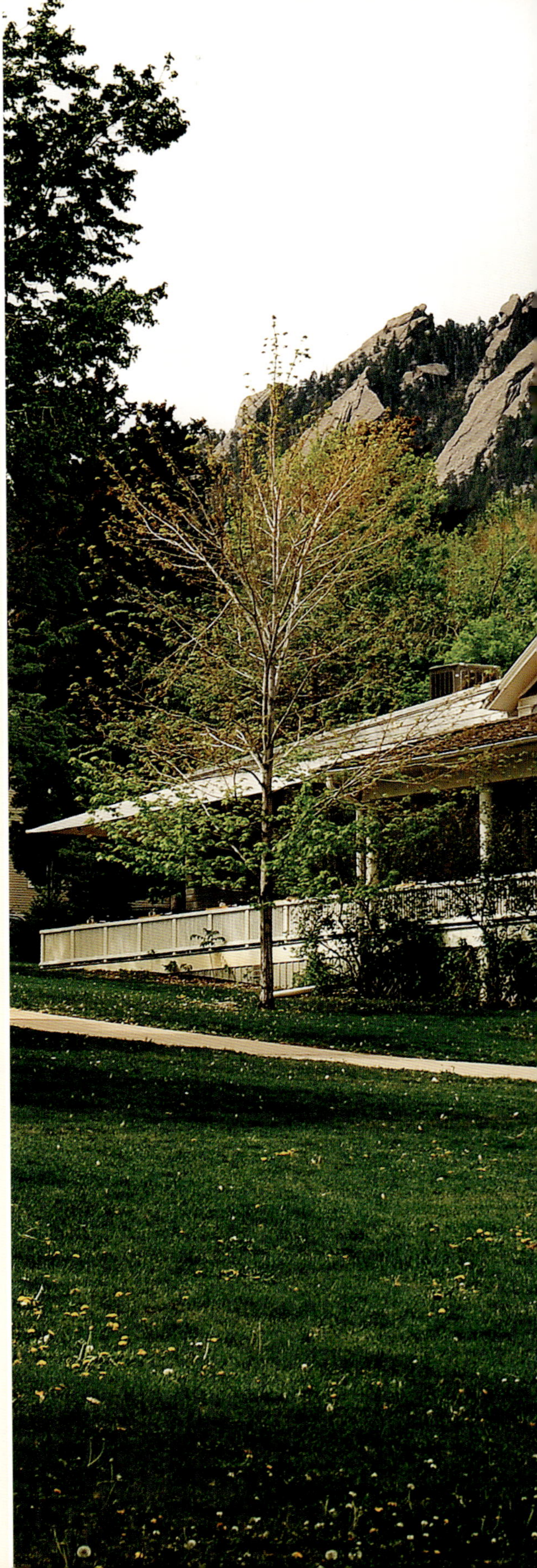

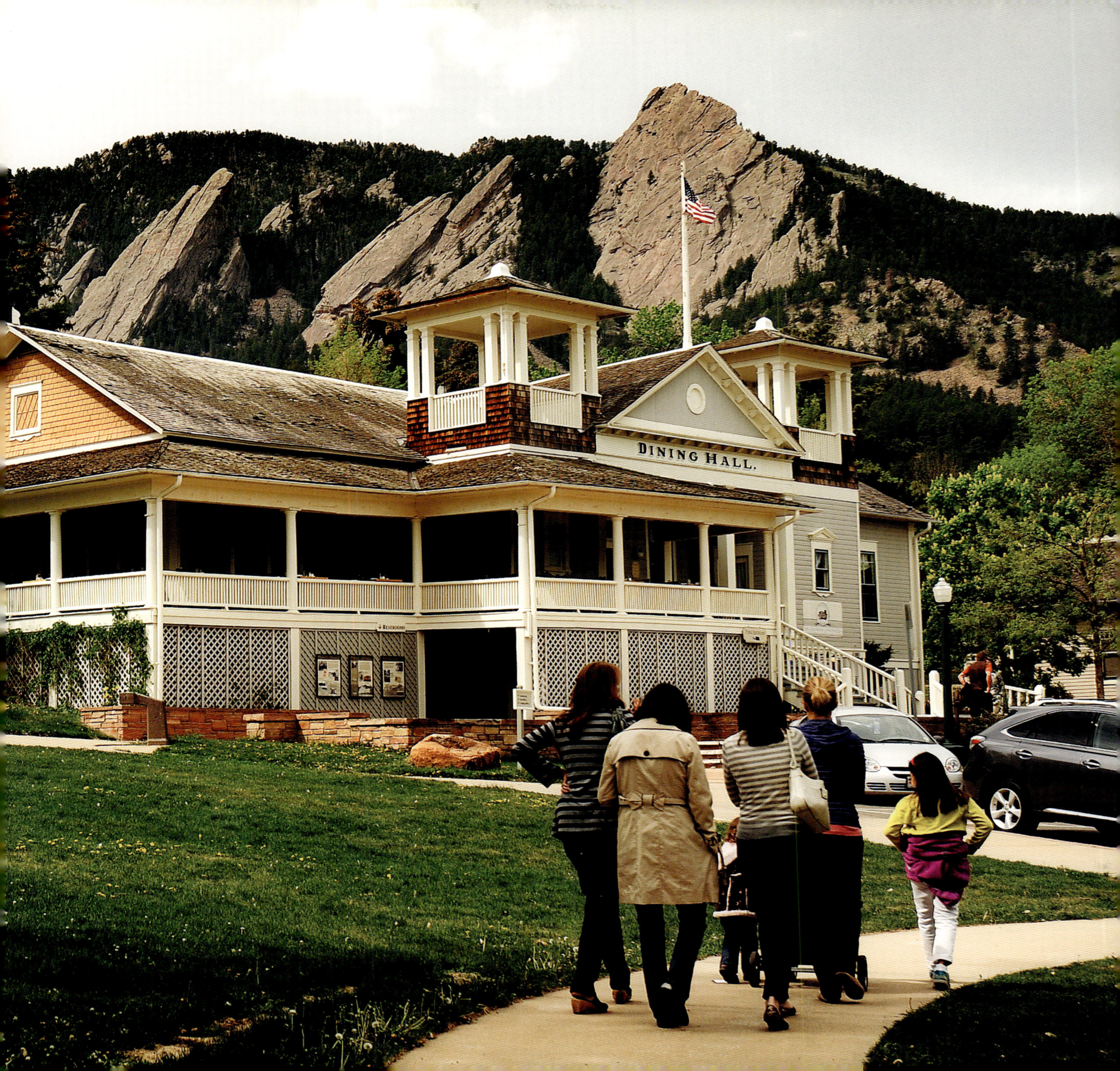
DINING HALL.
RESTROOMS

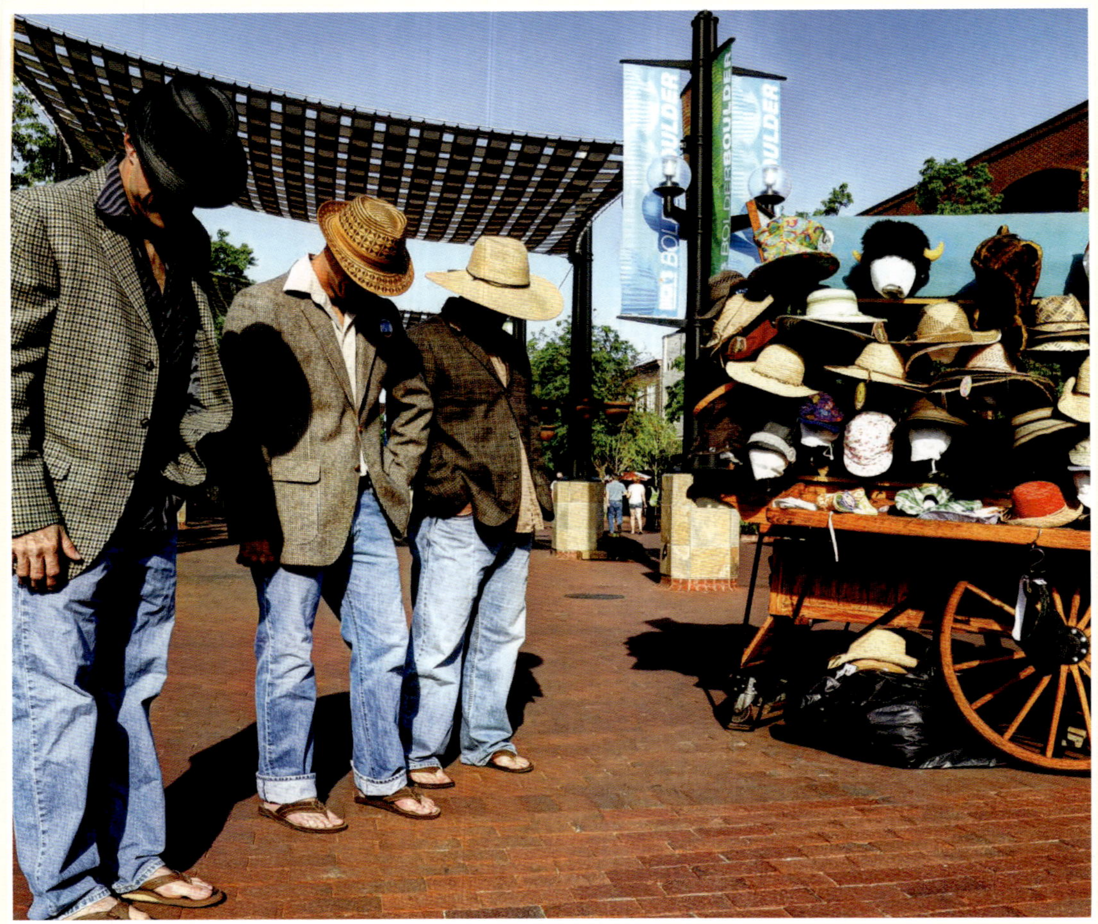

ABOVE: Vendors are popular on the Pearl Street Mall. This one, specializing in hats, set up shop in front of the Boulder County Courthouse.

RIGHT: Moe's, a bagel shop, began when a New York transplant to Boulder had a yearning for the perfect East Coast bagel. Now, with three Boulder locations and one in Denver, Moe's Broadway Bagel has enough variations to please even the most discriminating bagel connoisseur.

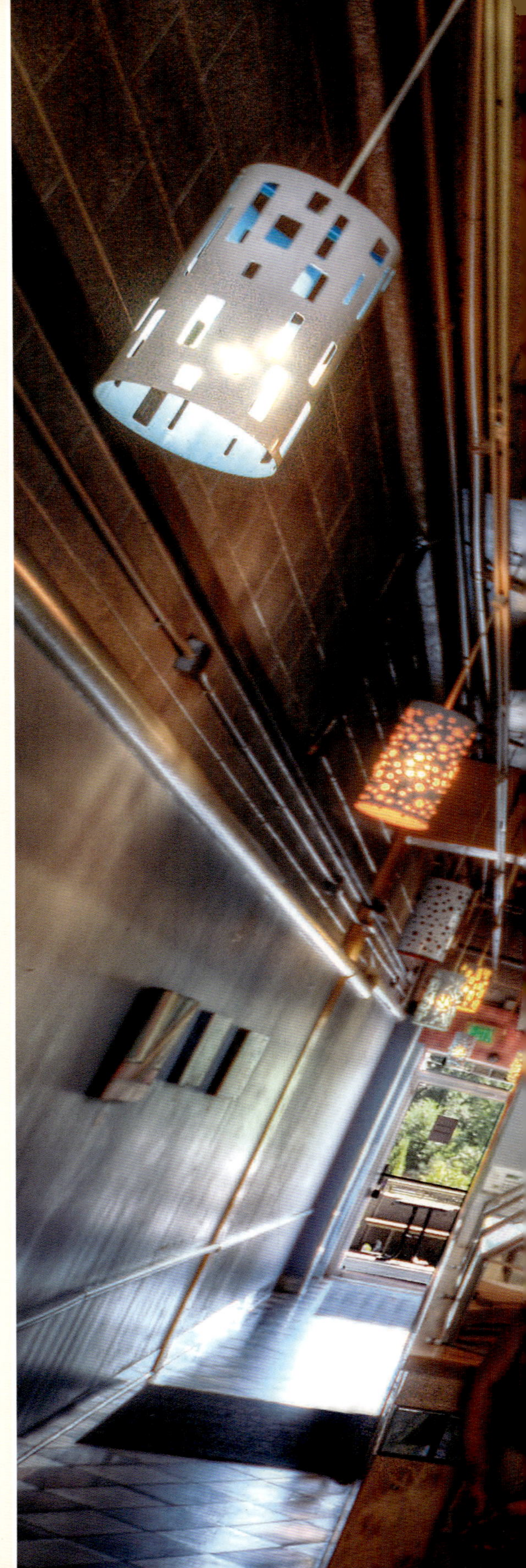

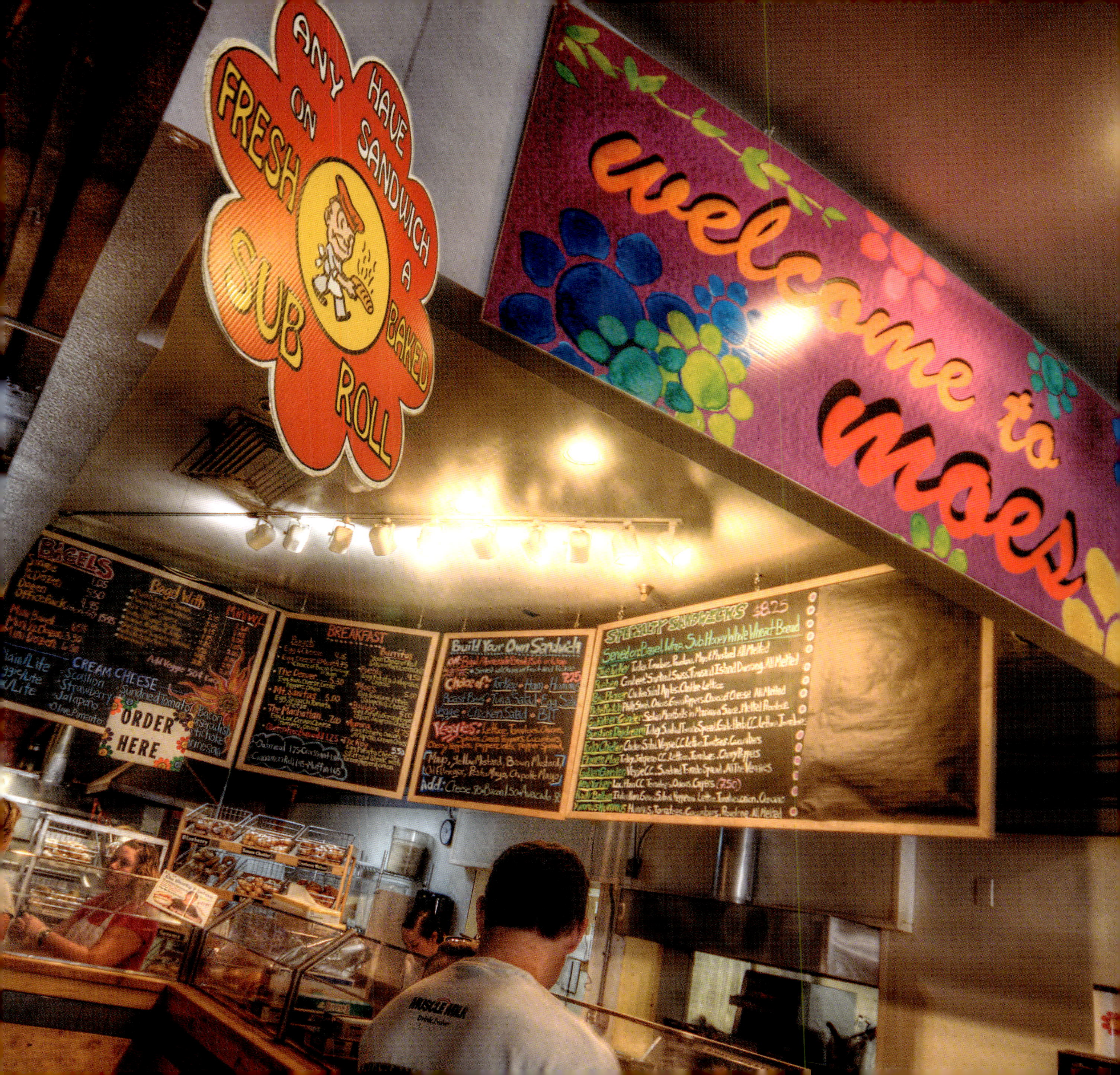
HAVE ANY SANDWICH ON A FRESH BAKED SUB ROLL
welcome to moes
BAGELS
Bagel With
BREAKFAST
Build Your Own Sandwich
SPECIALTY SANDWICHES $8.25
CREAM CHEESE
ORDER HERE
MUSCLE MILK

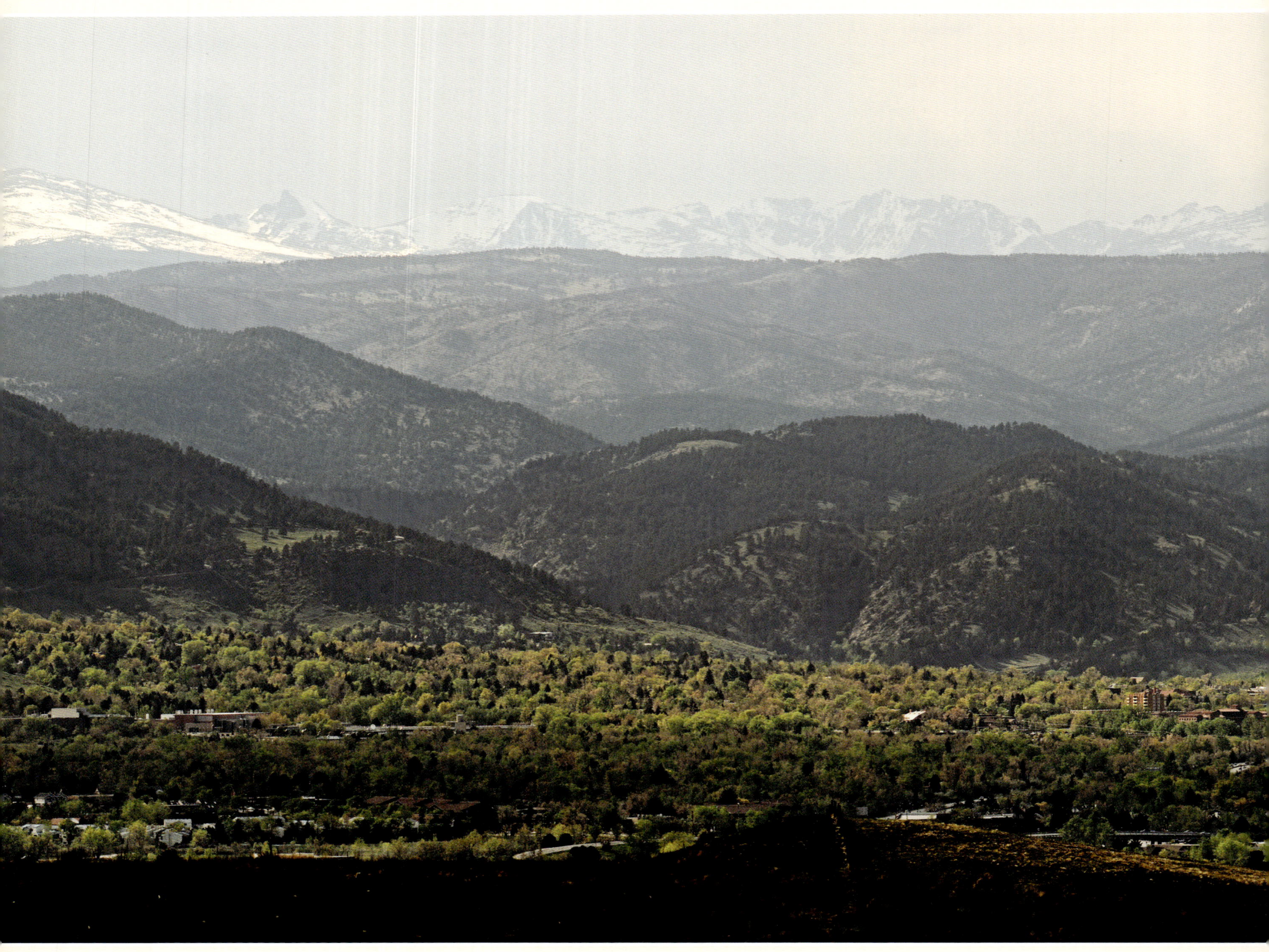

Tree-covered foothills and the snow-covered peaks of the Colorado Front Range provide a dramatic backdrop to the city of Boulder. Today, where the mountains meet the plains, more than 100,000 people make Boulder their home.

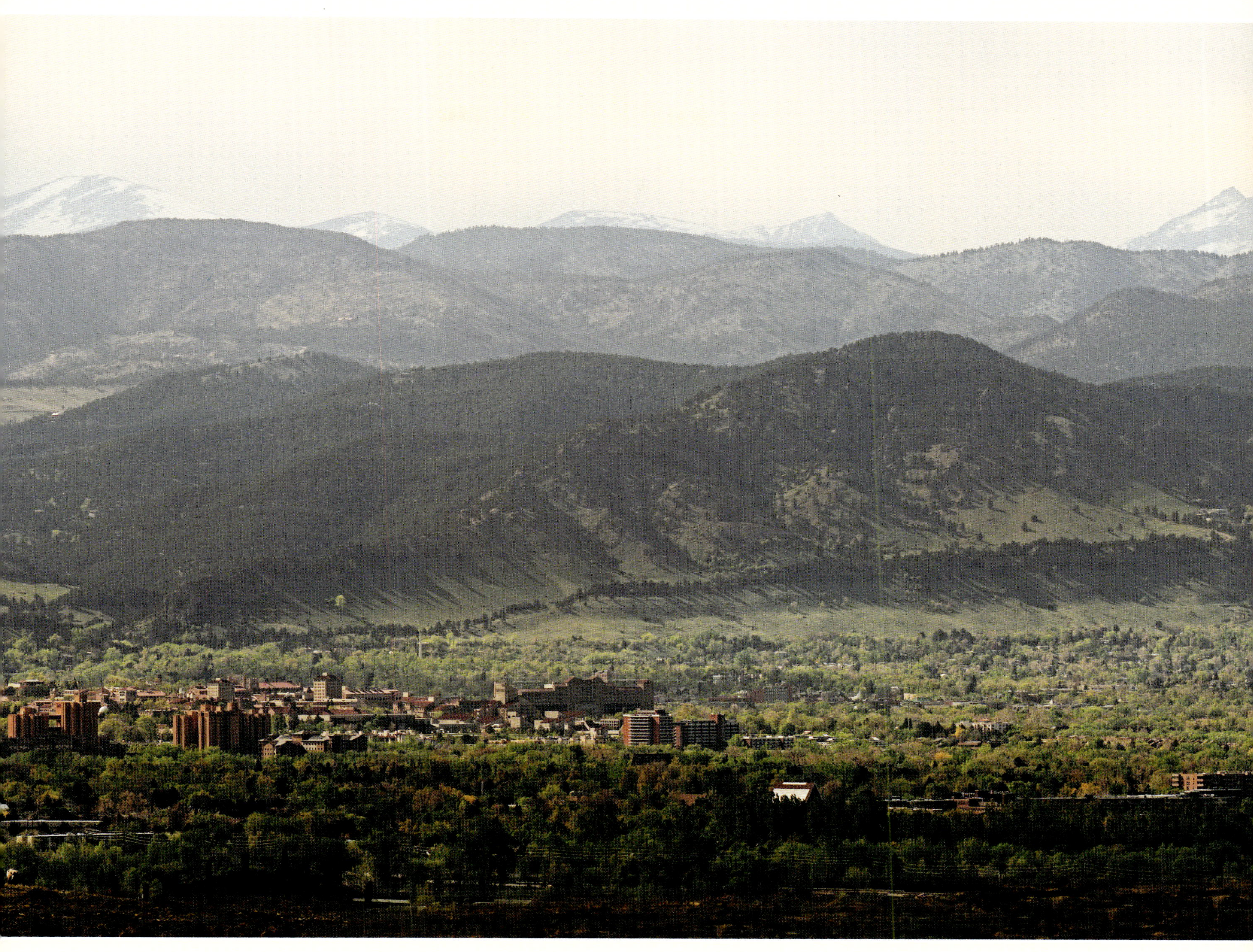

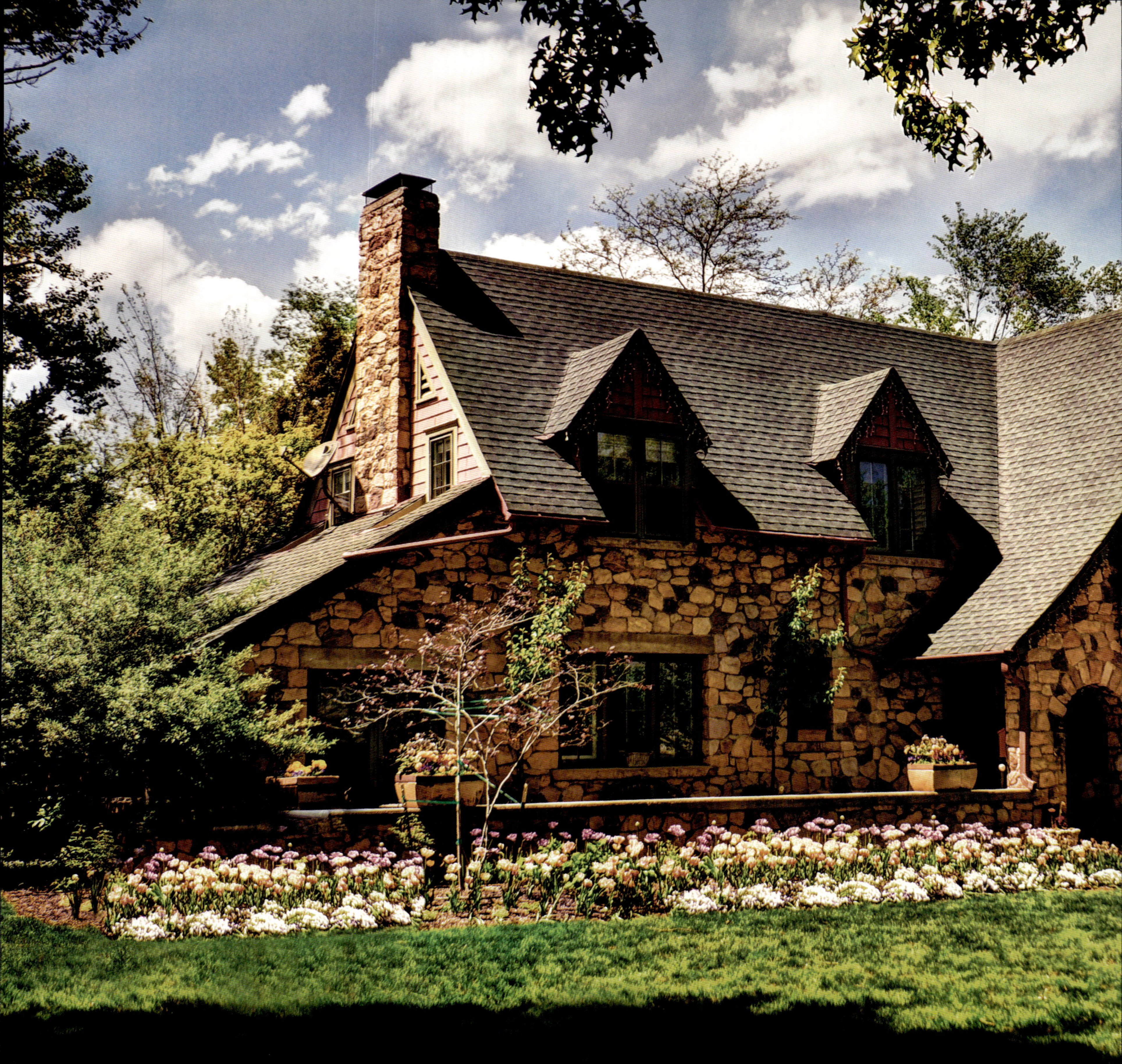

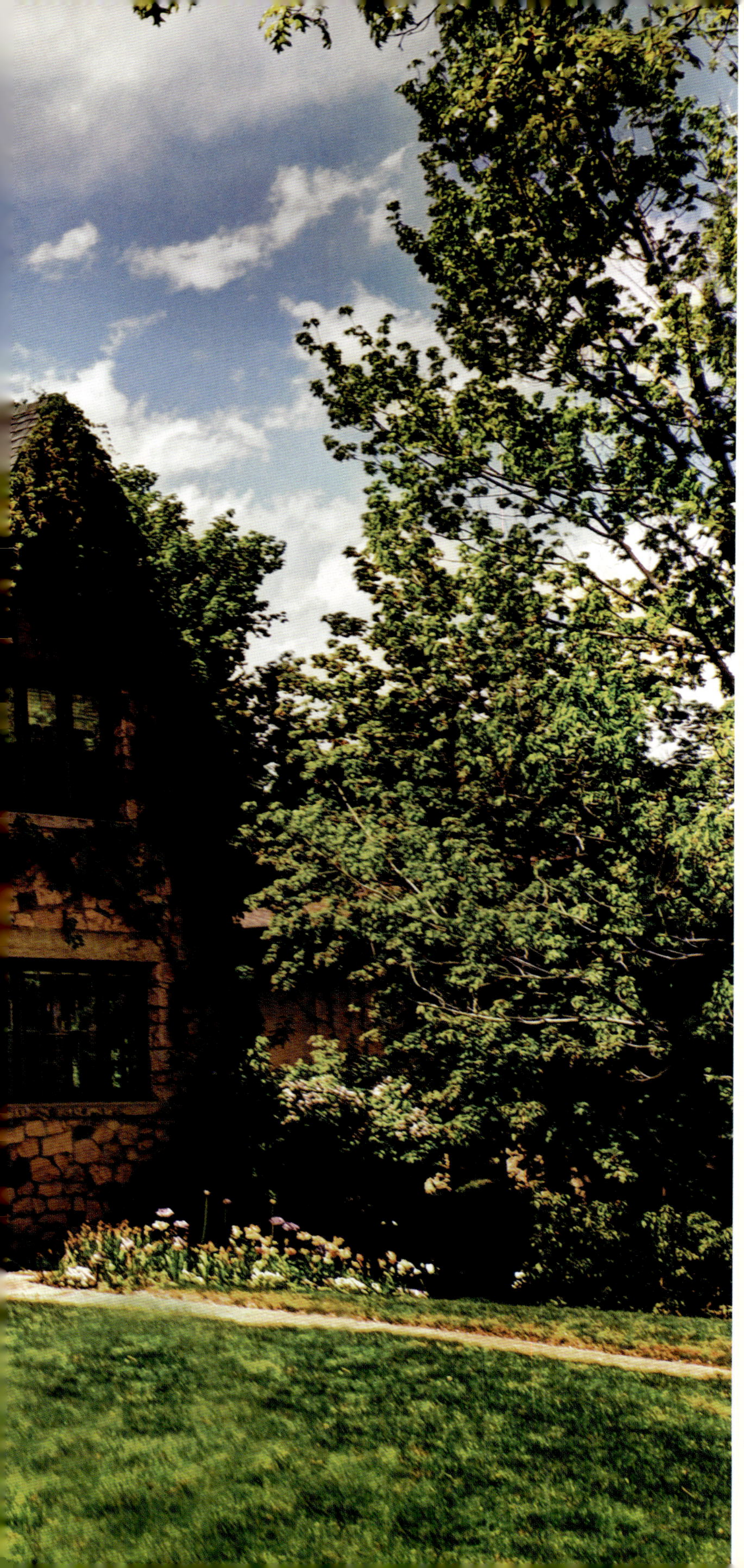

LEFT: This Tudor Revival–style house was designed by Boulder architect Glen H. Huntington and built of local stone in 1923. Its first owner was Ross Whitman, a member of the faculty of the University of Colorado's medical school.

BELOW: In 1903, after hired sharpshooter Tom Horn was (wrongfully) hanged for murder in Cheyenne, Wyoming, his brother brought his body to Boulder for burial. Horn's grave is in the southwestern section of Columbia Cemetery.

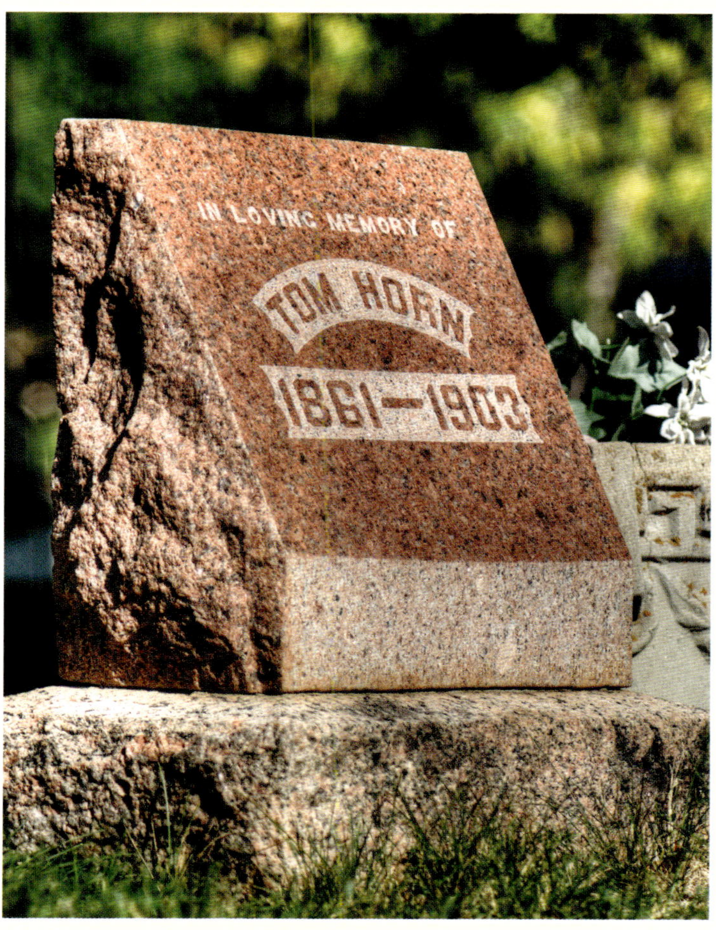

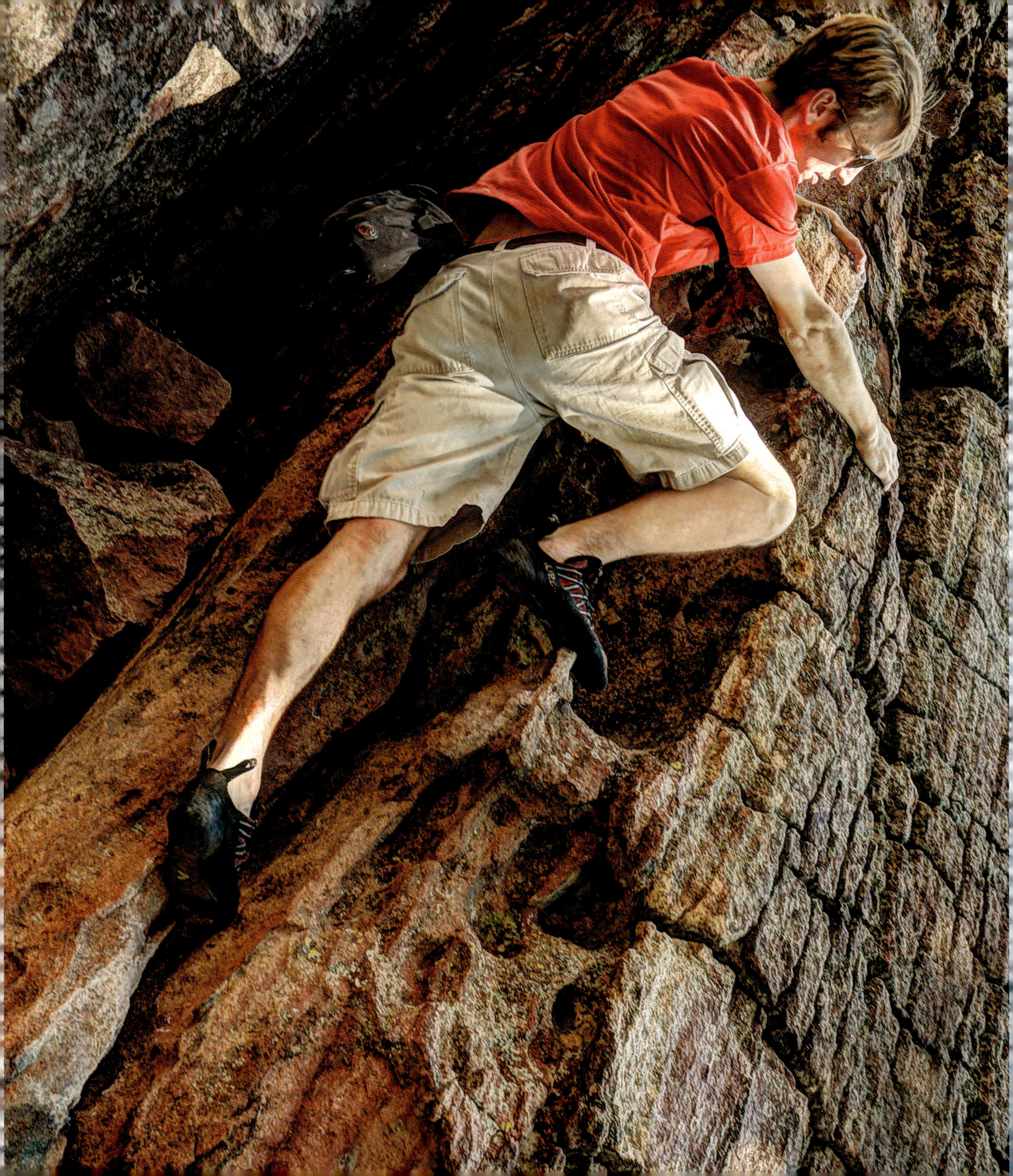

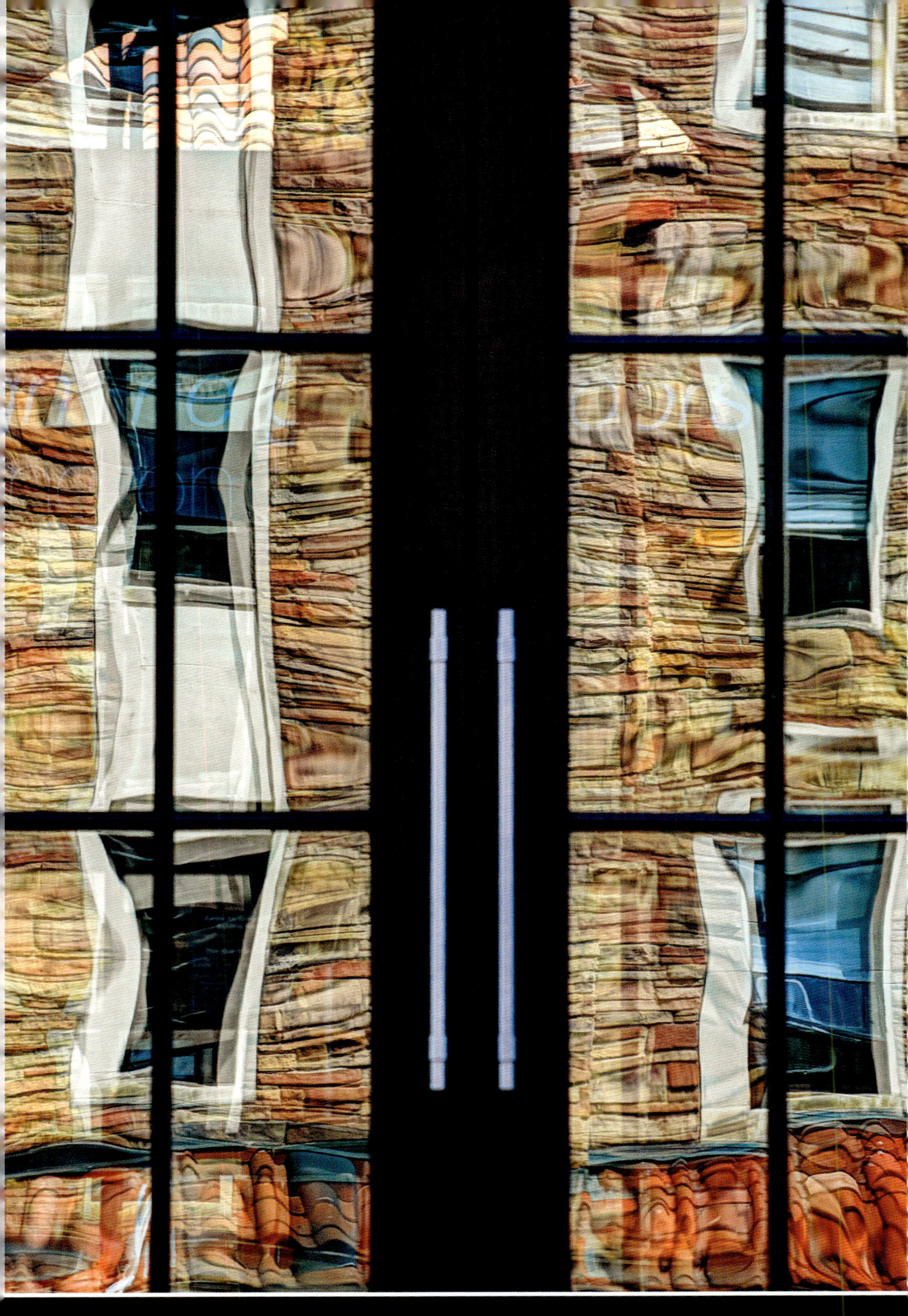

ABOVE: Locally quarried Lyons sandstone—distorted through windows at the University of Colorado—is a popular and colorful building material in Boulder.

FACING PAGE: Using the natural features of the rock, climber Jami Mohlenkamp free solos on the Second Flatiron. *Outside* magazine recently rated Boulder "America's Number One Sports Town in America."

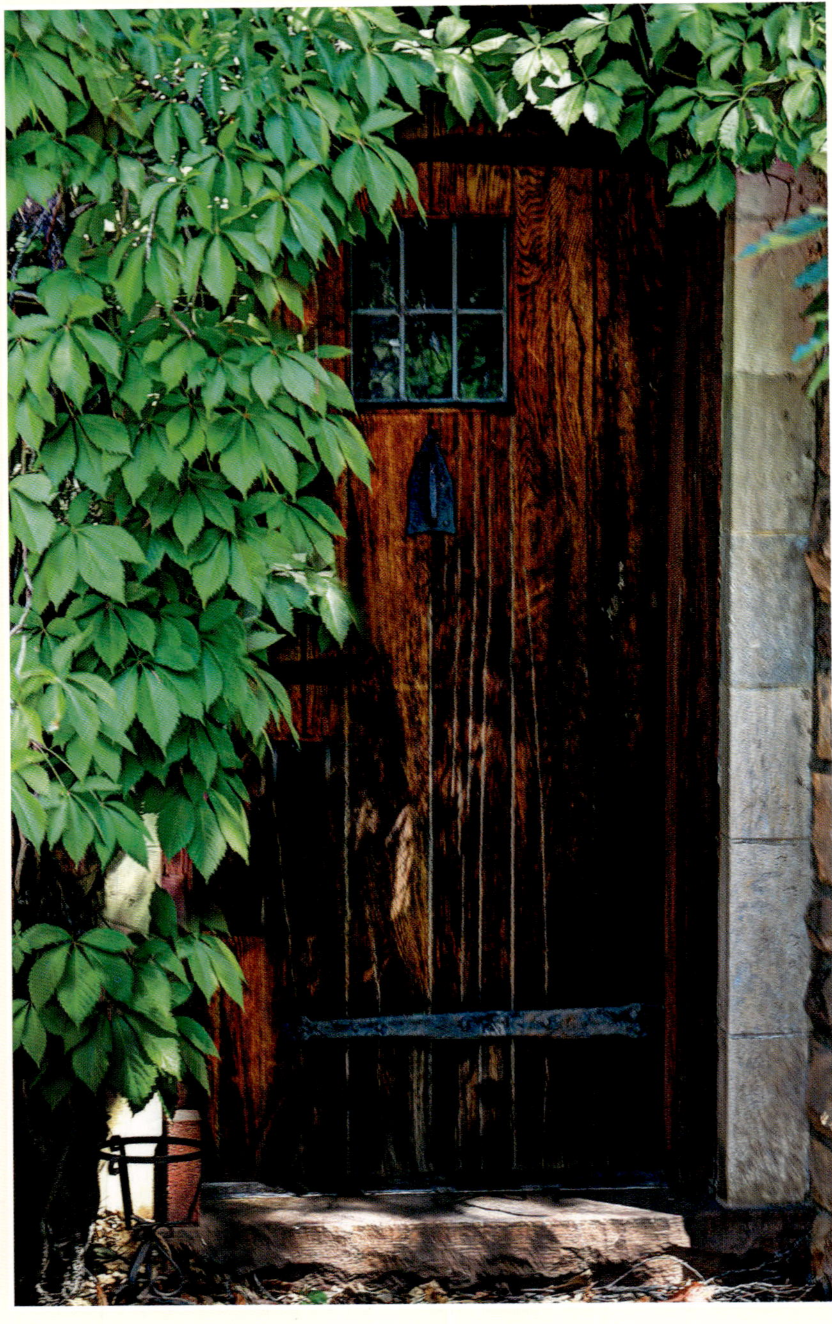

ABOVE: Boulder has a solid historic preservation ordinance, ensuring that architectural details of its historic buildings remain in place for future generations.

RIGHT: A student stretches out for a quick nap, taking advantage of the lush, green grass.

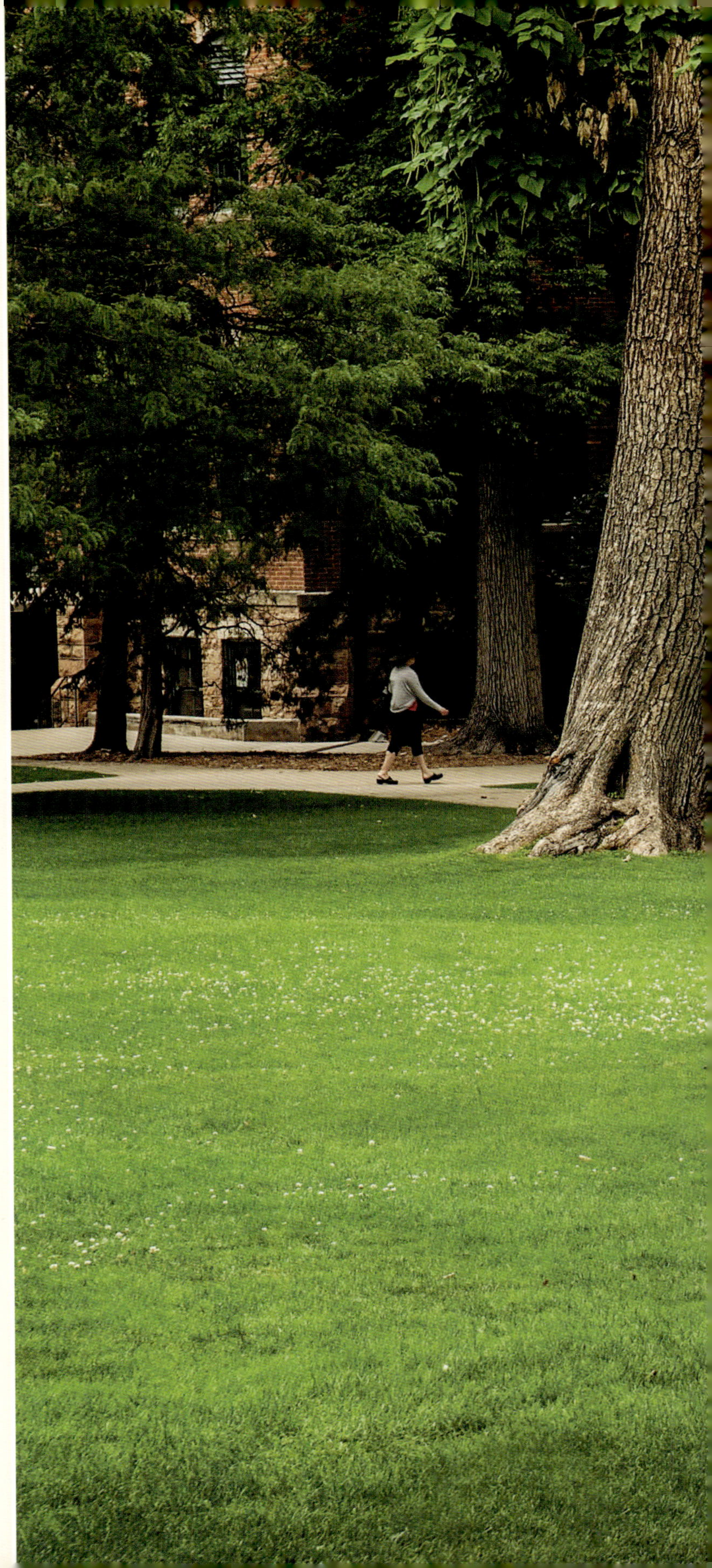

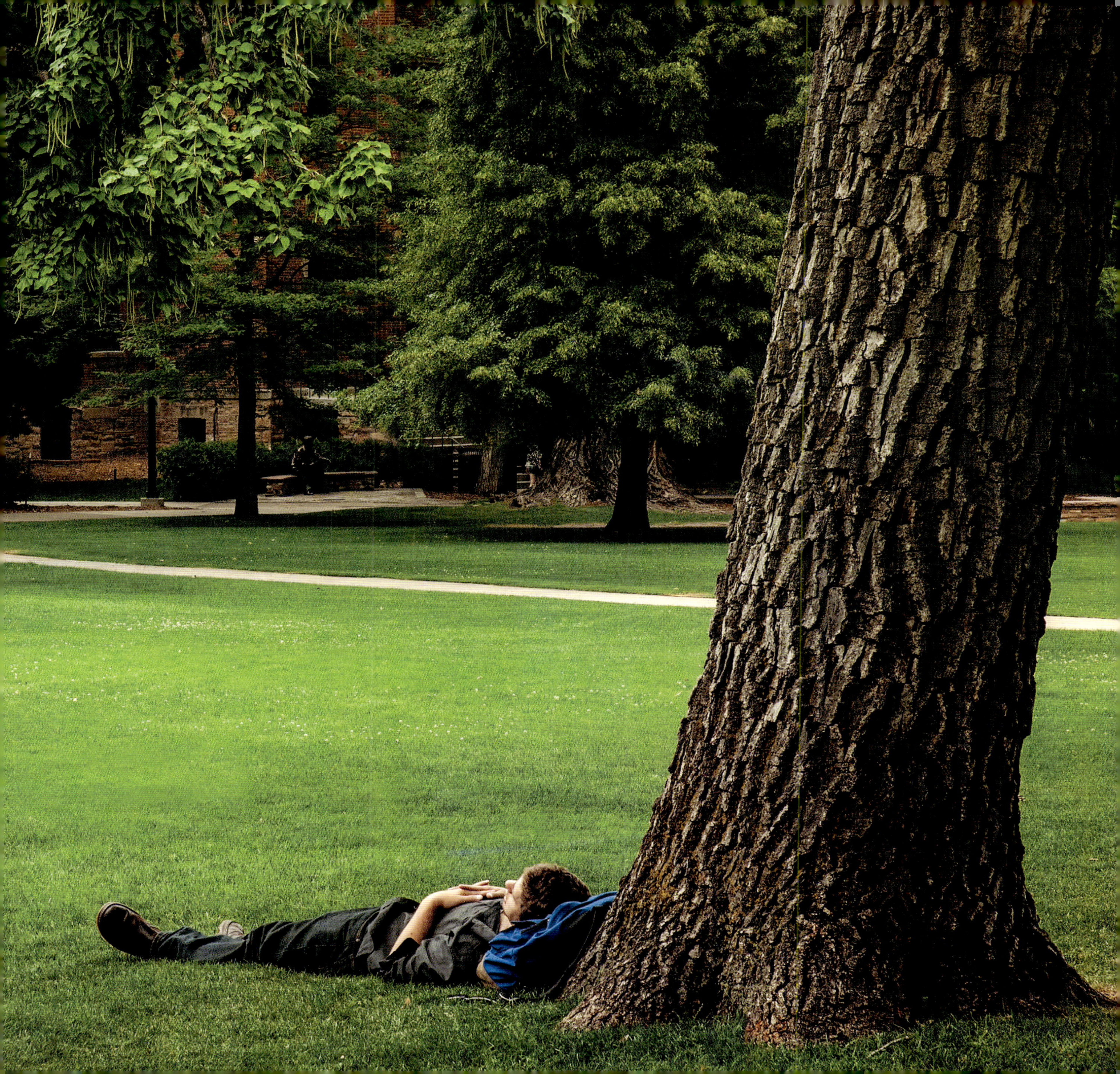

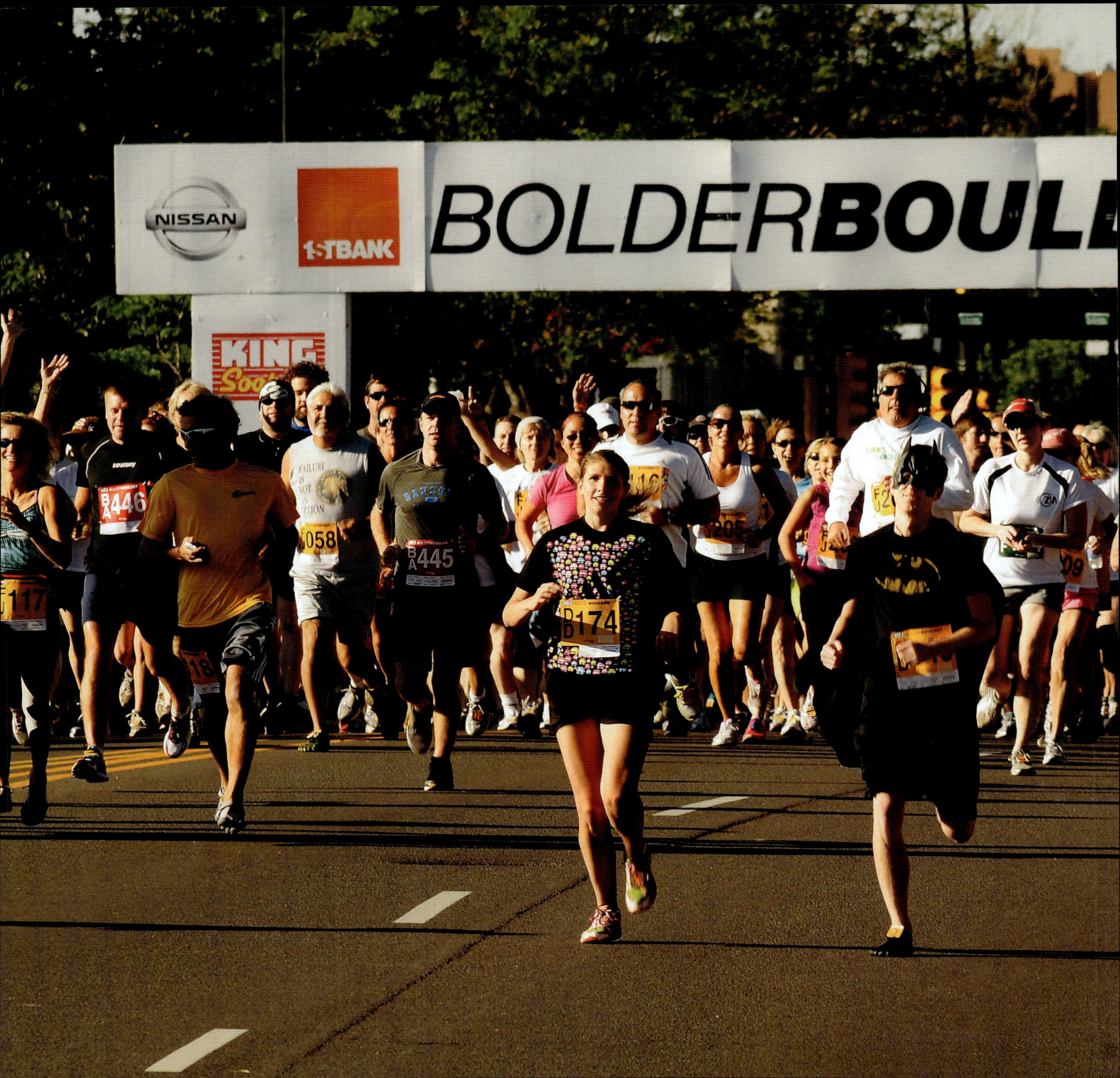

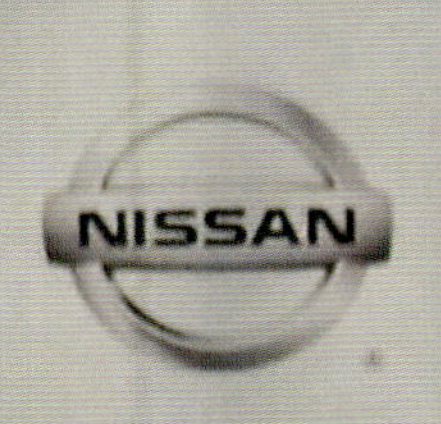
NISSAN

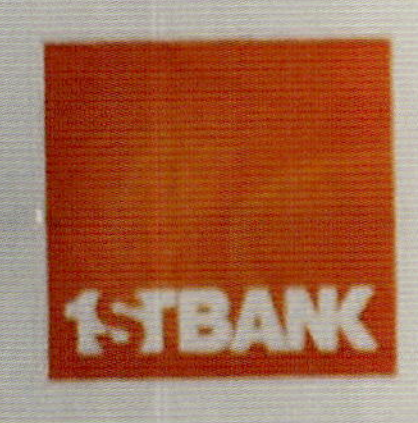
1STBANK

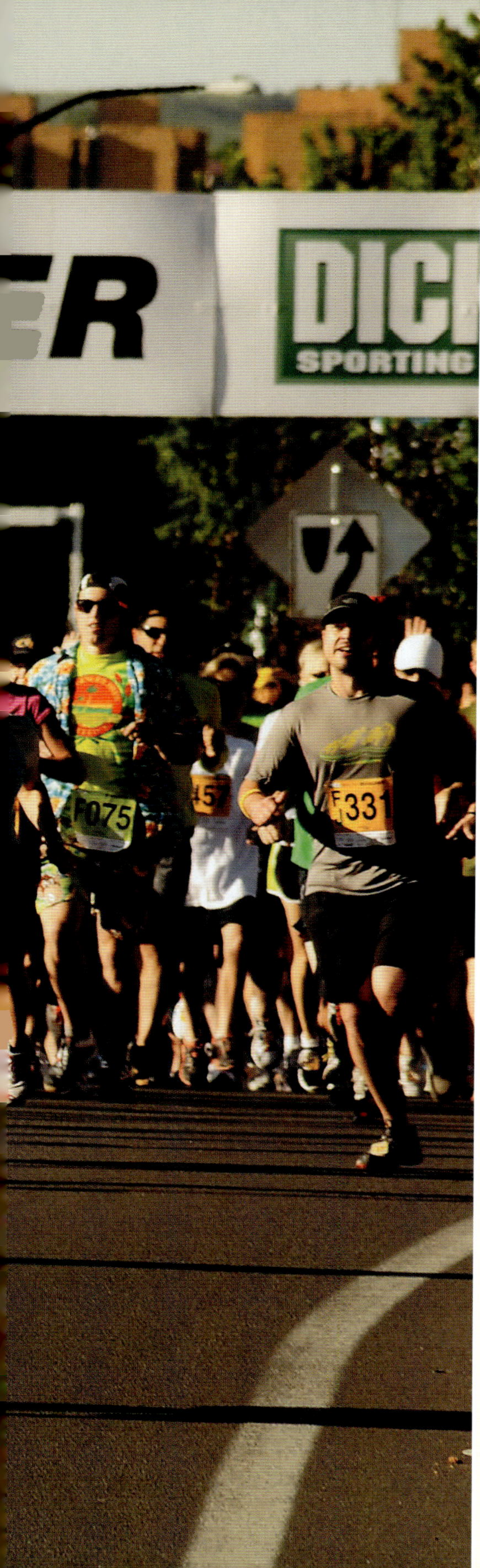

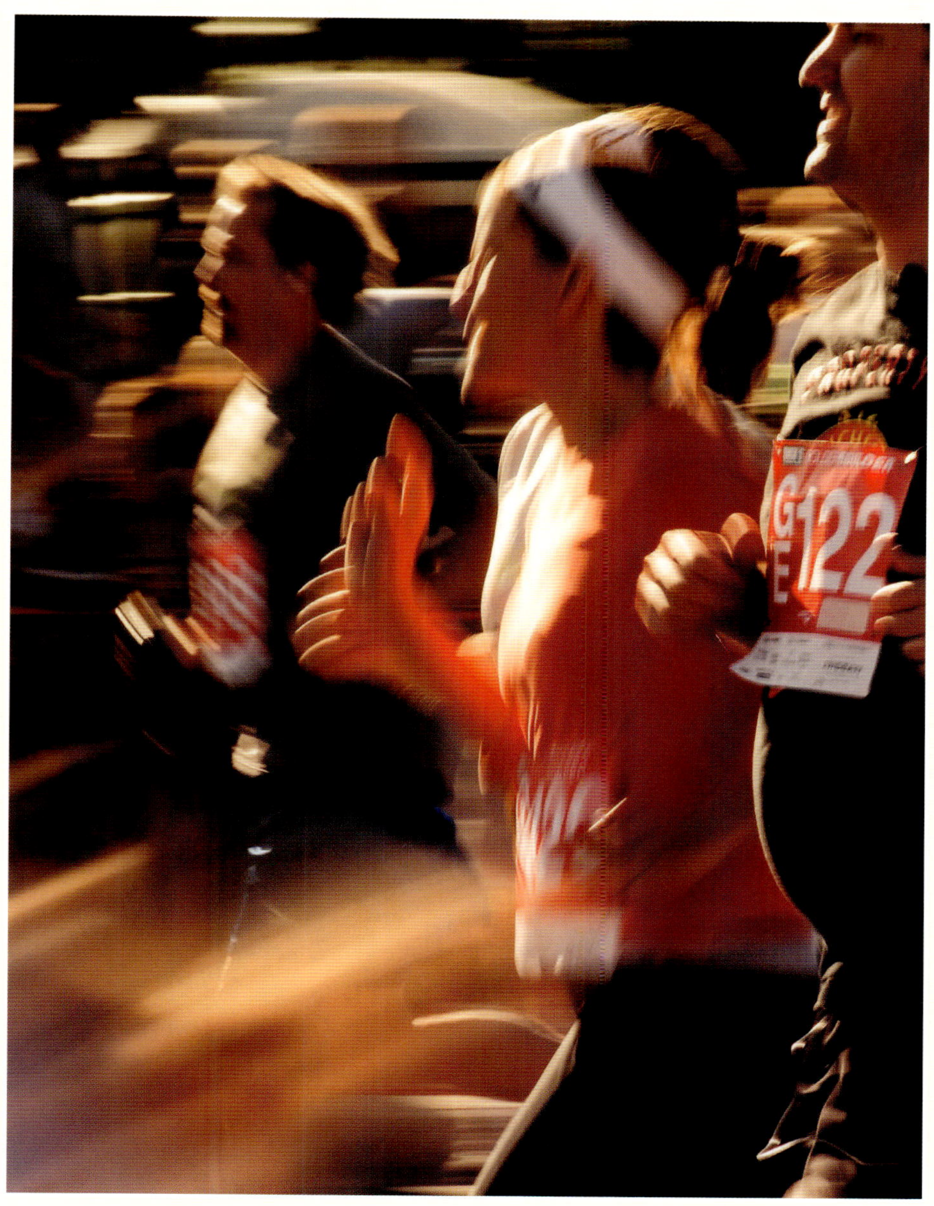

ABOVE AND LEFT: Every Memorial Day since 1979, runners, walkers, and wheelchair racers compete in the Bolder Boulder 10-kilometer road race. In recent years, participants have numbered more than 50,000.

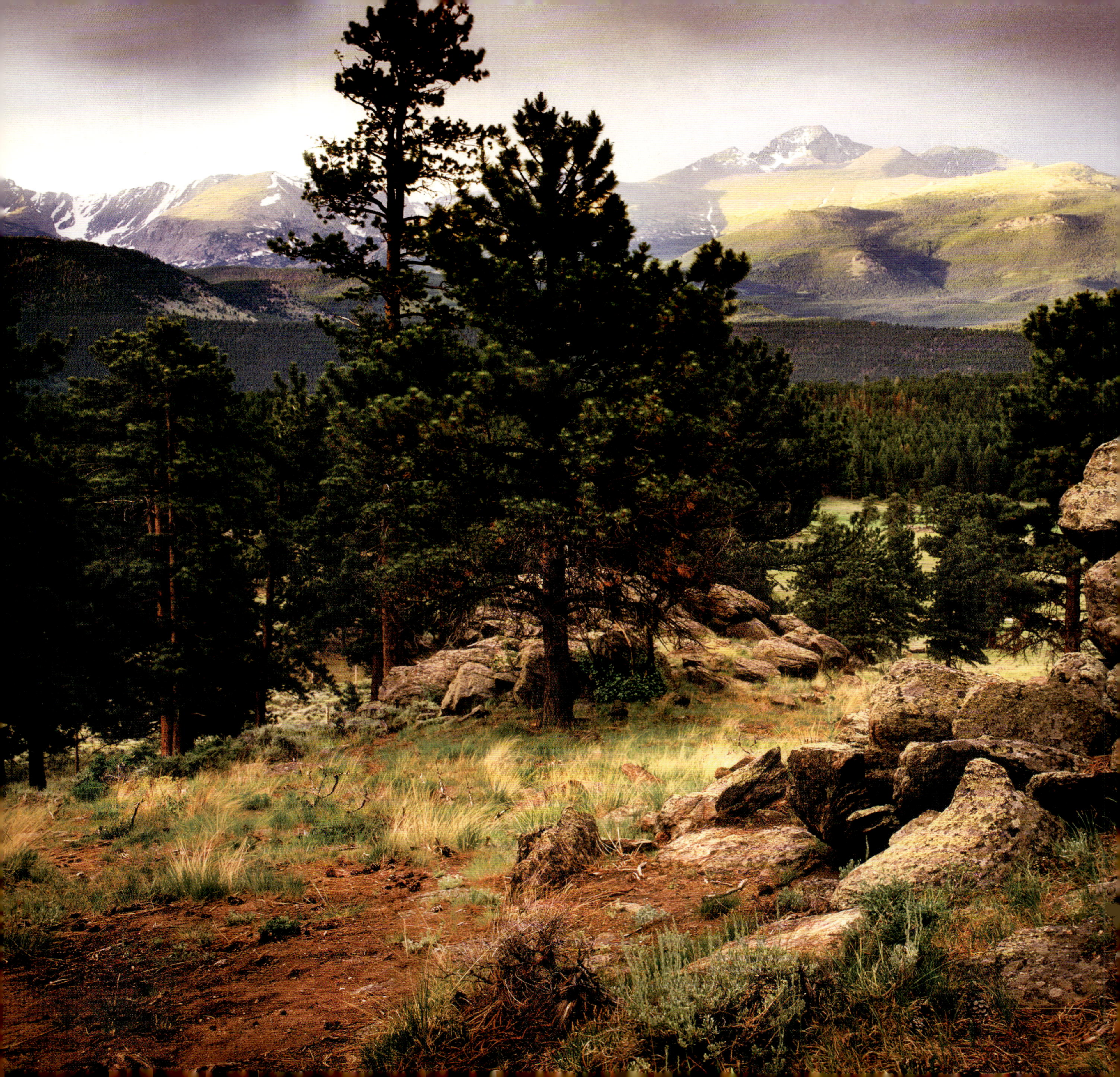

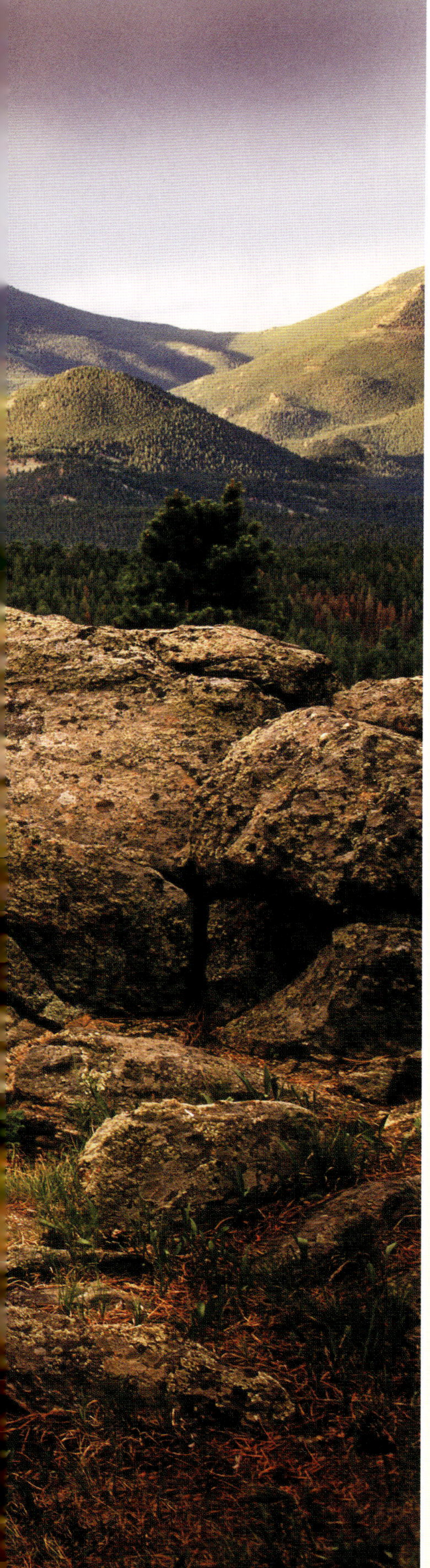

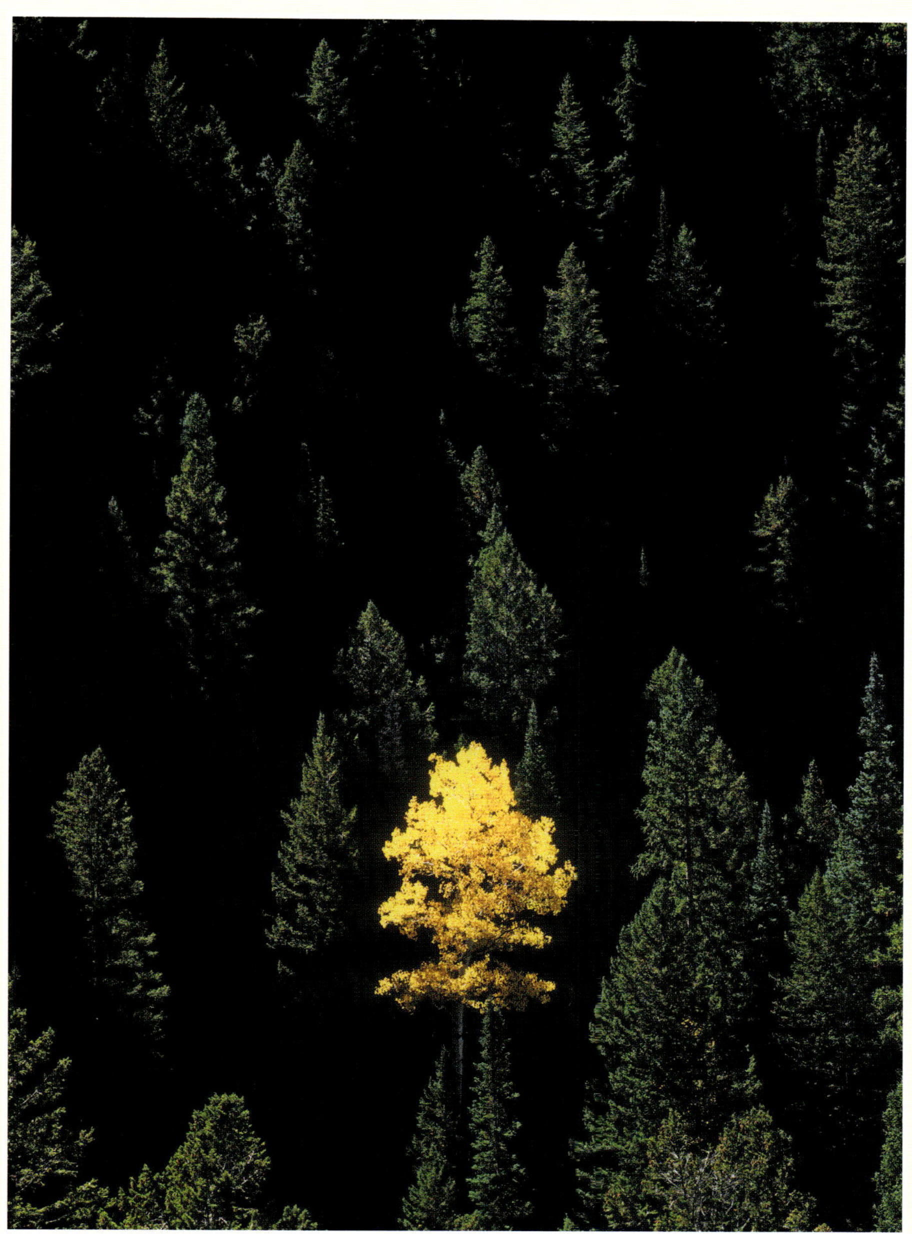

ABOVE: A brilliant yellow aspen stands alone in a forest of evergreens.

LEFT: Catching the day's first rays of sun, Longs Peak, at 14,259 feet in elevation, sits just within the northwestern boundary of Boulder County. Although Colorado has 55 peaks that are more than 14,000 feet in elevation, the only other fourteeners on the Front Range are Grays Peak, Torreys Peak, Pikes Peak, Mount Bierstadt, and Mount Evans.

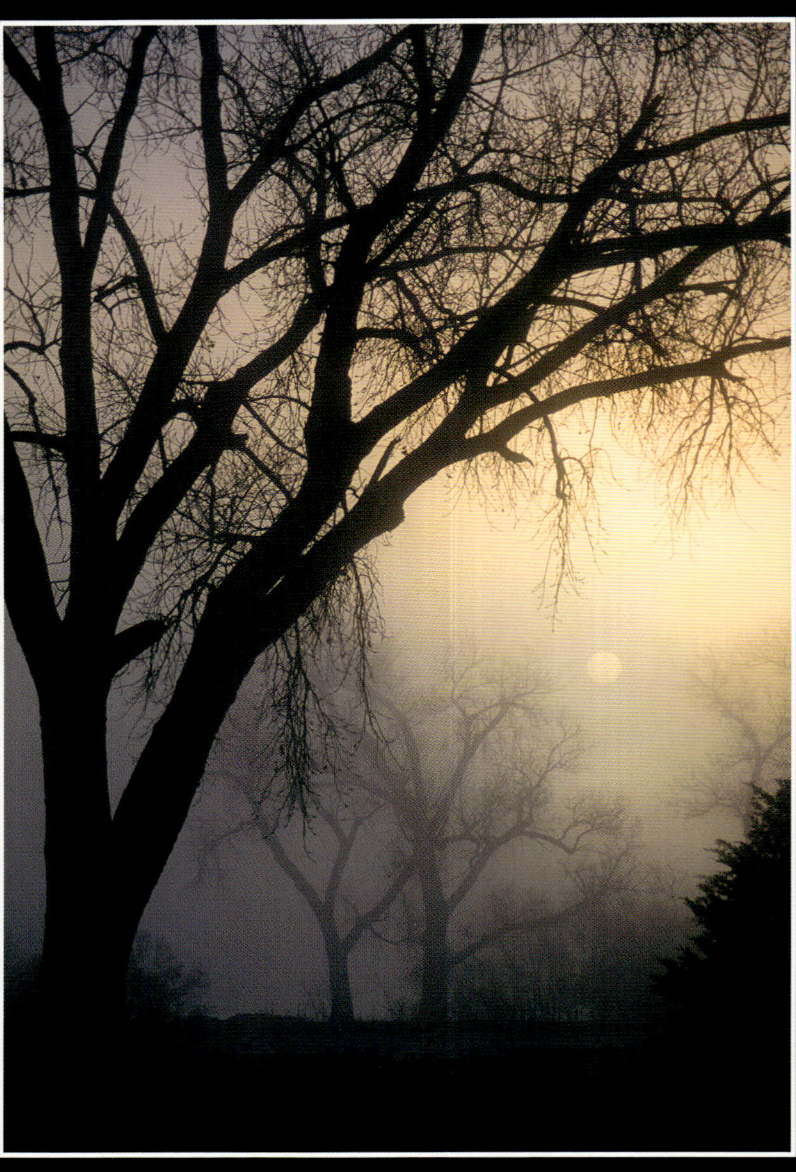

ABOVE: Foggy mornings in Boulder are few and far between.

RIGHT: Sunlight cuts through the day's mist while softening the light in this cold spring scene.

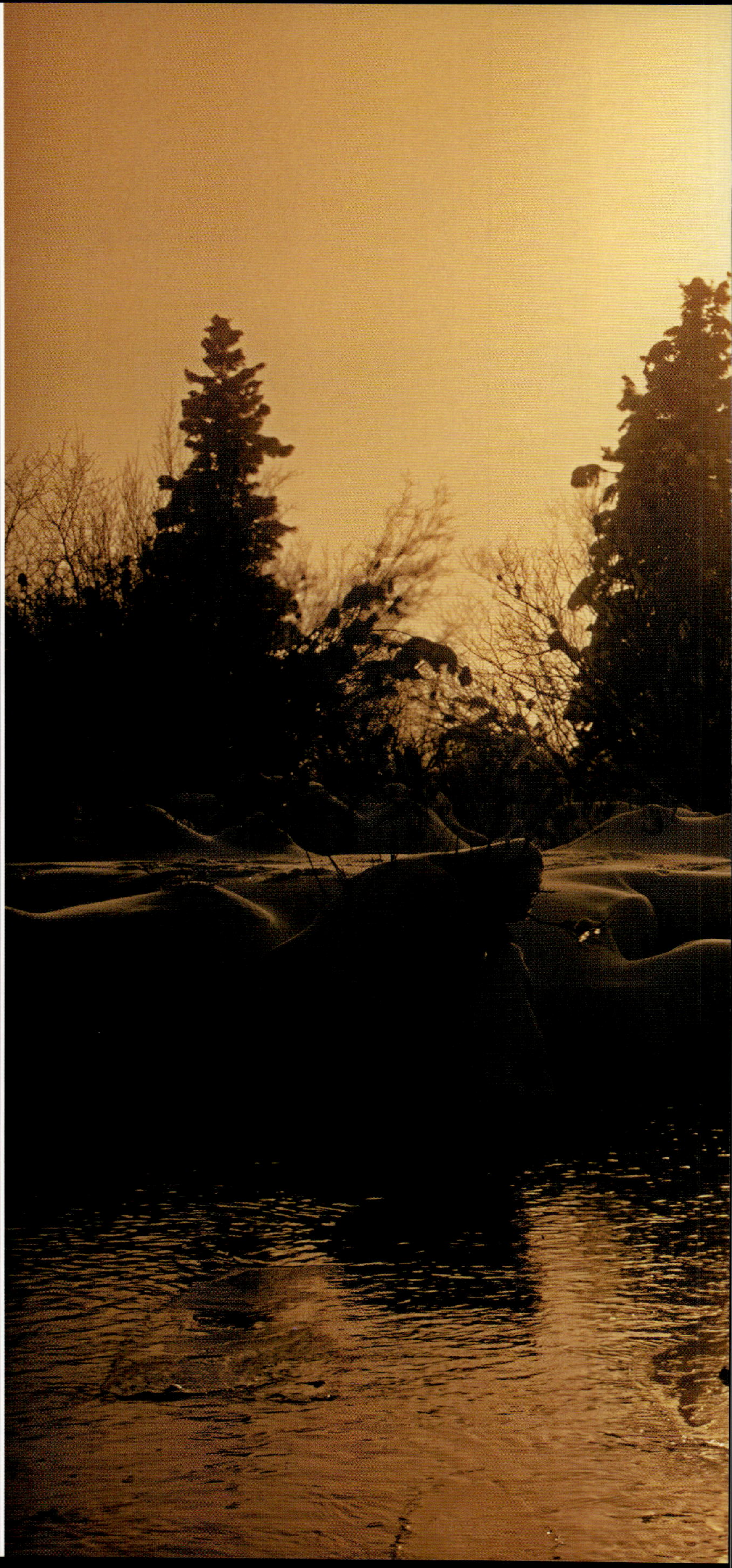

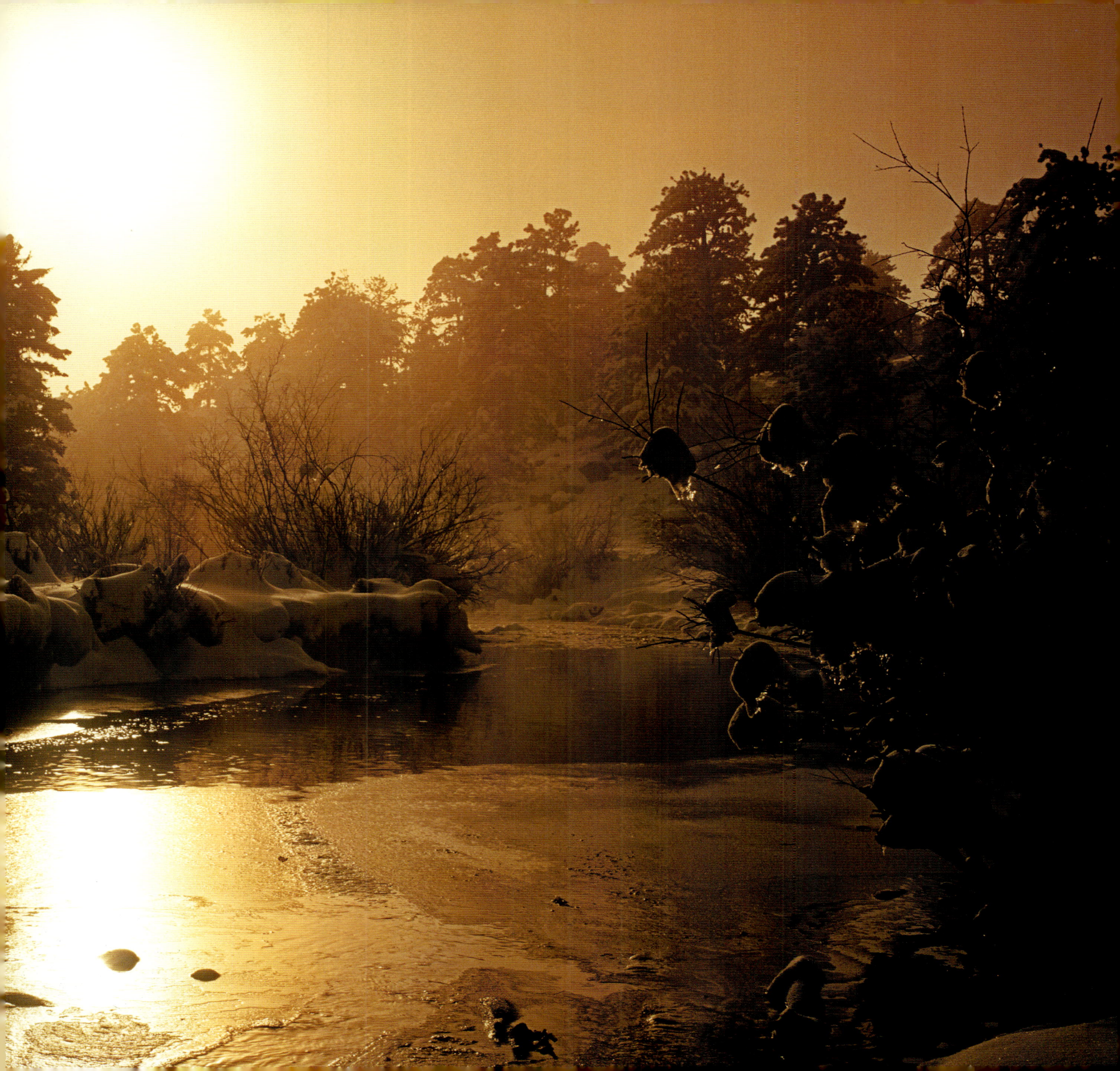

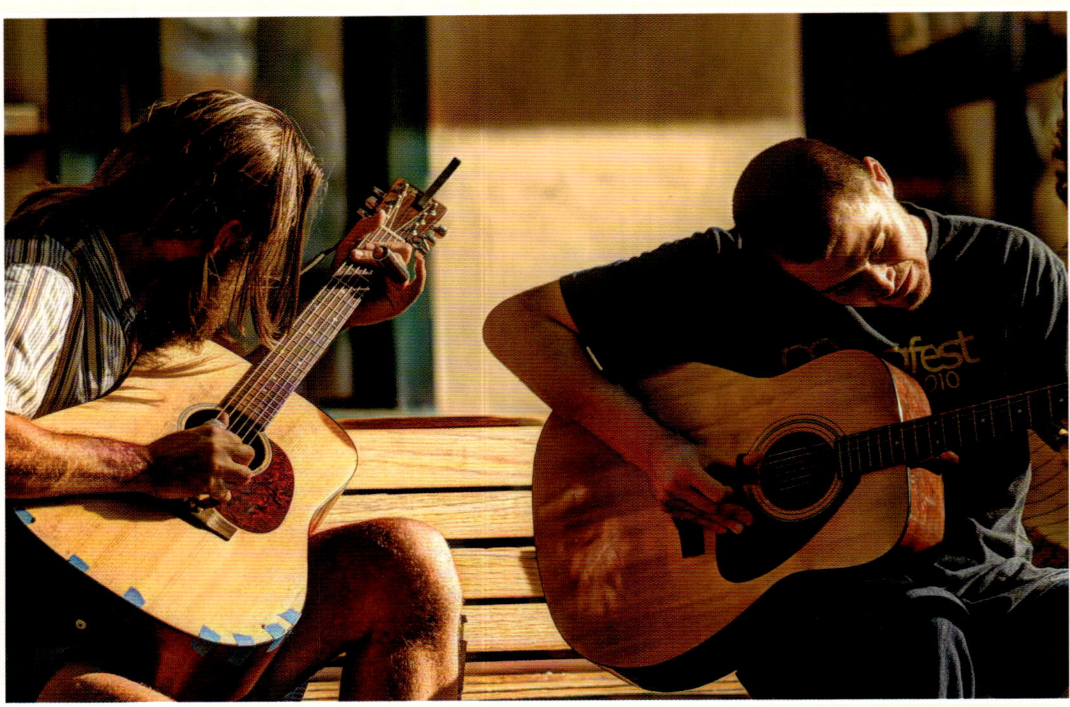

ABOVE: Bluegrass musicians and fans come to Lyons from all over the country.

RIGHT: Evening light illuminates Lyons, a small town in northern Boulder County. Within the past decade, the town has emerged as the bluegrass mecca of the West. Lyons is home to roots-music giant Planet Bluegrass, producer of events that include the Telluride Bluegrass Festival.

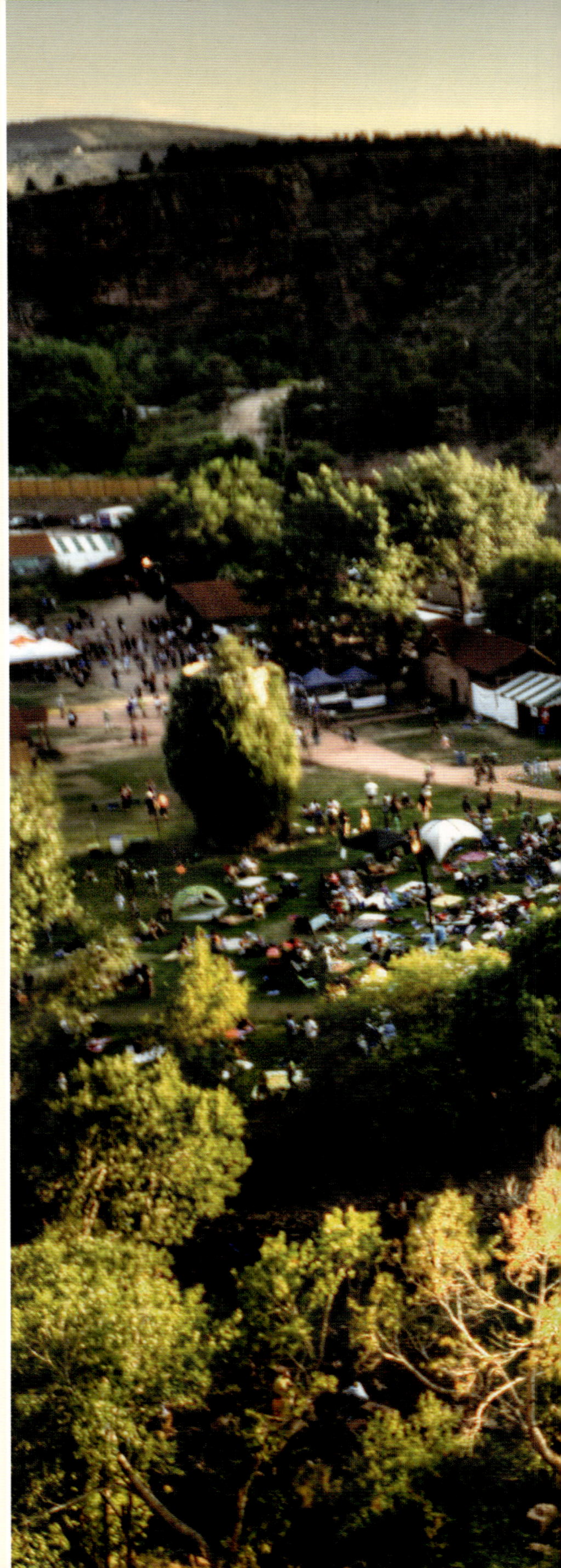

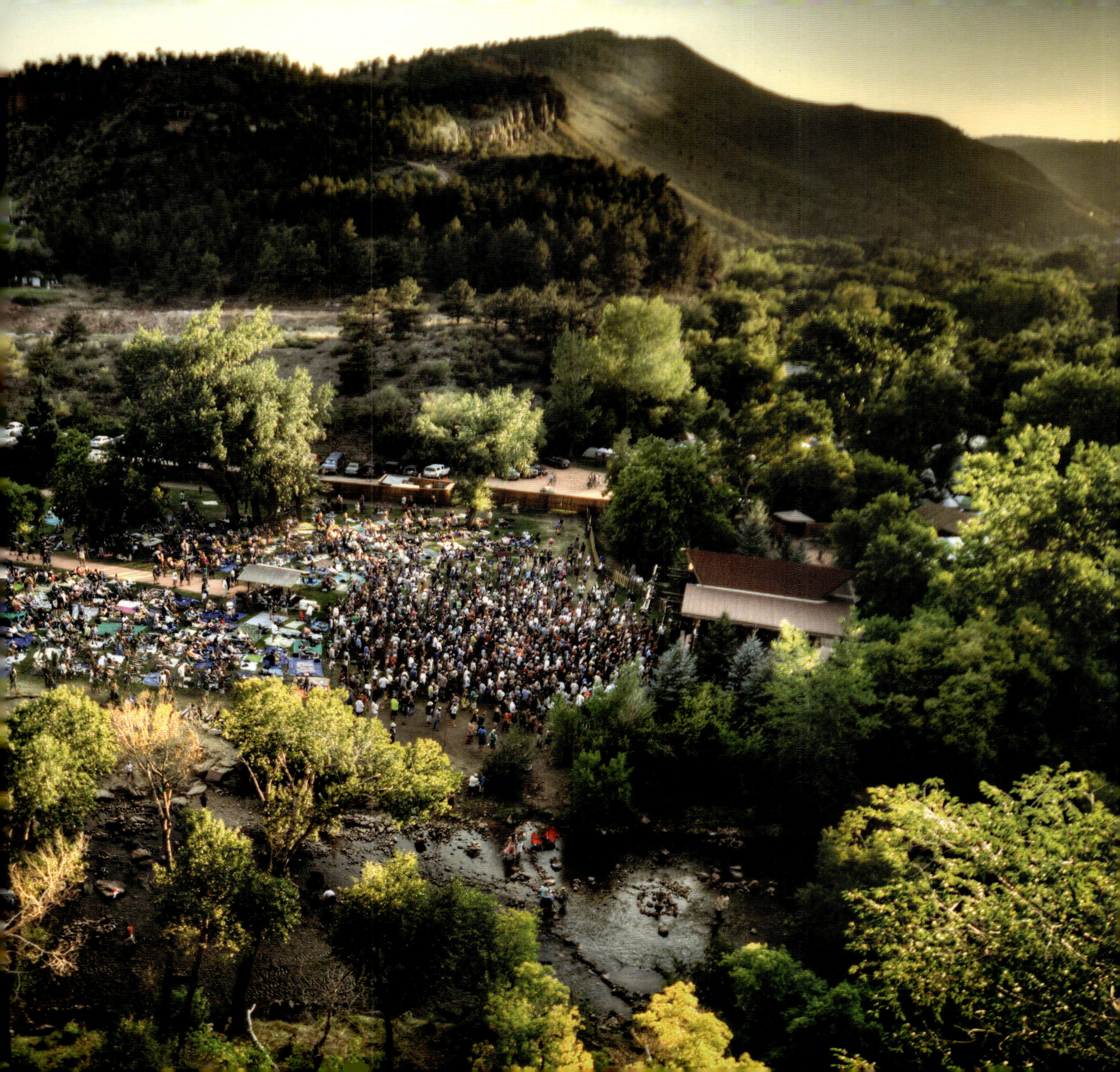

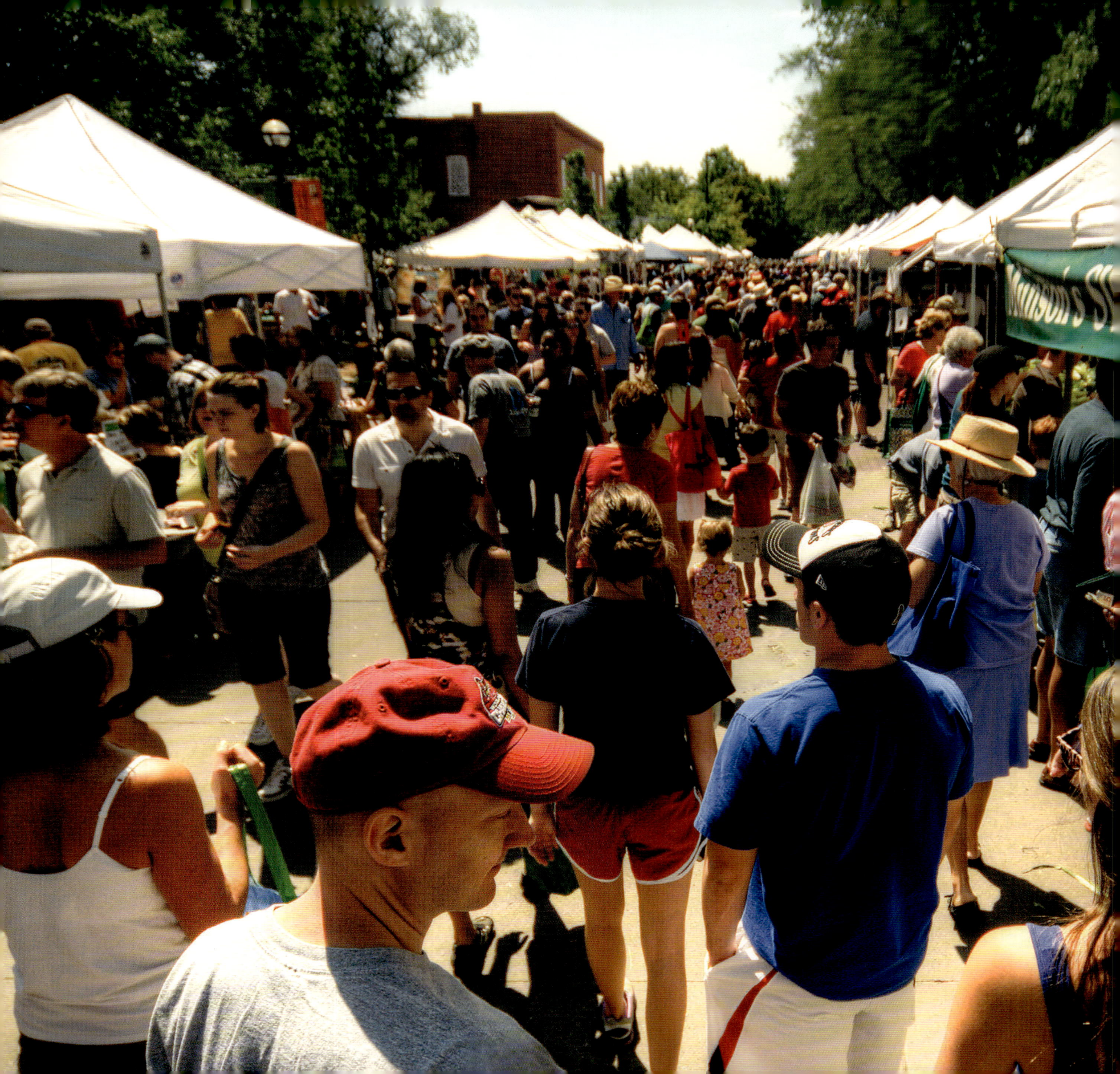

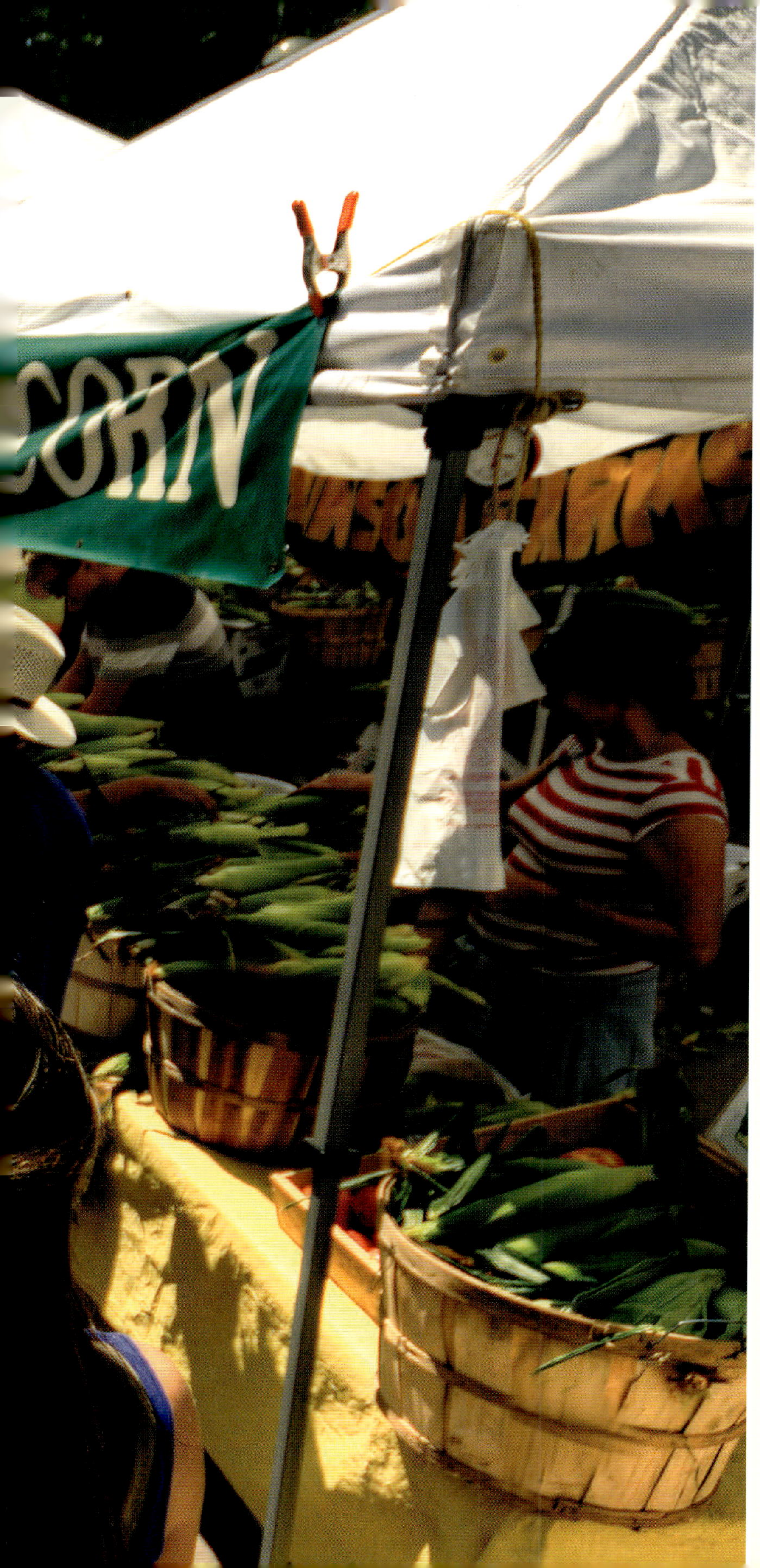

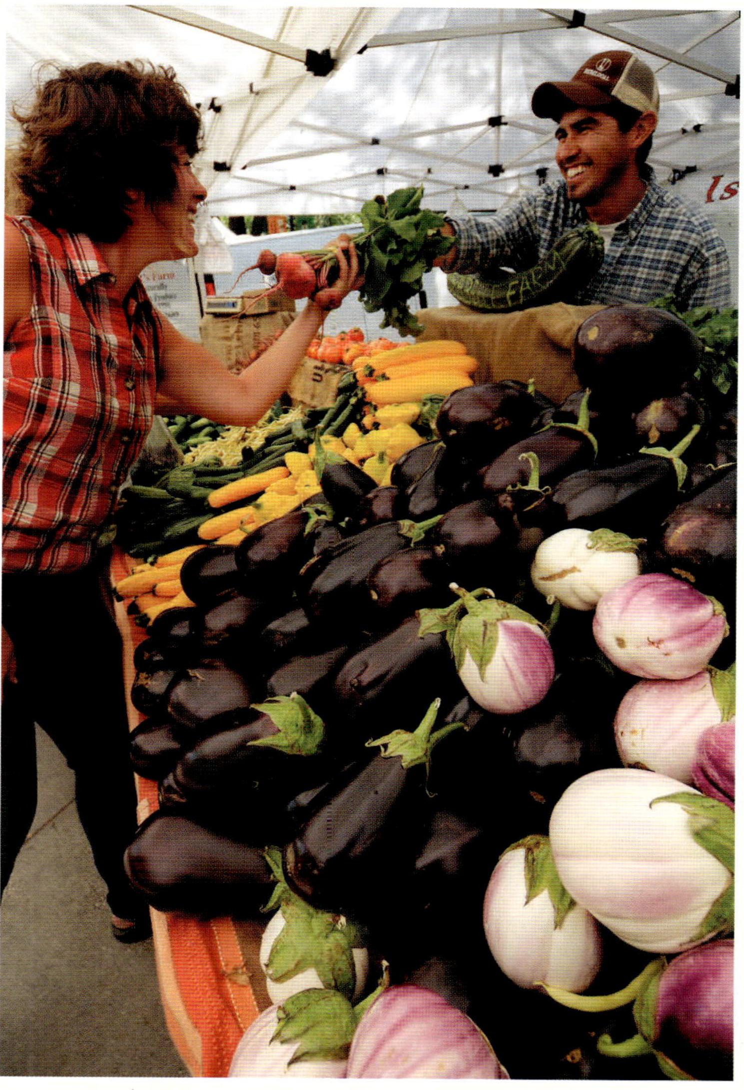

ABOVE: This shopper takes advantage of a bountiful harvest that is as fresh as could be.

LEFT: From mid-spring to mid-fall, the Boulder County Farmers' Market is a community-gathering place where local farmers sell vegetables, meats, fruits, flowers, plants, wines, and gourmet cheeses that they grow and produce.

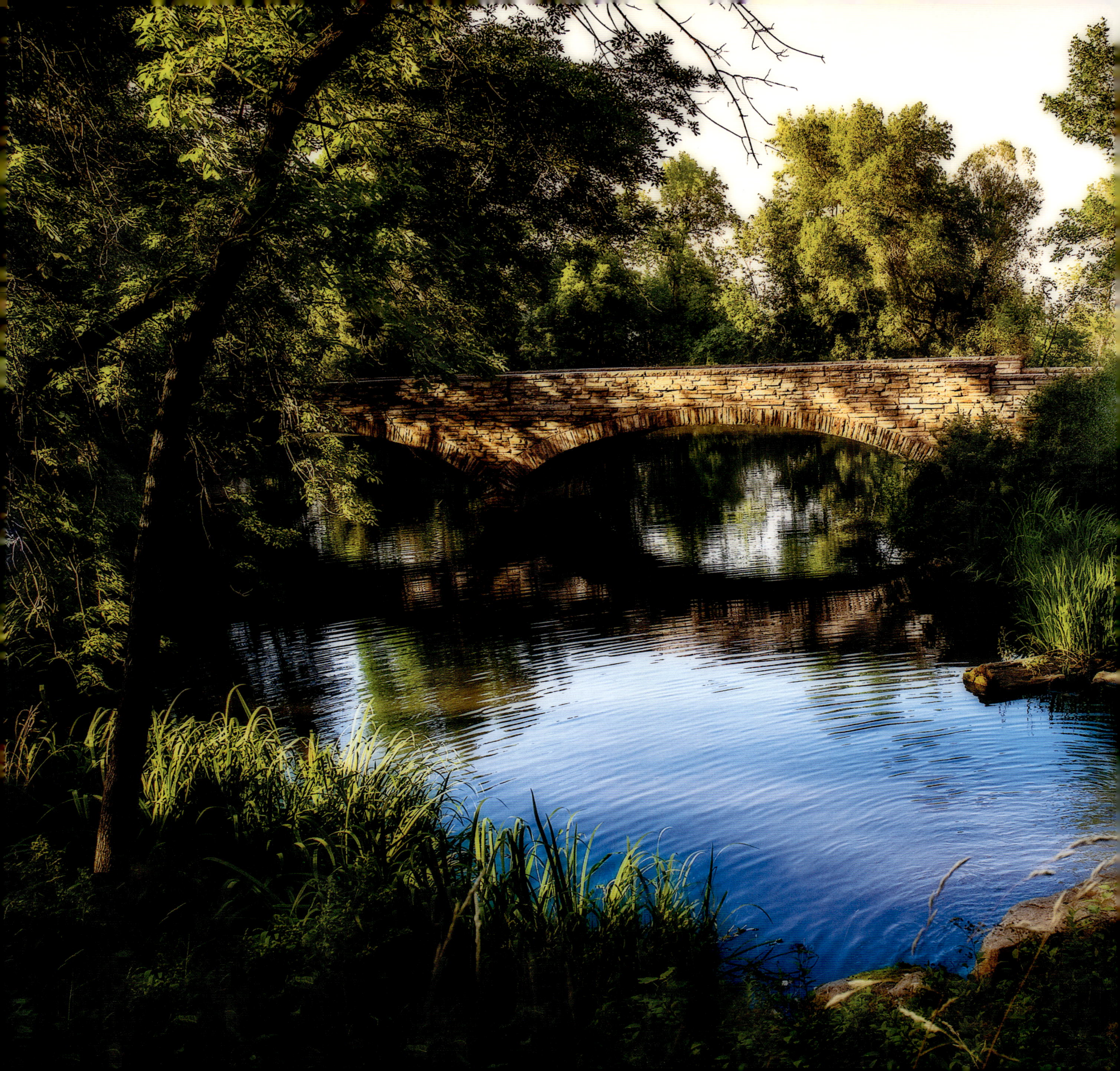

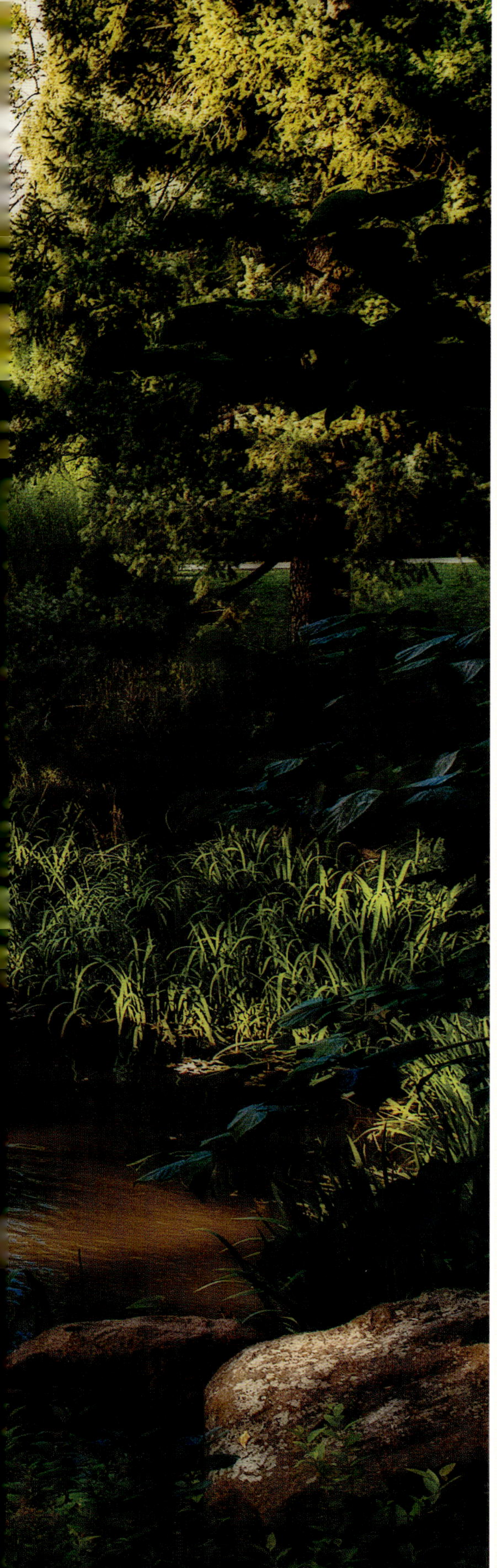

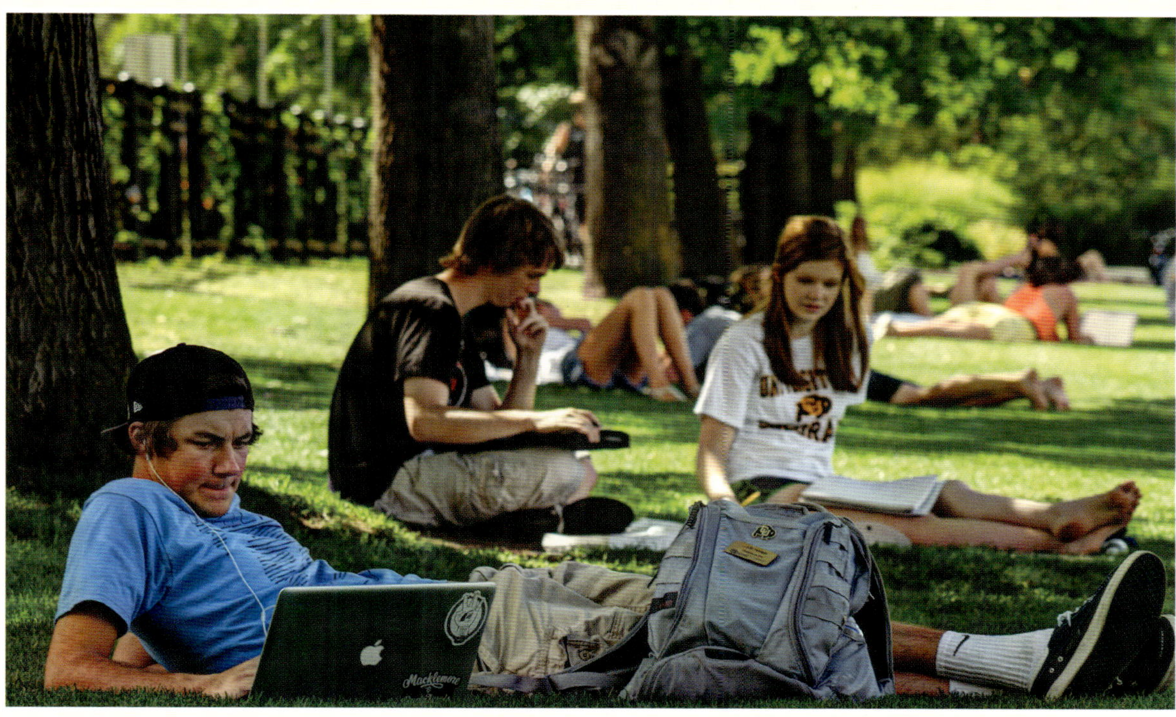

ABOVE: Today's University of Colorado-Boulder students relax and study on a lush campus, but it hasn't always been green. In CU's early days, the land was a barren mesa; every tree growing on the campus today was planted since the university's founding in 1877.

LEFT: Varsity Pond, originally a dammed-up ravine, provides CU students, staffers, and the public an idyllic place to escape.

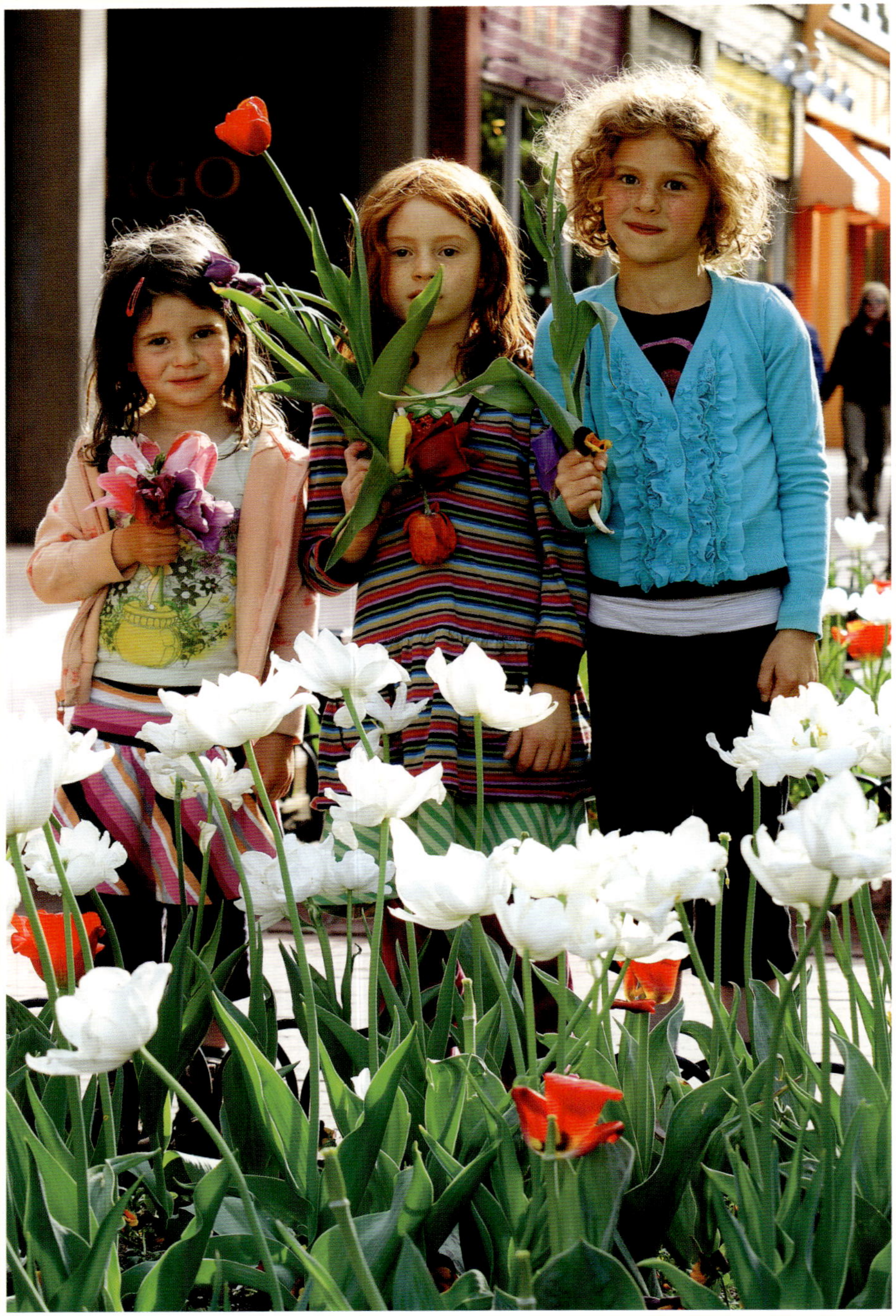

ABOVE: The sweet fragrance of tulips bring out admirers, and the efforts of the City of Boulder's Parks and Recreation Department pay off every spring when tulips burst into bloom on the Pearl Street Mall. Annually, the city staff plants 15,000 bulbs imported from Holland.

RIGHT: The first wheat crop in Boulder County was harvested in 1860. Although agriculture no longer is a large part of Boulder's economy, wheat and other crops are still grown in the county today.

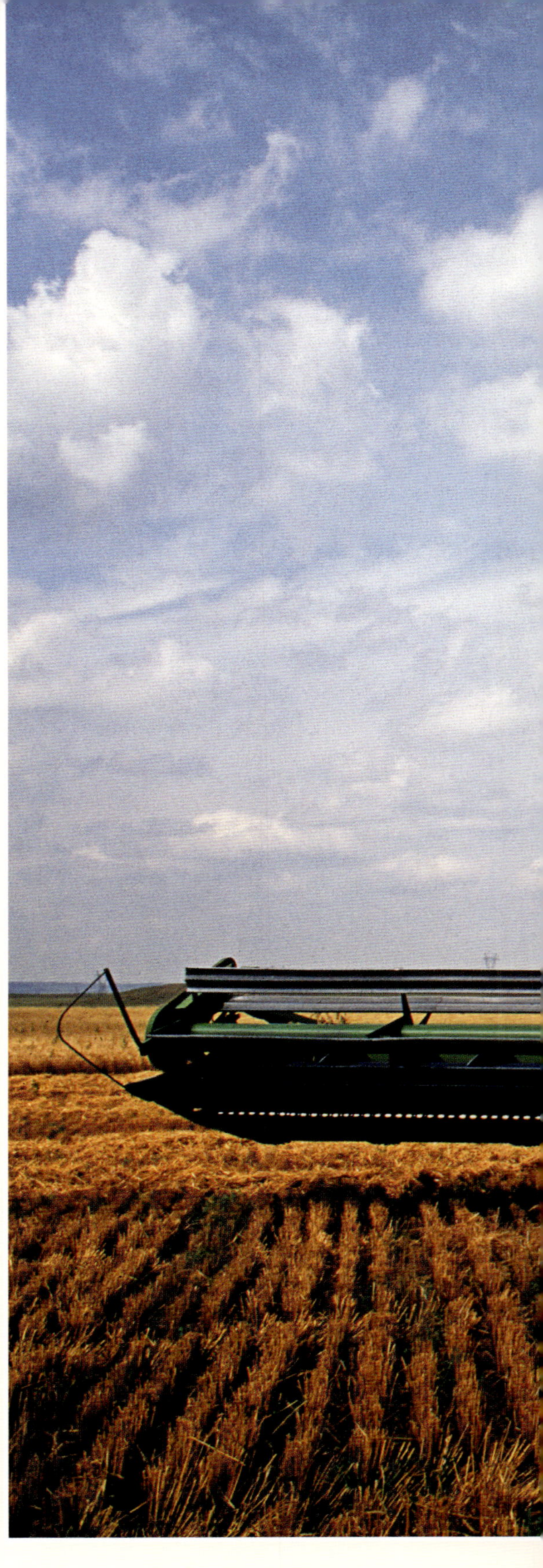

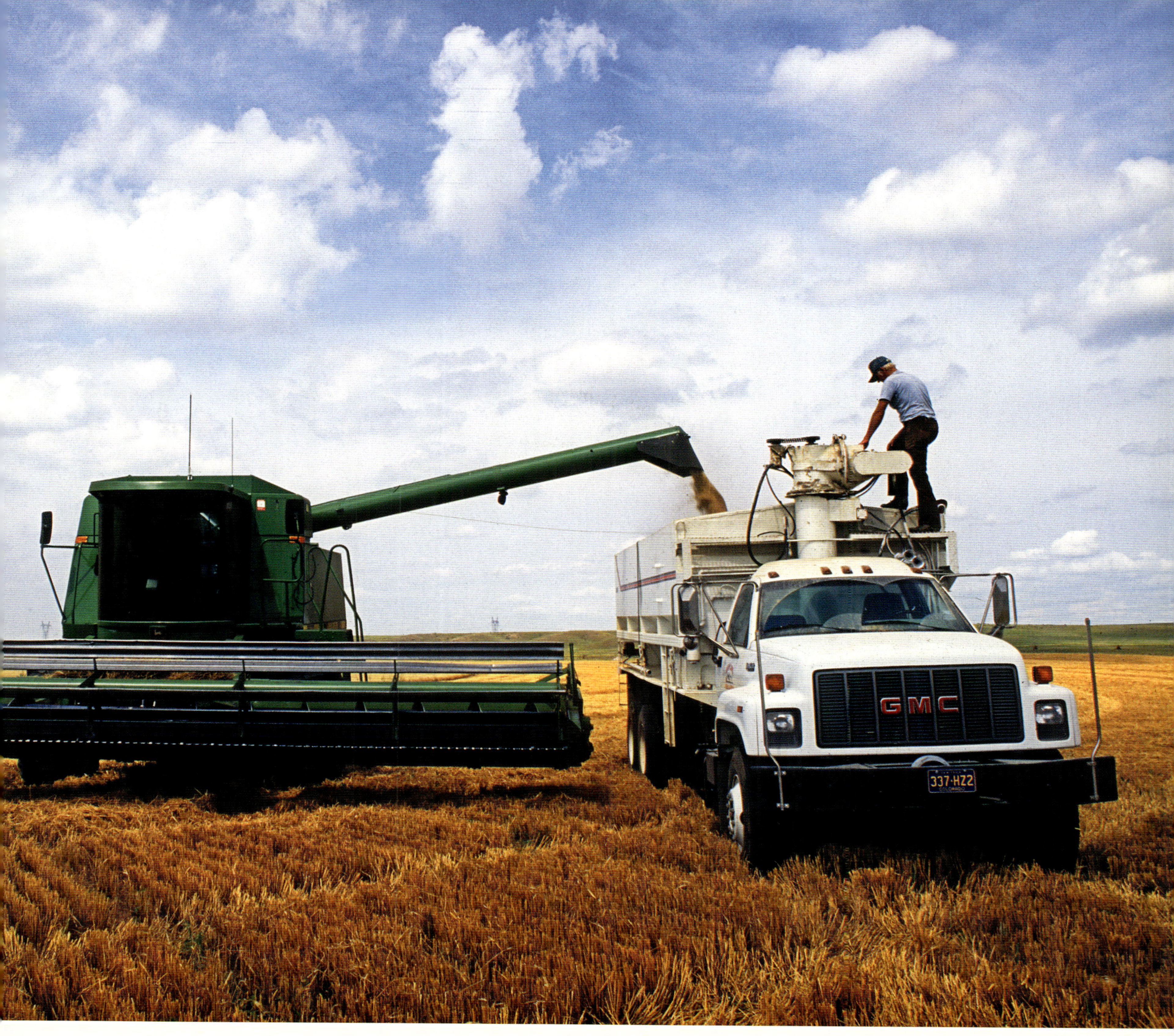
GMC
337·HZ2

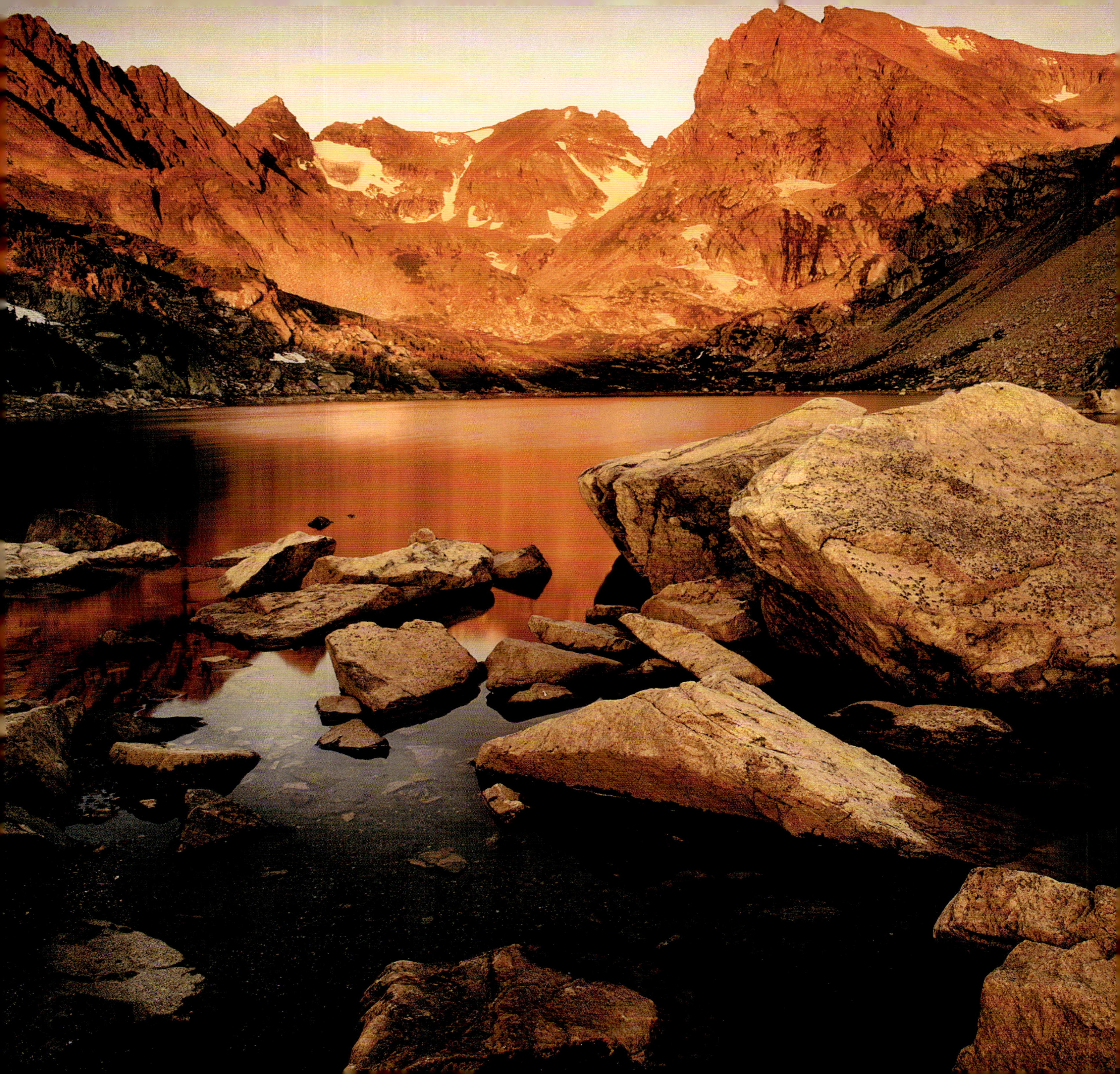

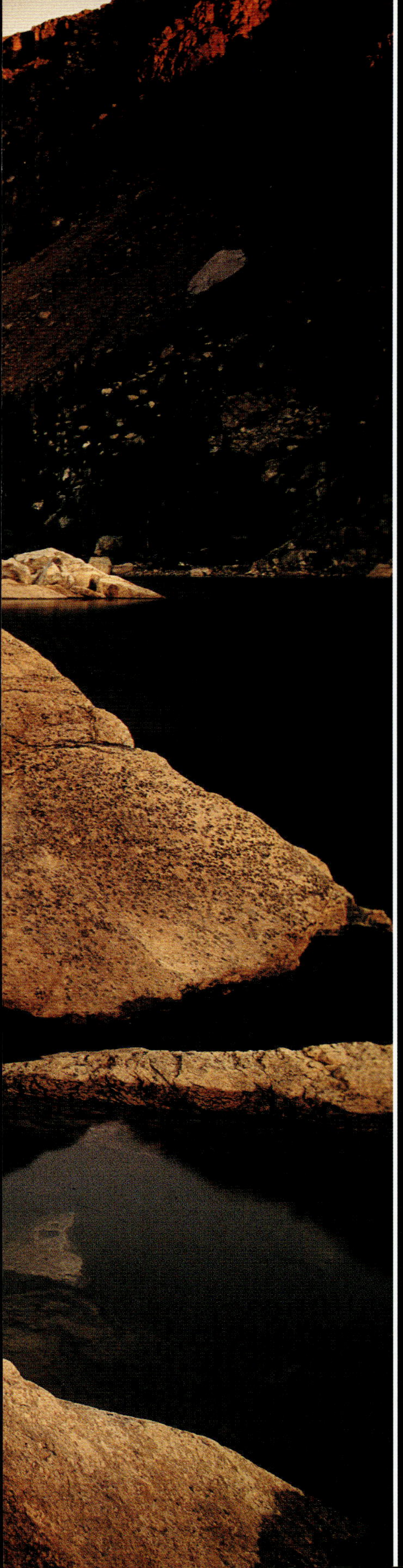

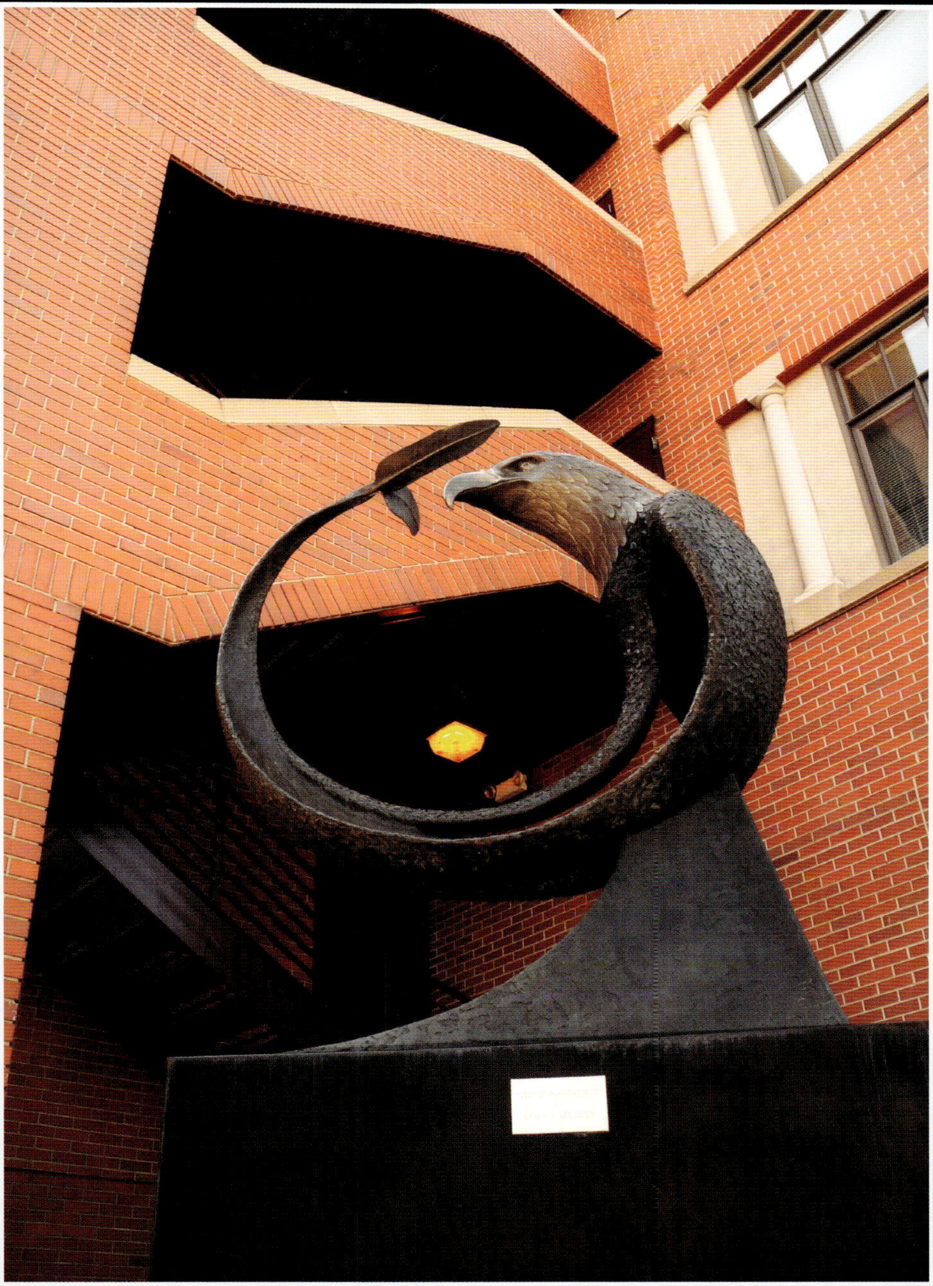

ABOVE: Boulder is adorned with art such as this intriguing sculpture—*Standing Proud* by Chuck Weaver.

LEFT: Lake Isabelle is a paternoster lake—uppermost in a chain of lakes carved out by the Isabelle Glacier. The lake is accessed by the Long Lake Trailhead in the Brainard Lake Recreation Area, west of Ward.

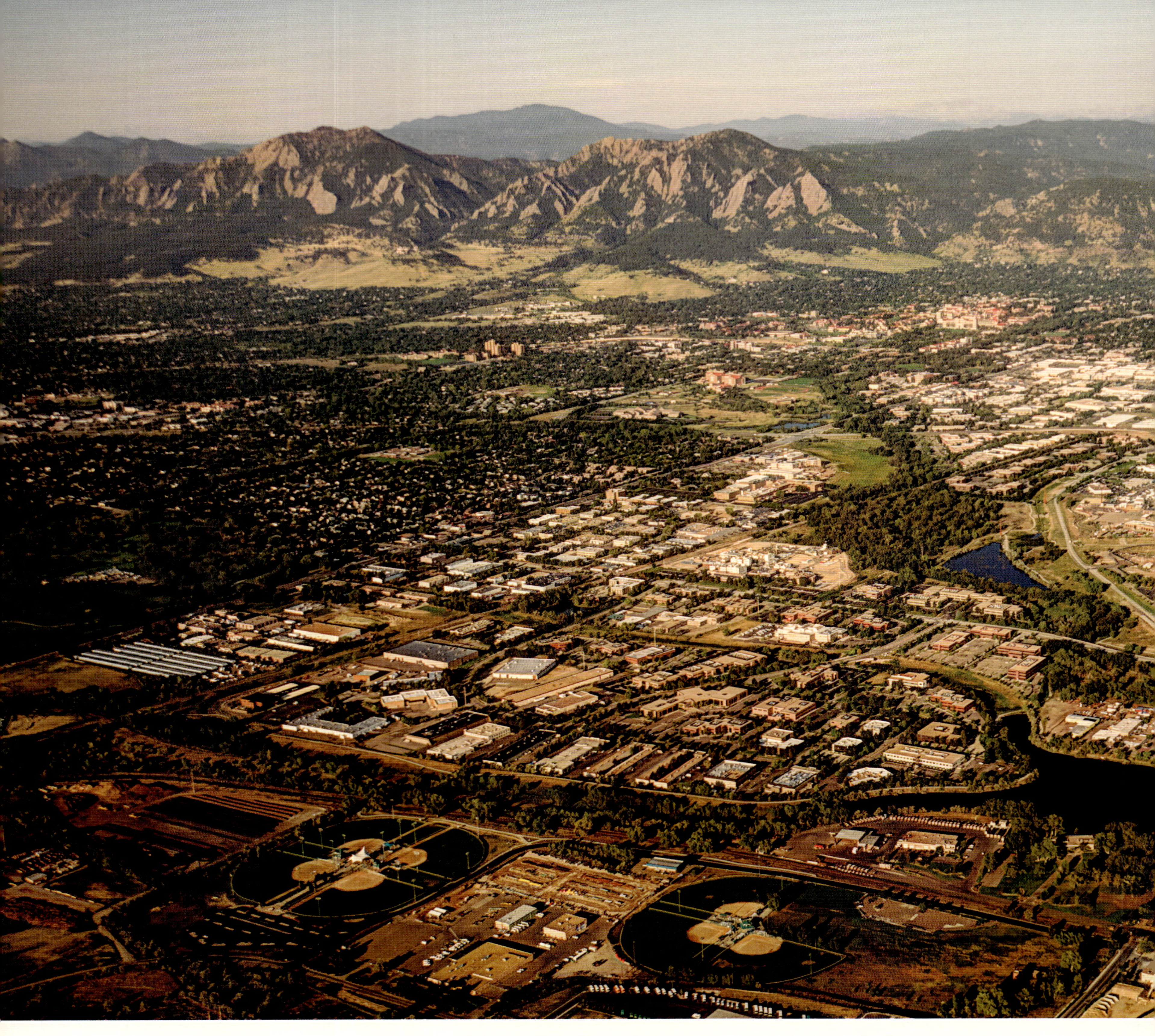

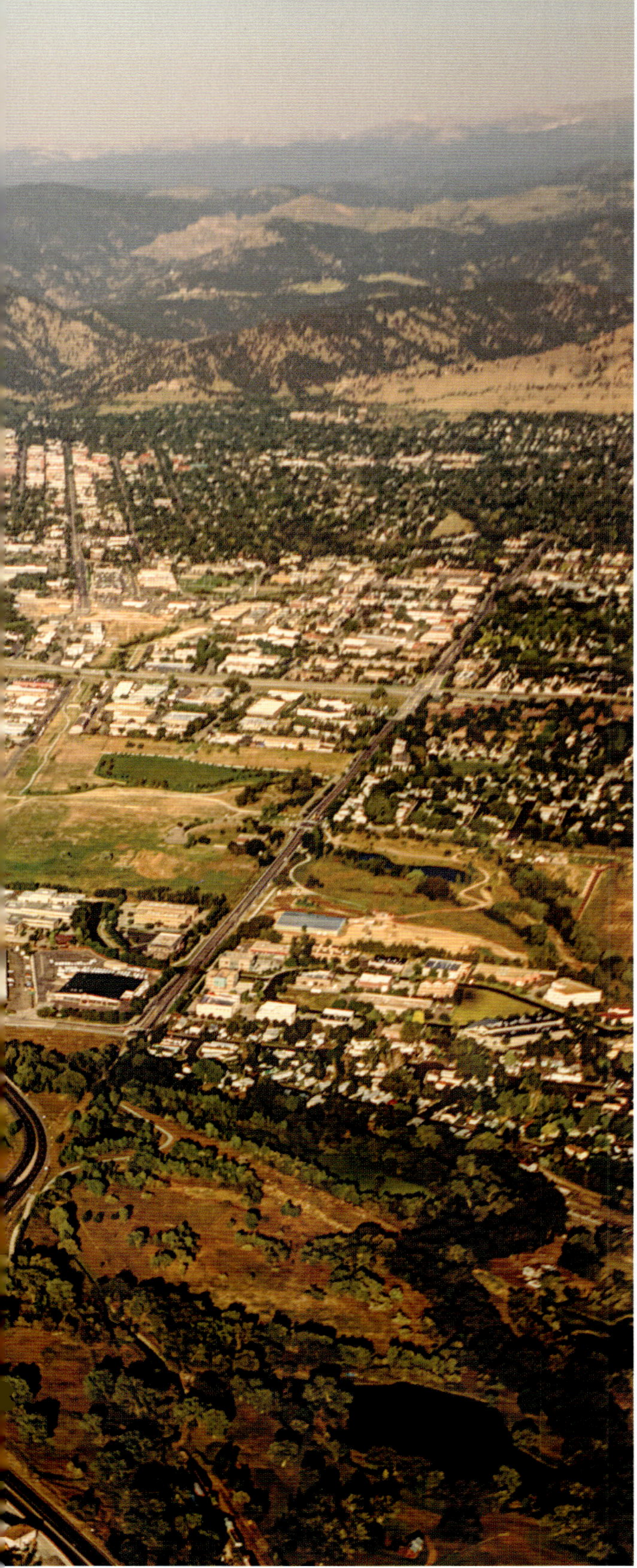

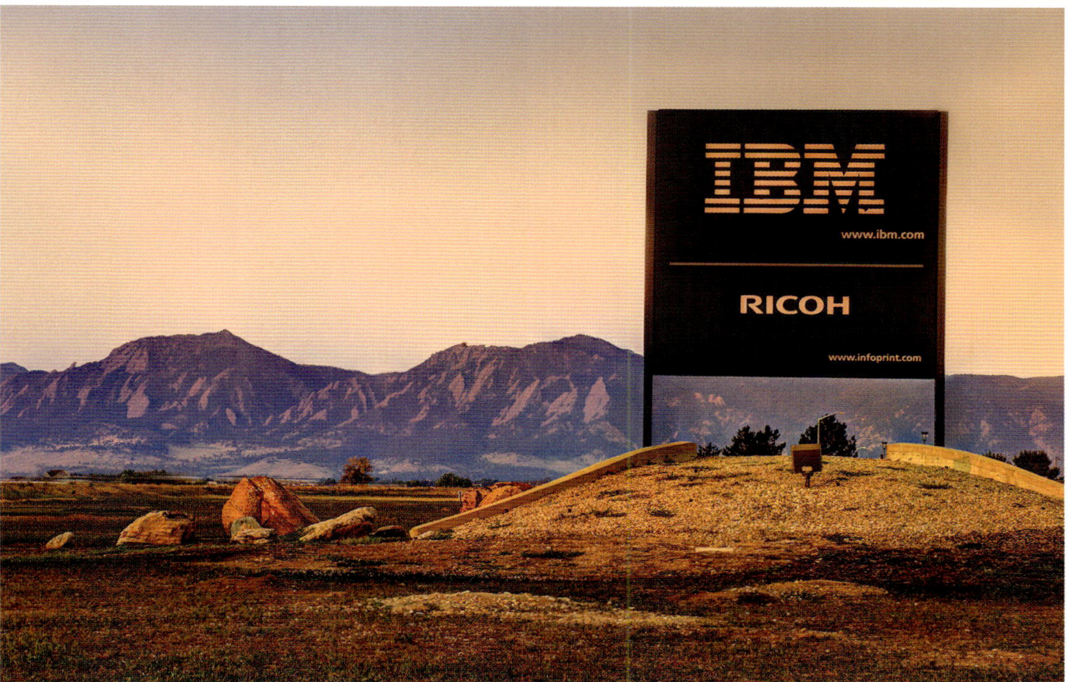

ABOVE: Opened in 1965, IBM-Boulder remains a primary location for the corporation. Its 470-acre campus is home to IBM's largest commercial data center complex in the world.

LEFT: Pearl Parkway snakes through the right foreground in this view of Boulder. Beyond the city are the Flatirons, then the foothills, and, finally, the Front Range of the Rocky Mountains along the Continental Divide.

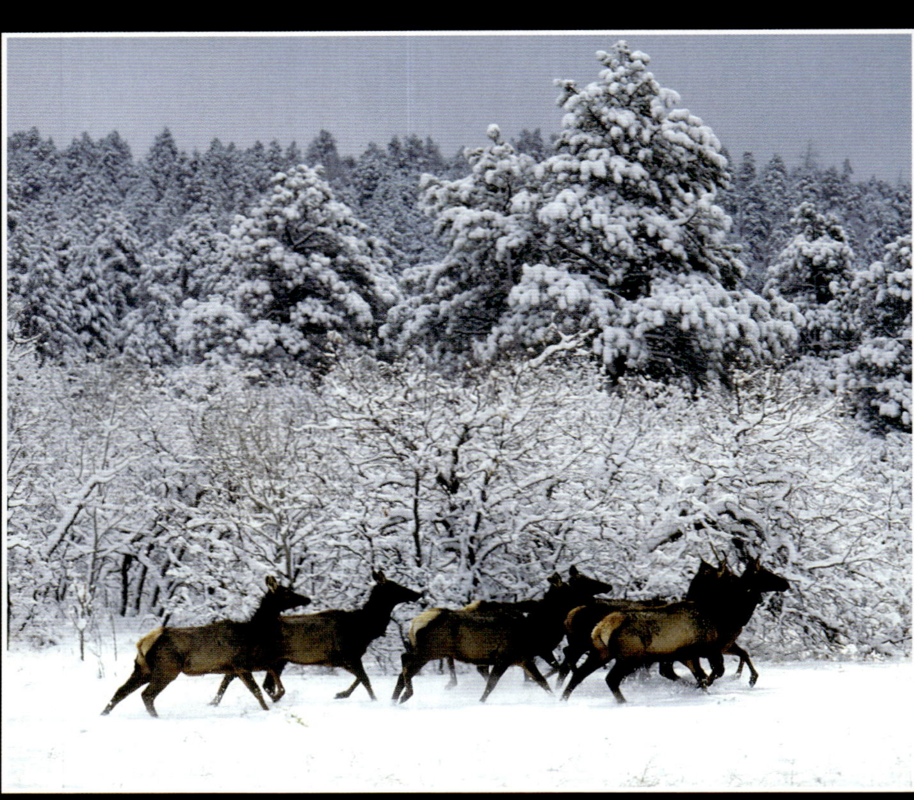

ABOVE: Elk race across a snow-covered meadow in the foothills west of Boulder.

RIGHT: A fresh snowfall adds to Boulder's beauty, especially when the sun comes out the next day. Here, heavily laden evergreens frame the First, Second, and Third Flatirons (right to left).

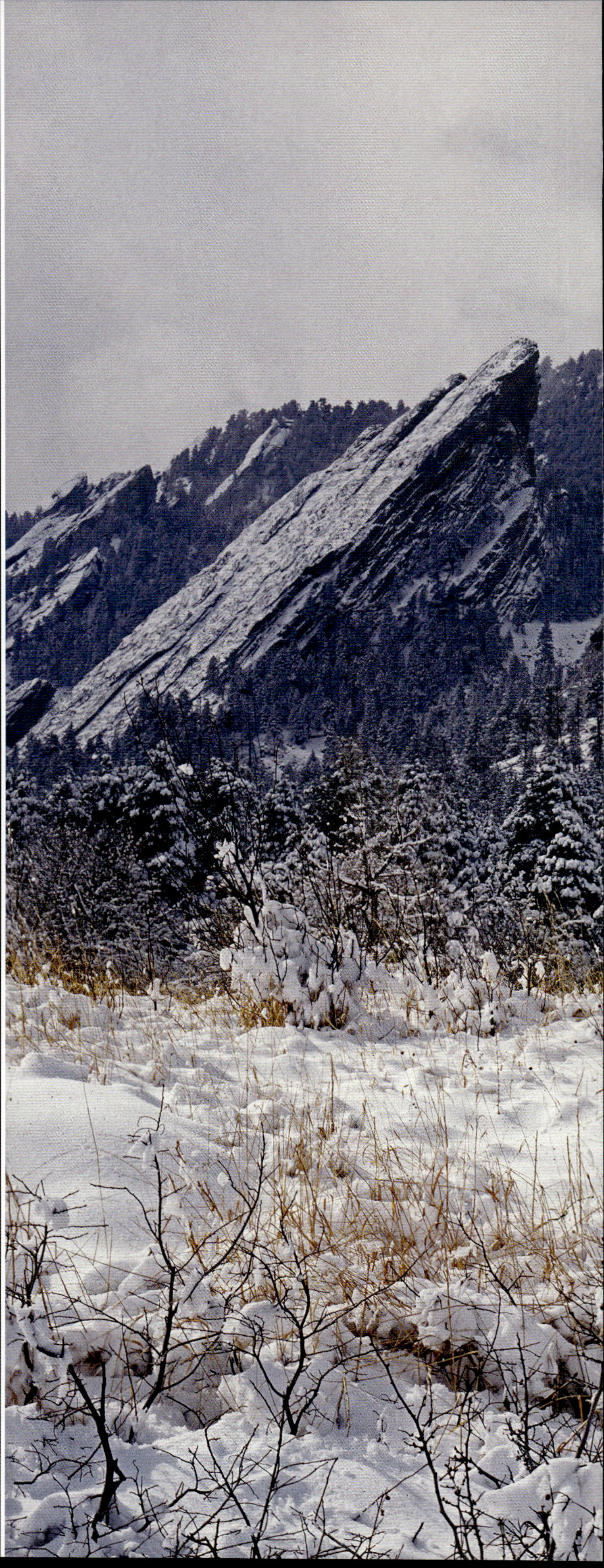

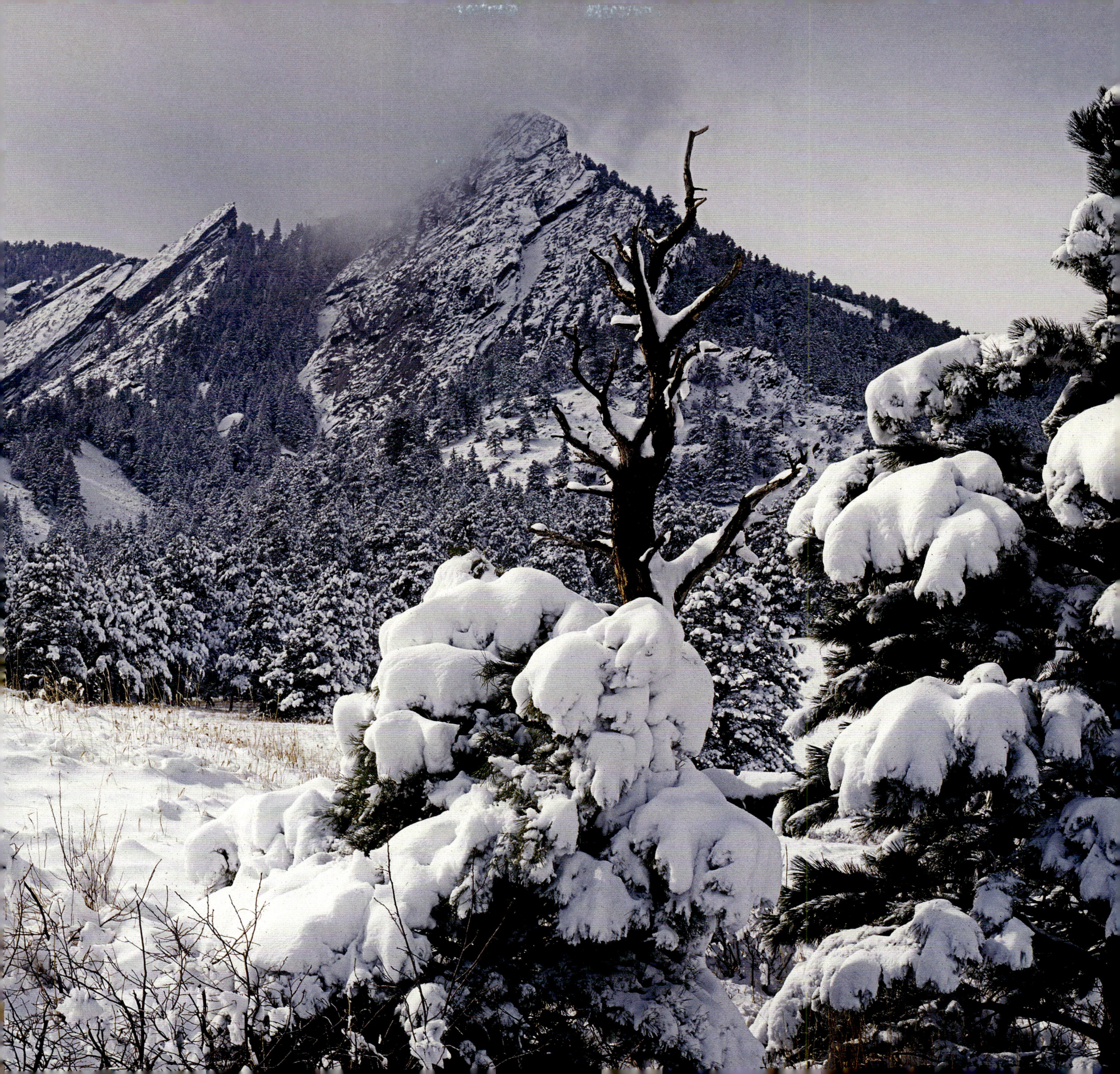

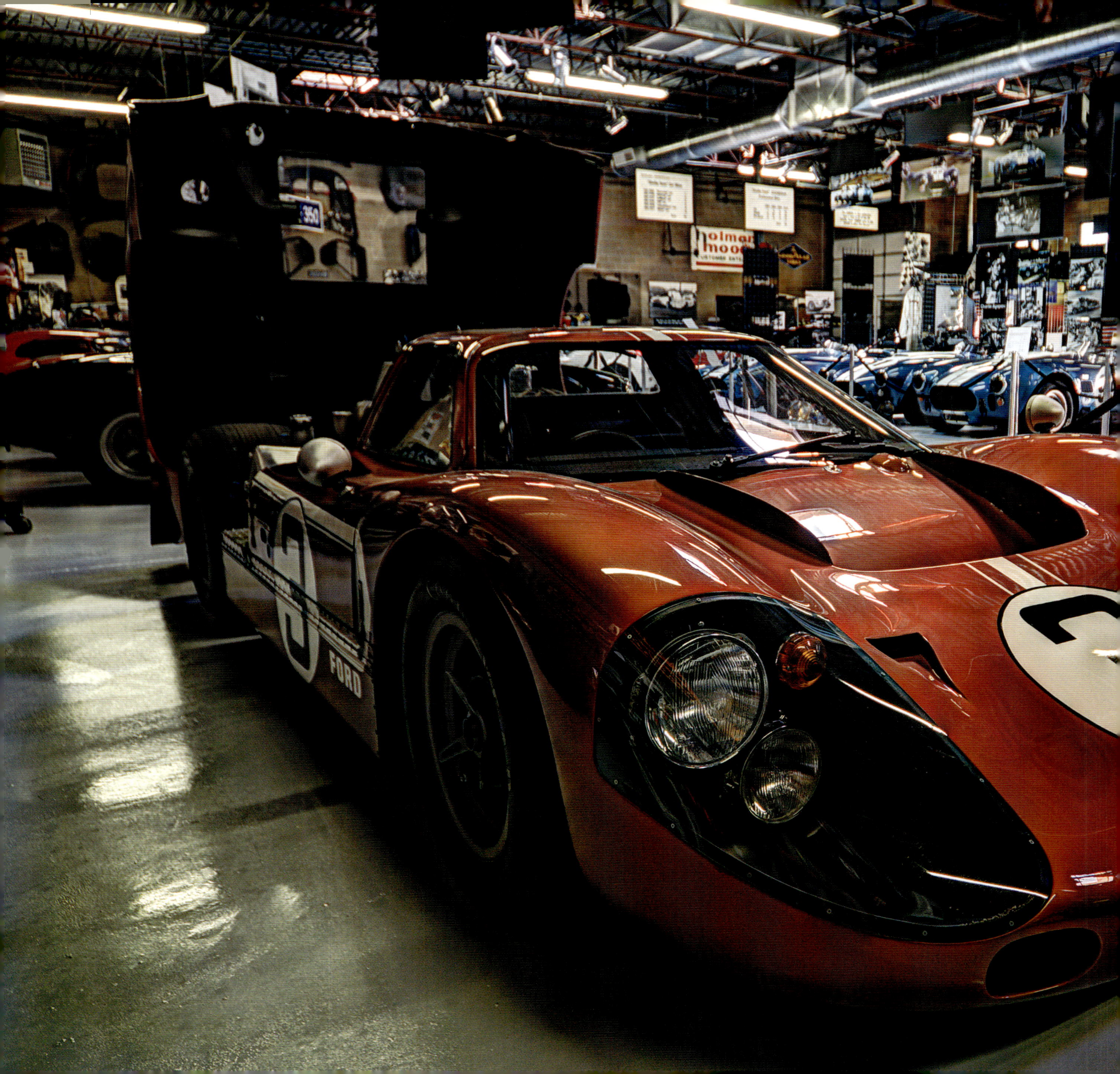
FORD

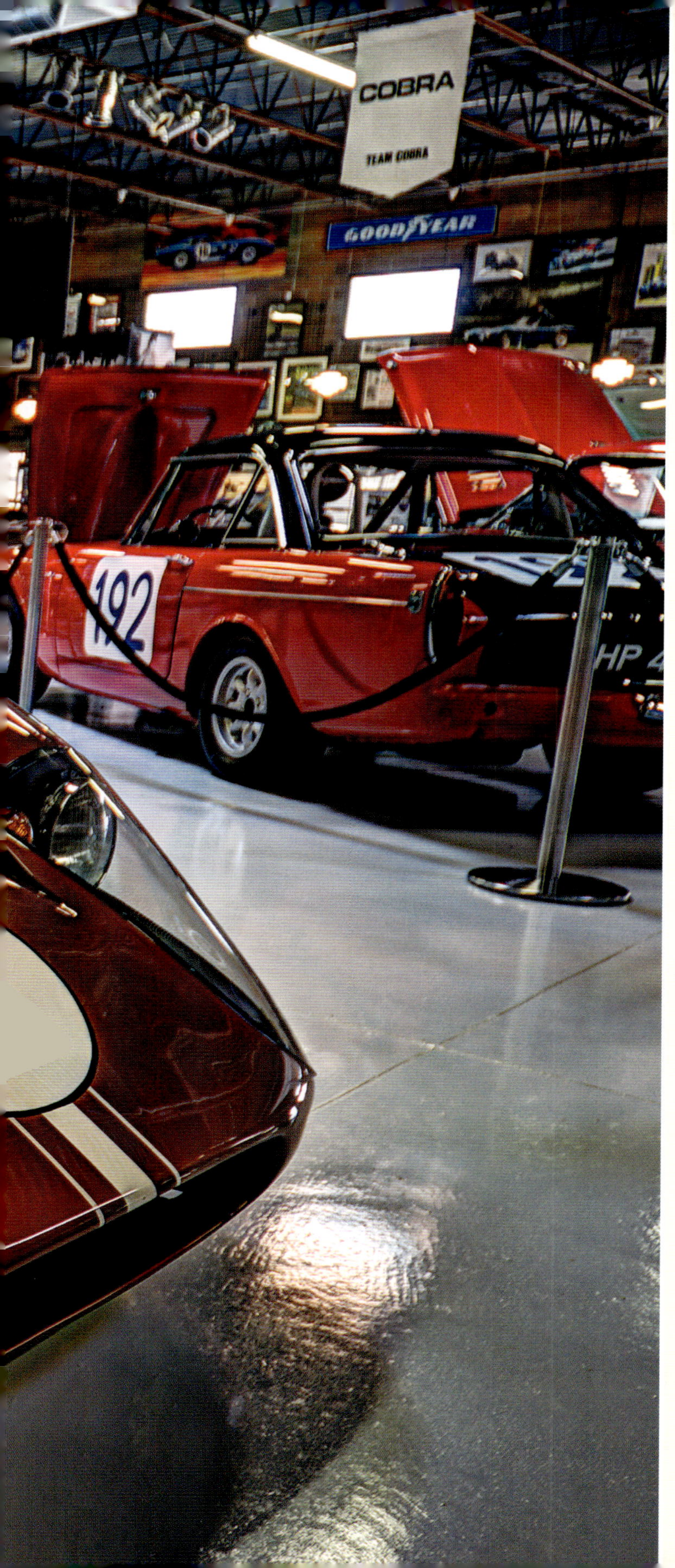

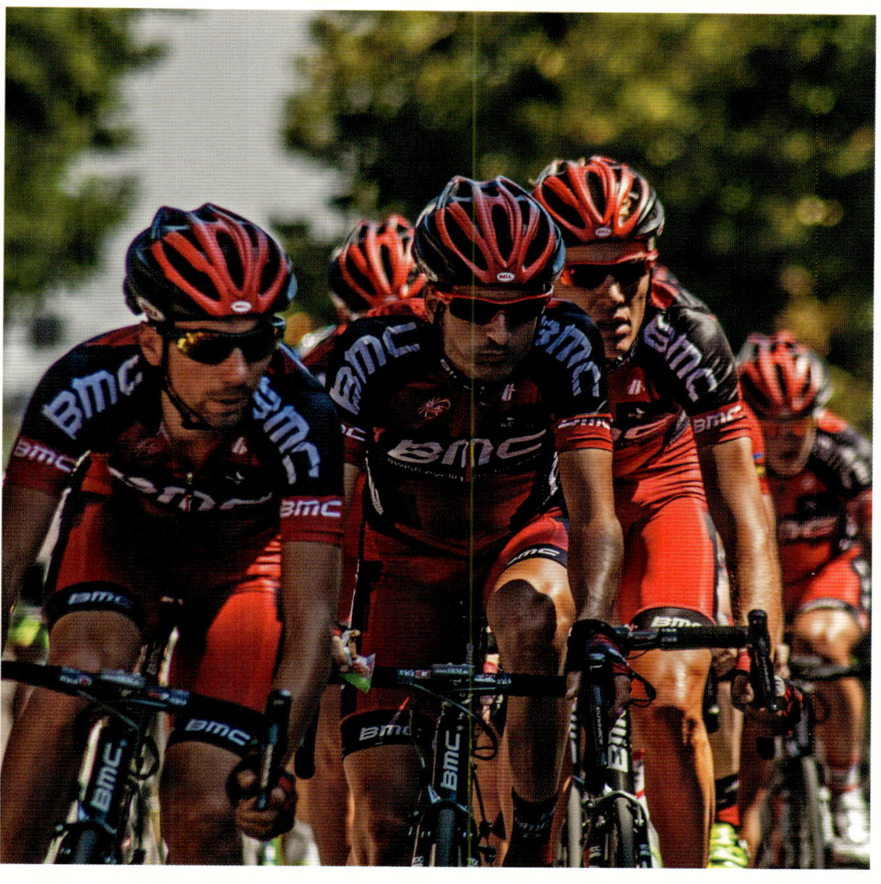

ABOVE: Biking is big in Boulder and got even bigger with the advent of the USA Pro Cycling Challenge and its epic finish on Flagstaff Mountain, west of the city.

LEFT: The Shelby American Collection is a unique and extensive collection of racing cars featuring Shelby Cobras, Shelby GT 350s, and Ford GT 40s, as well as historical records and memorabilia. The museum is dedicated to the preservation of Shelby American automobiles and conveys the Shelby American team story to the public.

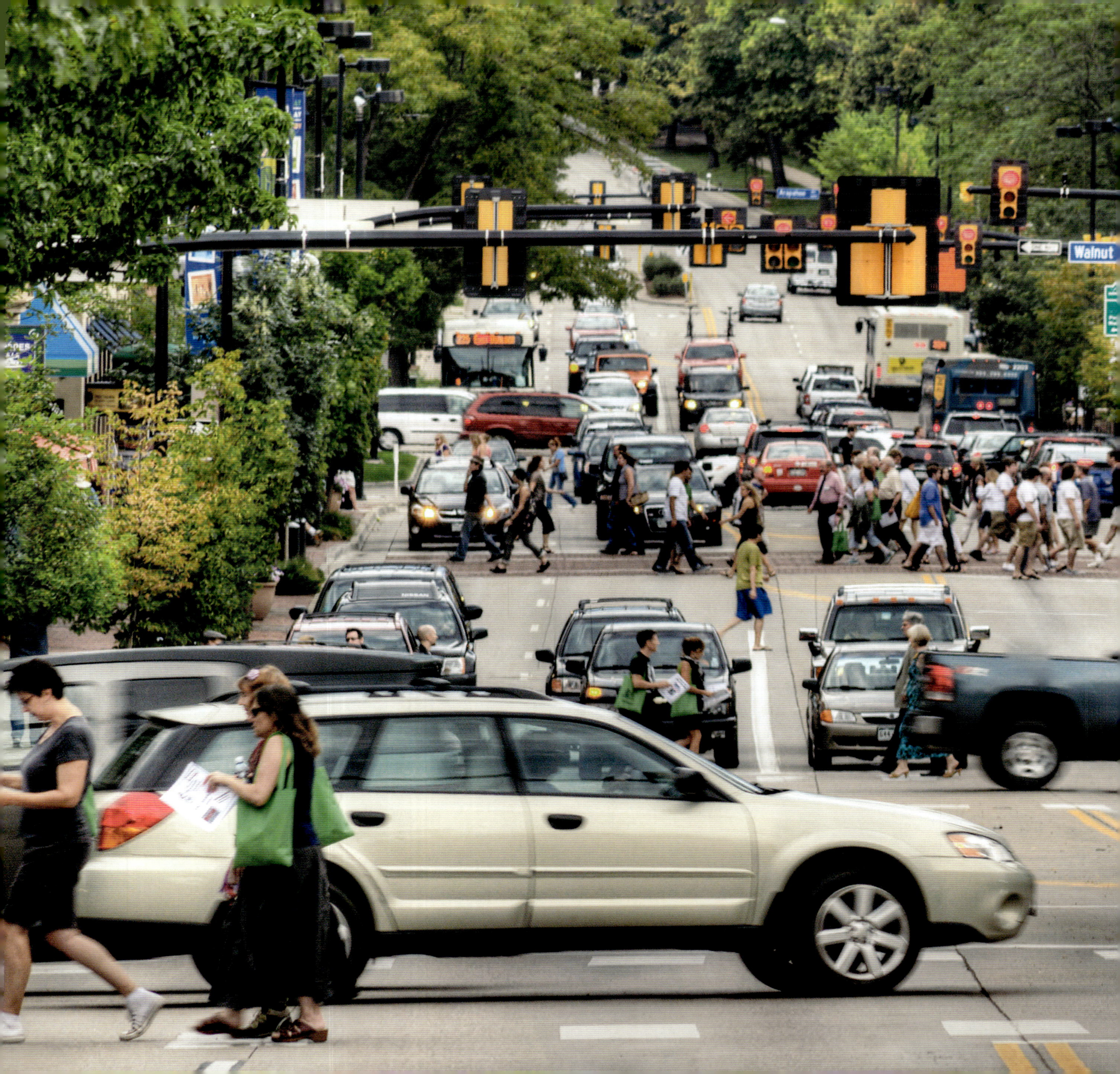
Walnut

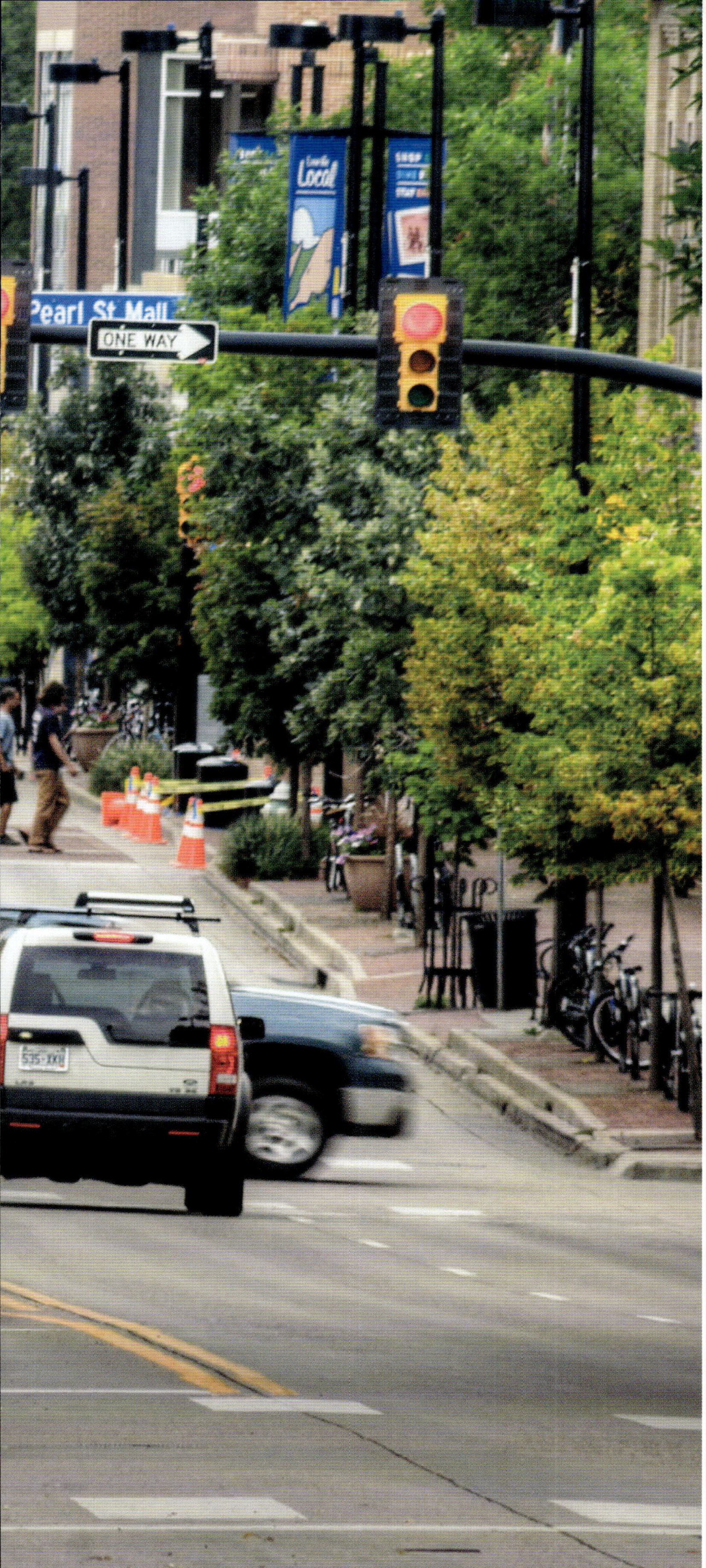

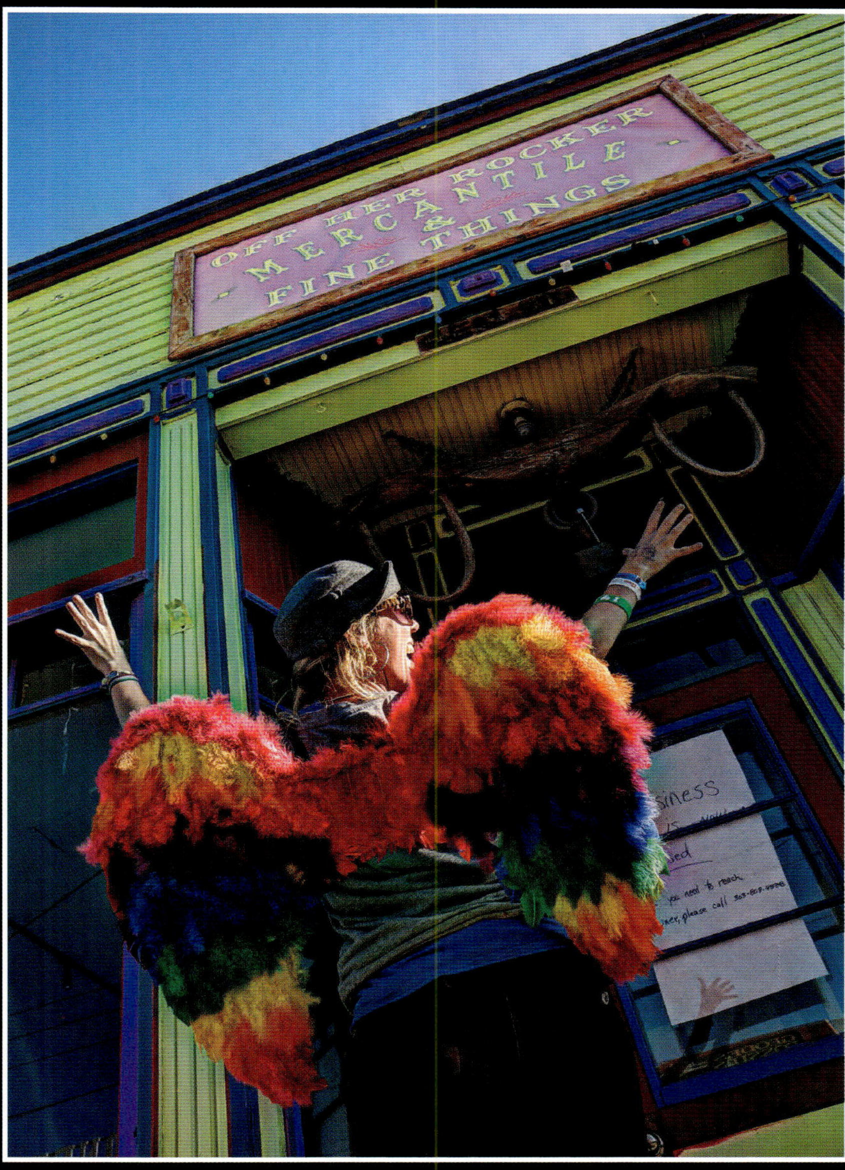

ABOVE: This "angel," in front of a retail shop in the mountain town of Nederland, just flew in, looking for a bargain.

LEFT: Broadway is Boulder's main north–south artery and intersects the Pearl Street Mall.

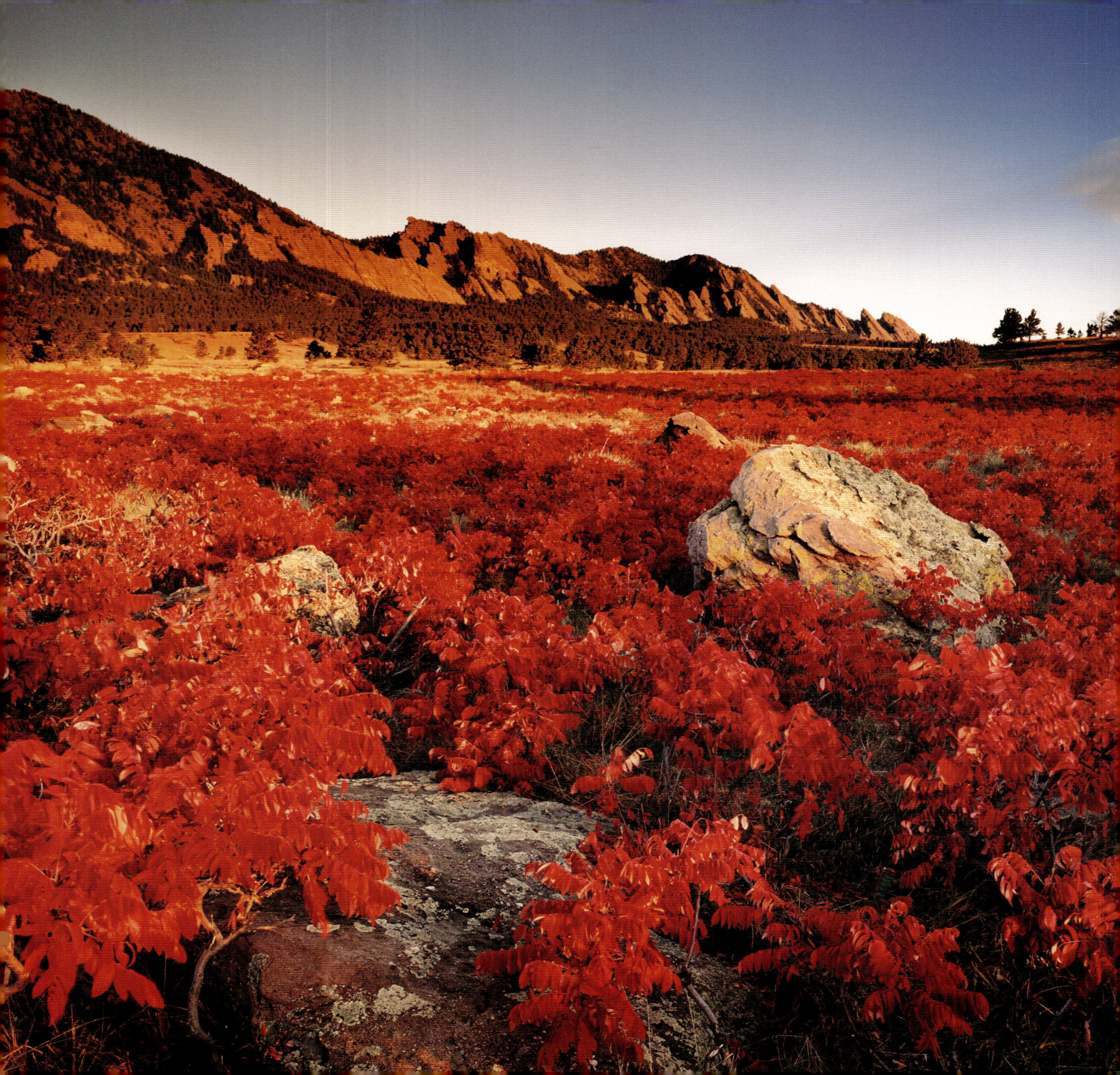

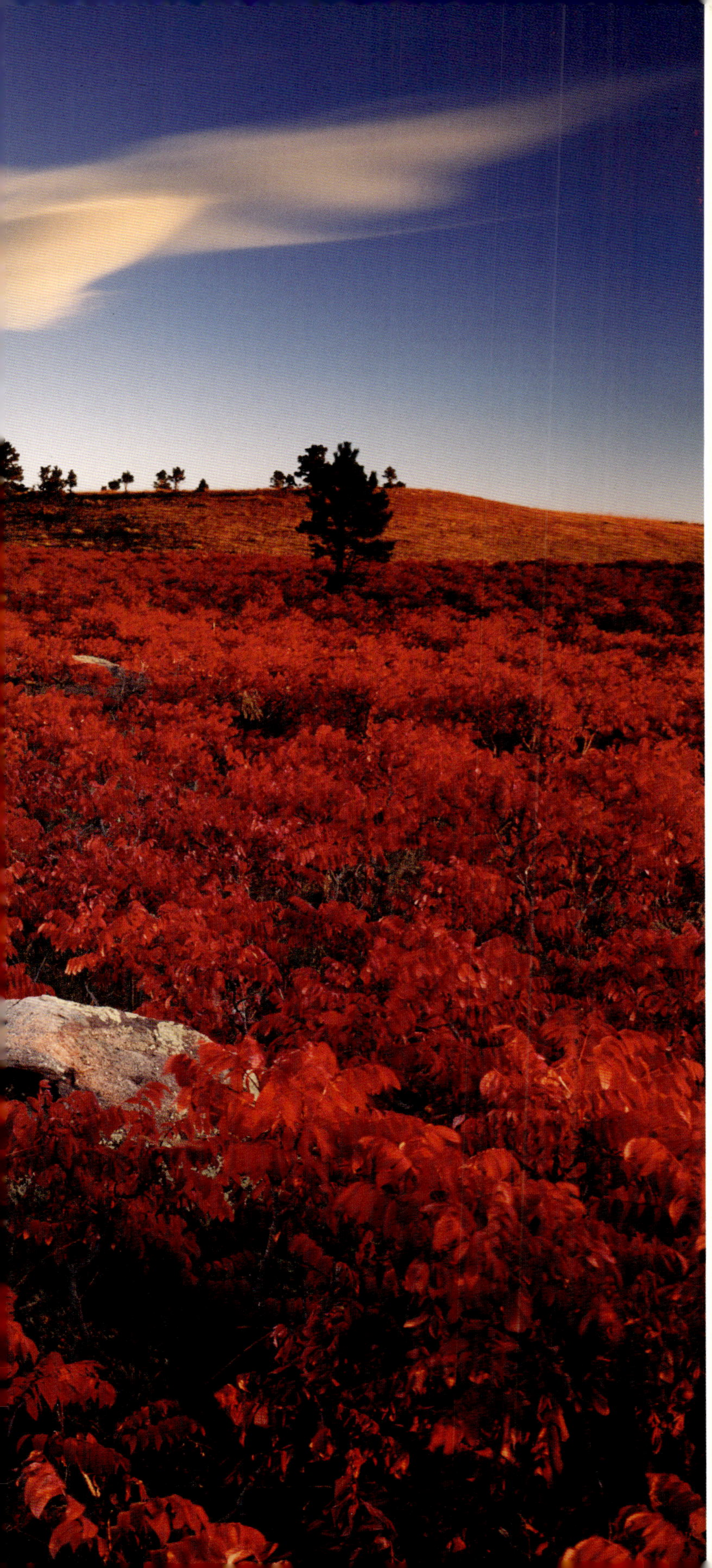

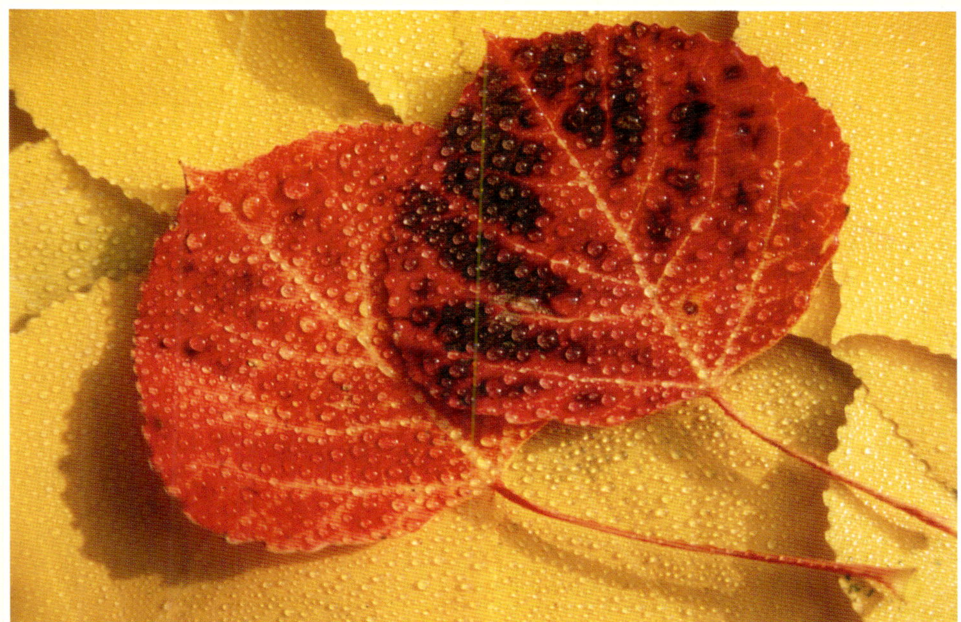

ABOVE: Aspen leaves, brilliantly colored, range from red to yellow.

LEFT: The coming of winter is starkly announced as smooth sumac turns bright red. The species was widely used among Native American tribes in making a root and leaf tea to treat diarrhea, dysentery, and mouth/throat ulcers.

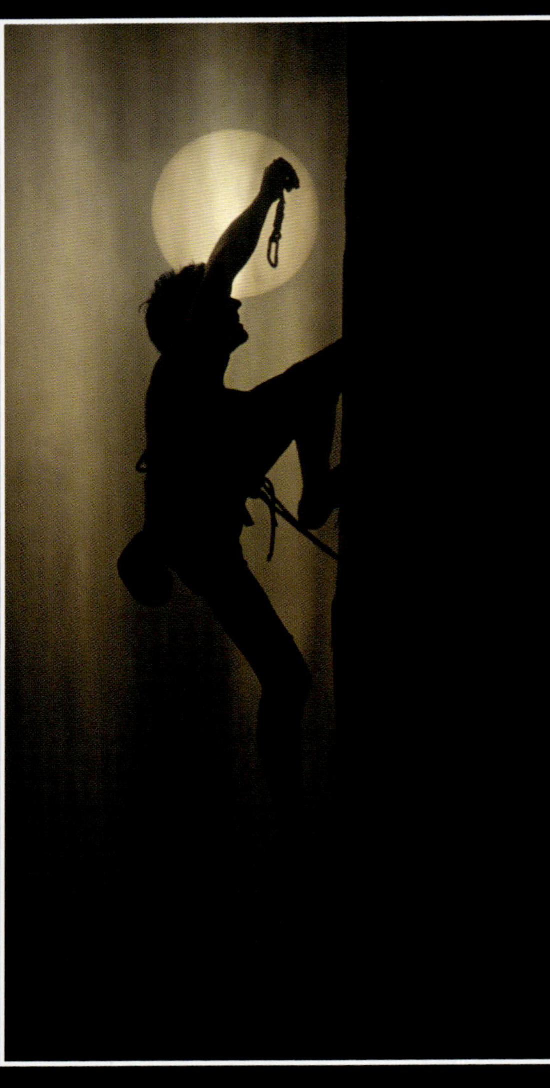

ABOVE: A climber is silhouetted against the sun.

RIGHT: A brilliant sunset accentuates Eldorado Canyon, which lures technical climbers from around the world and features more than 500 rock climbing routes.

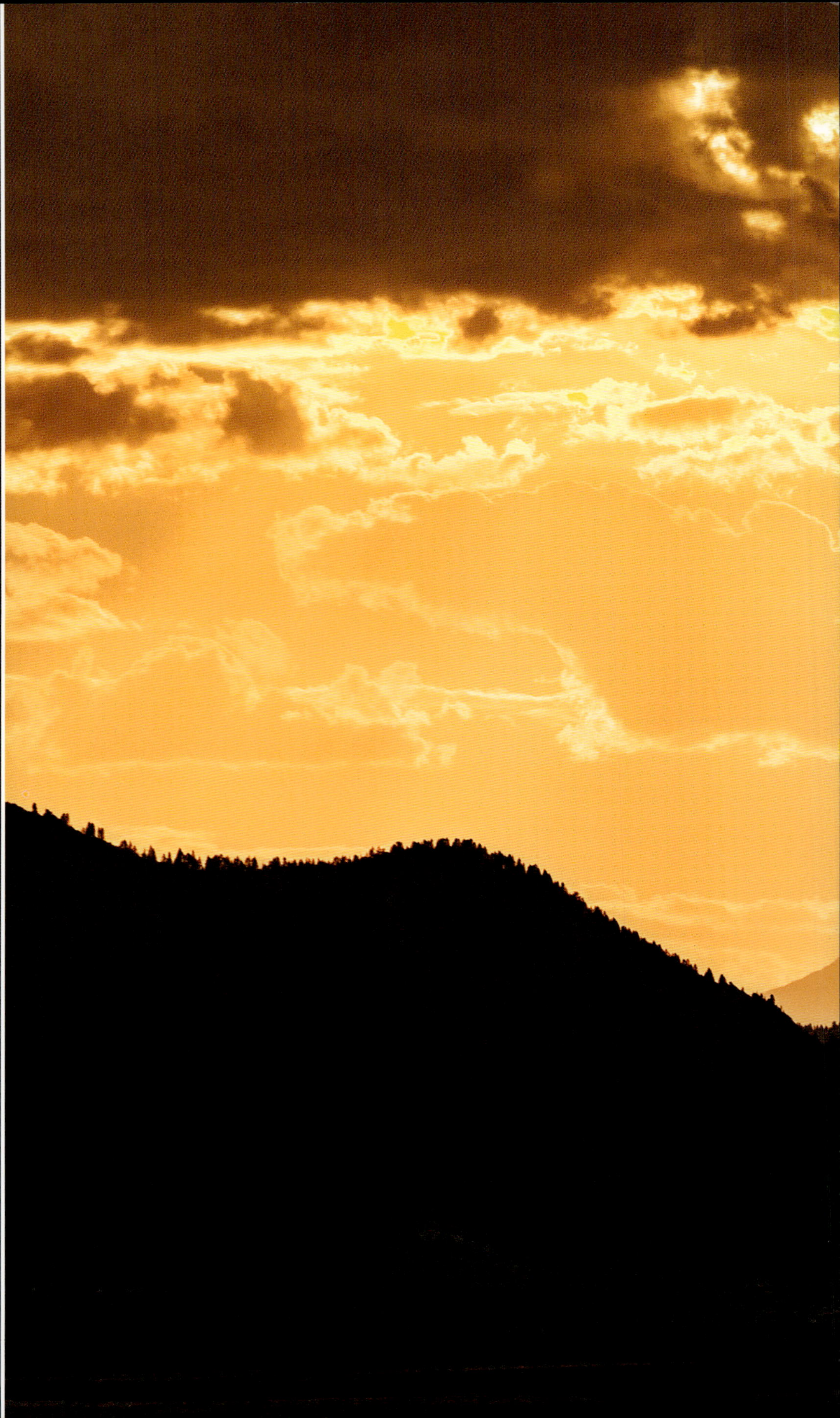

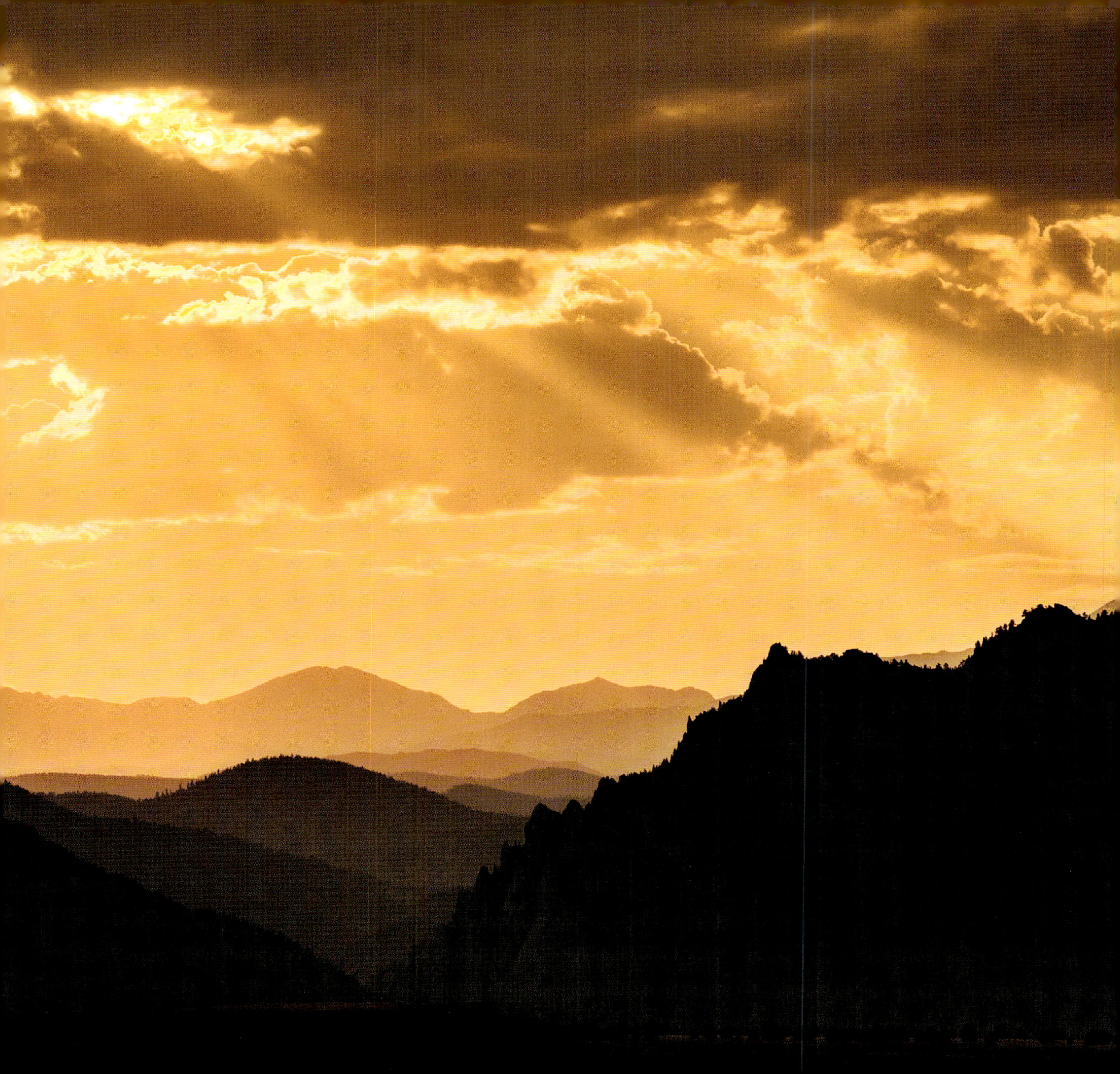

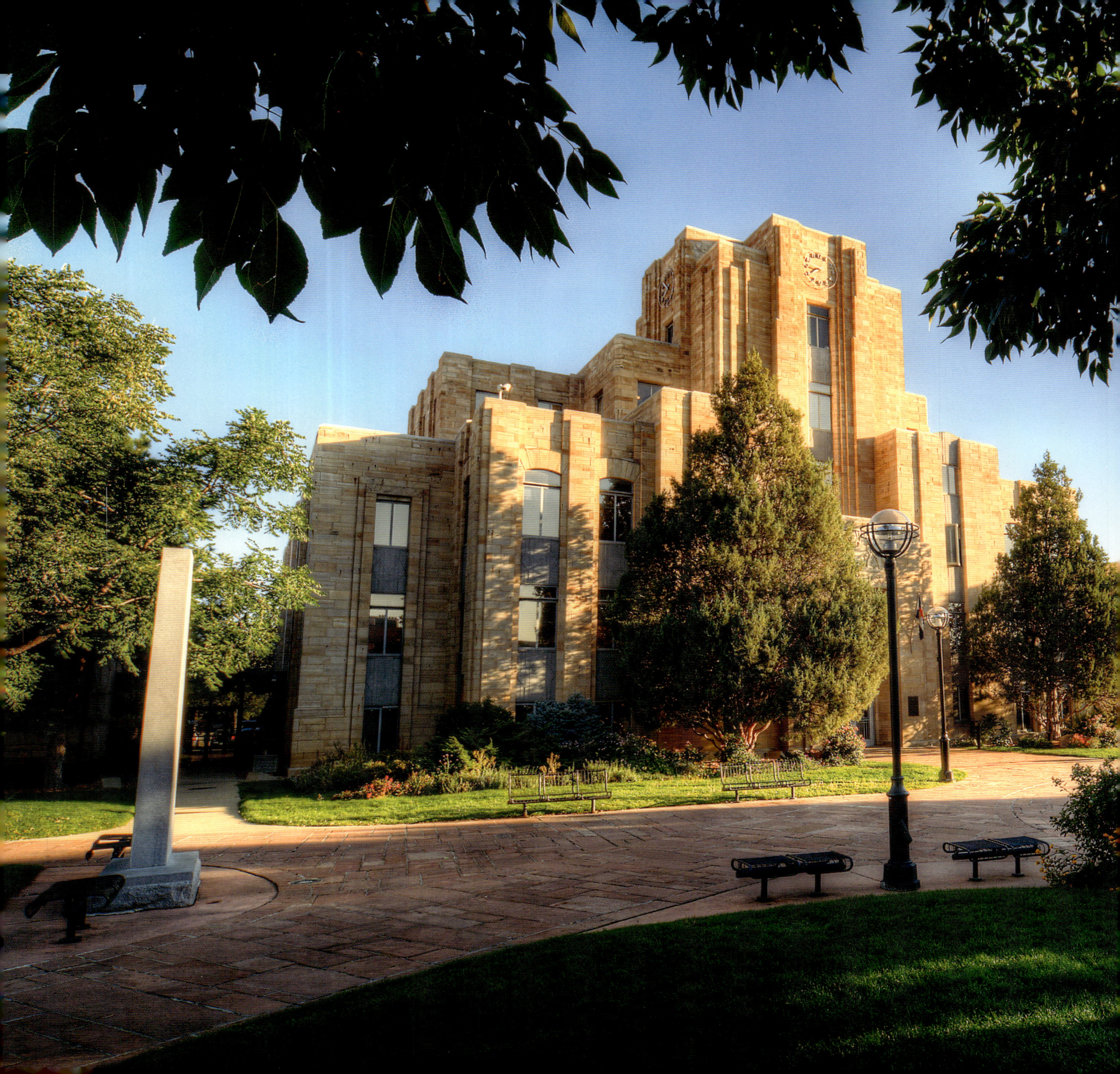

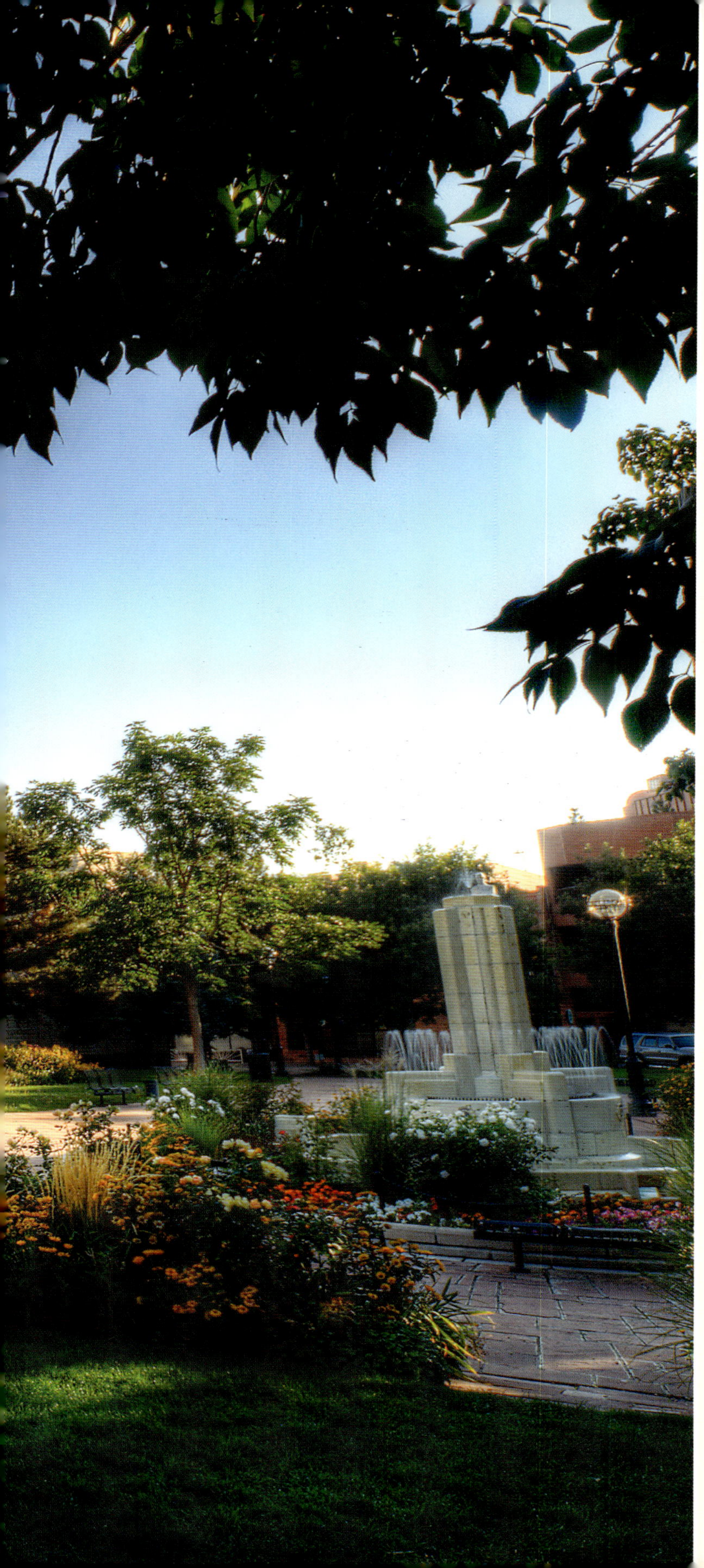

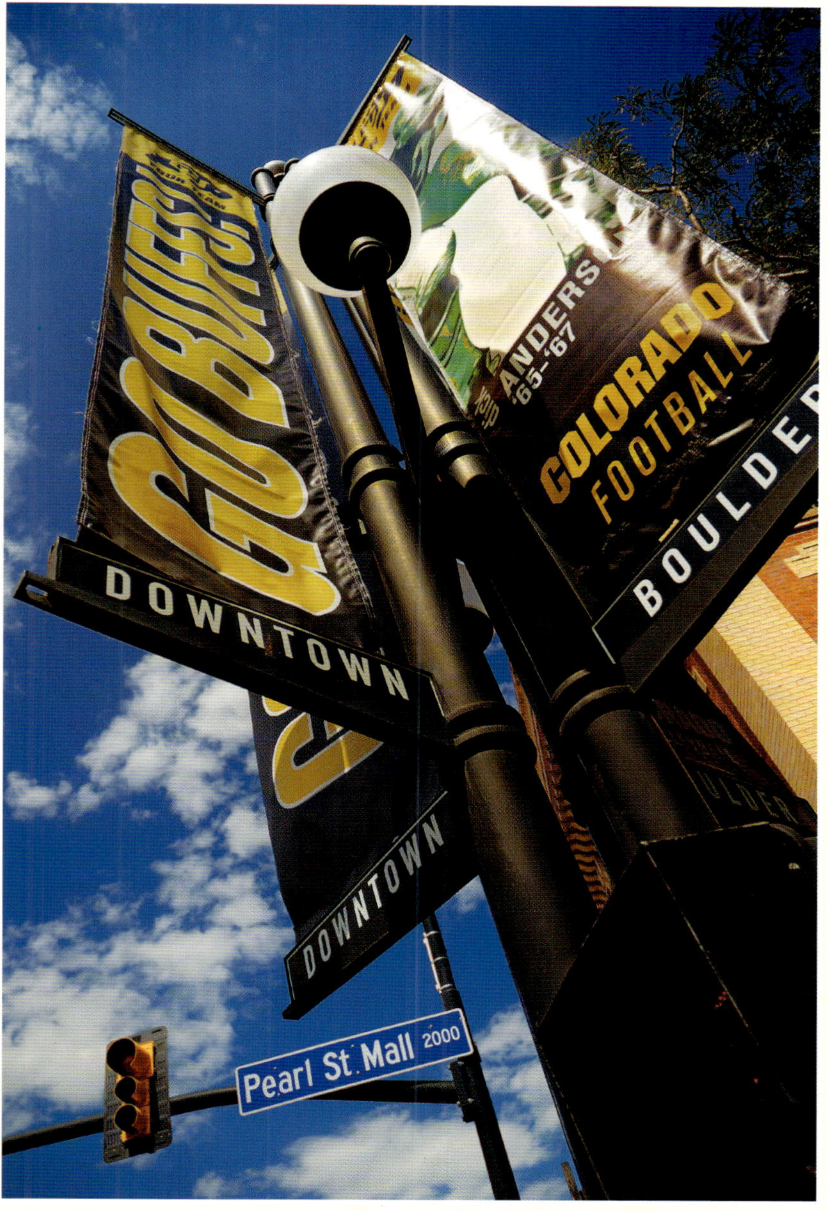

ABOVE: University of Colorado school spirit extends to downtown Boulder, where "Go Buffs" banners are prominently displayed on the Pearl Street Mall.

LEFT: The Art Deco–style Boulder County Courthouse was completed in 1934 on the site of its predecessor—a brick Victorian-era building that was destroyed by fire. On the left is Boulder's World War Memorial, and on the right is the restored Lions Club fountain.

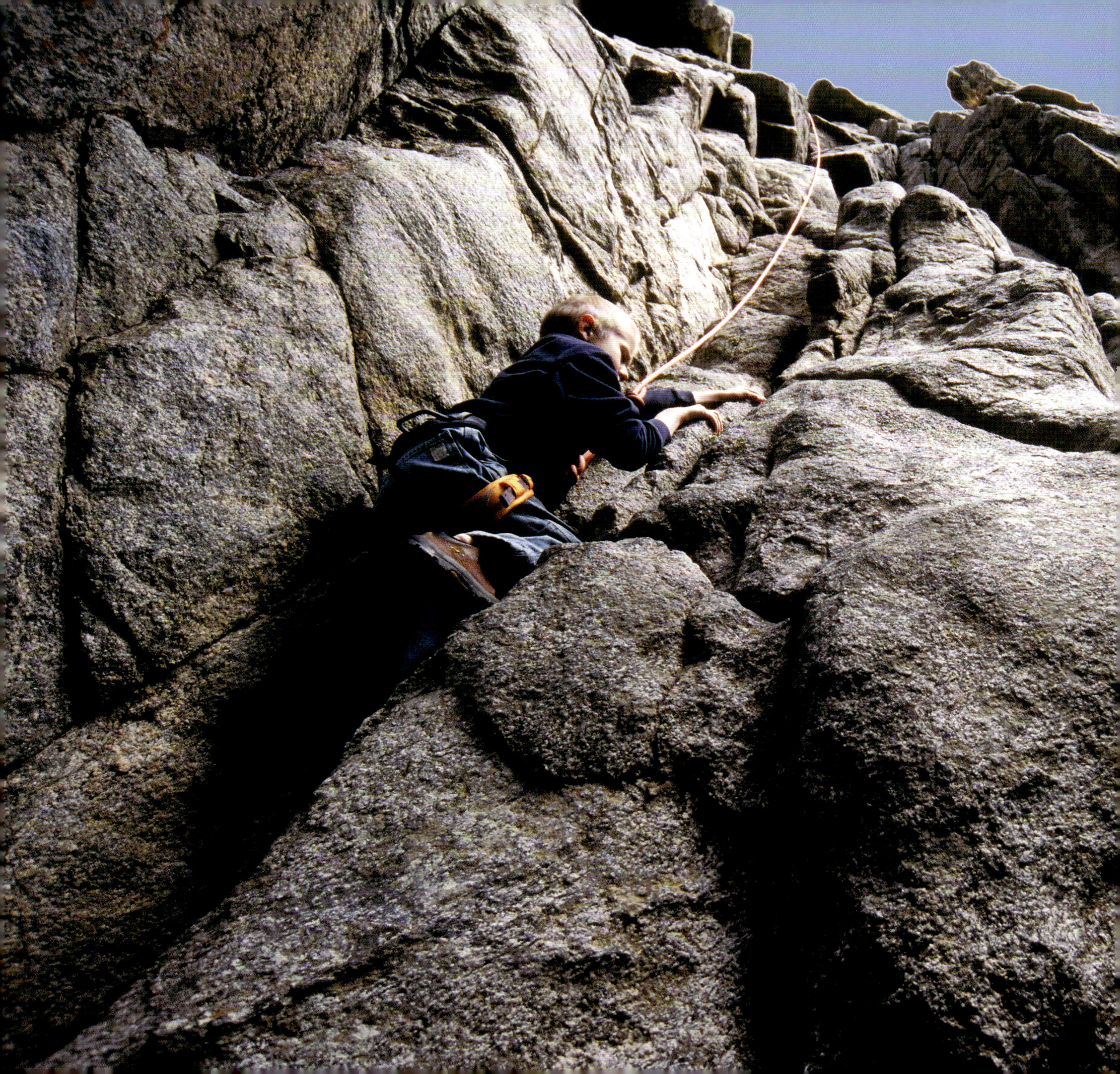

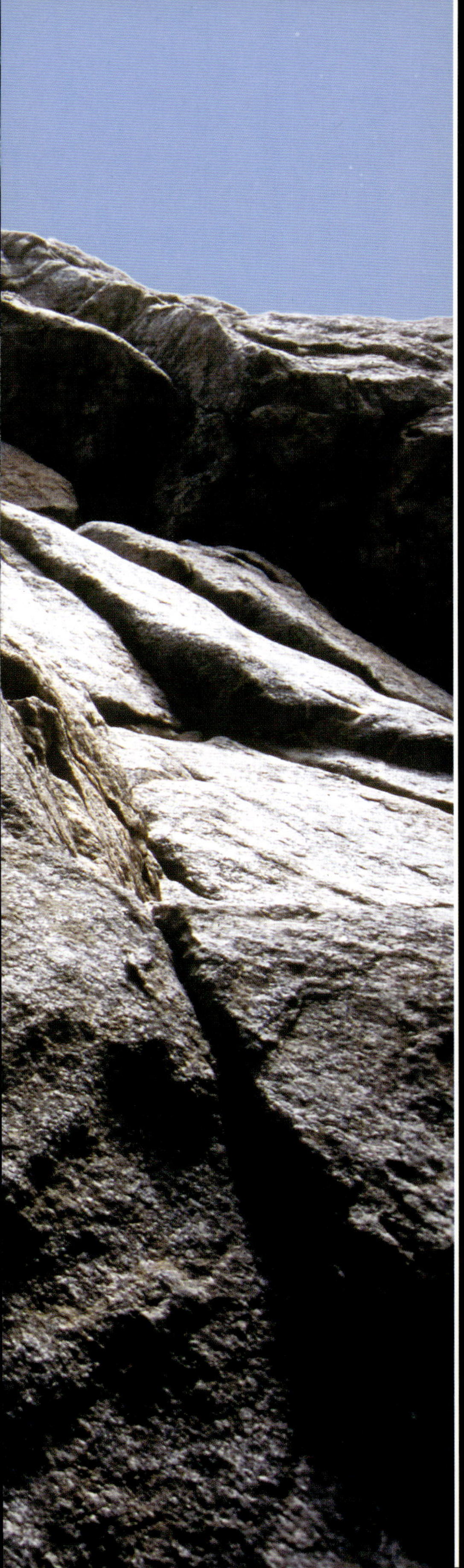

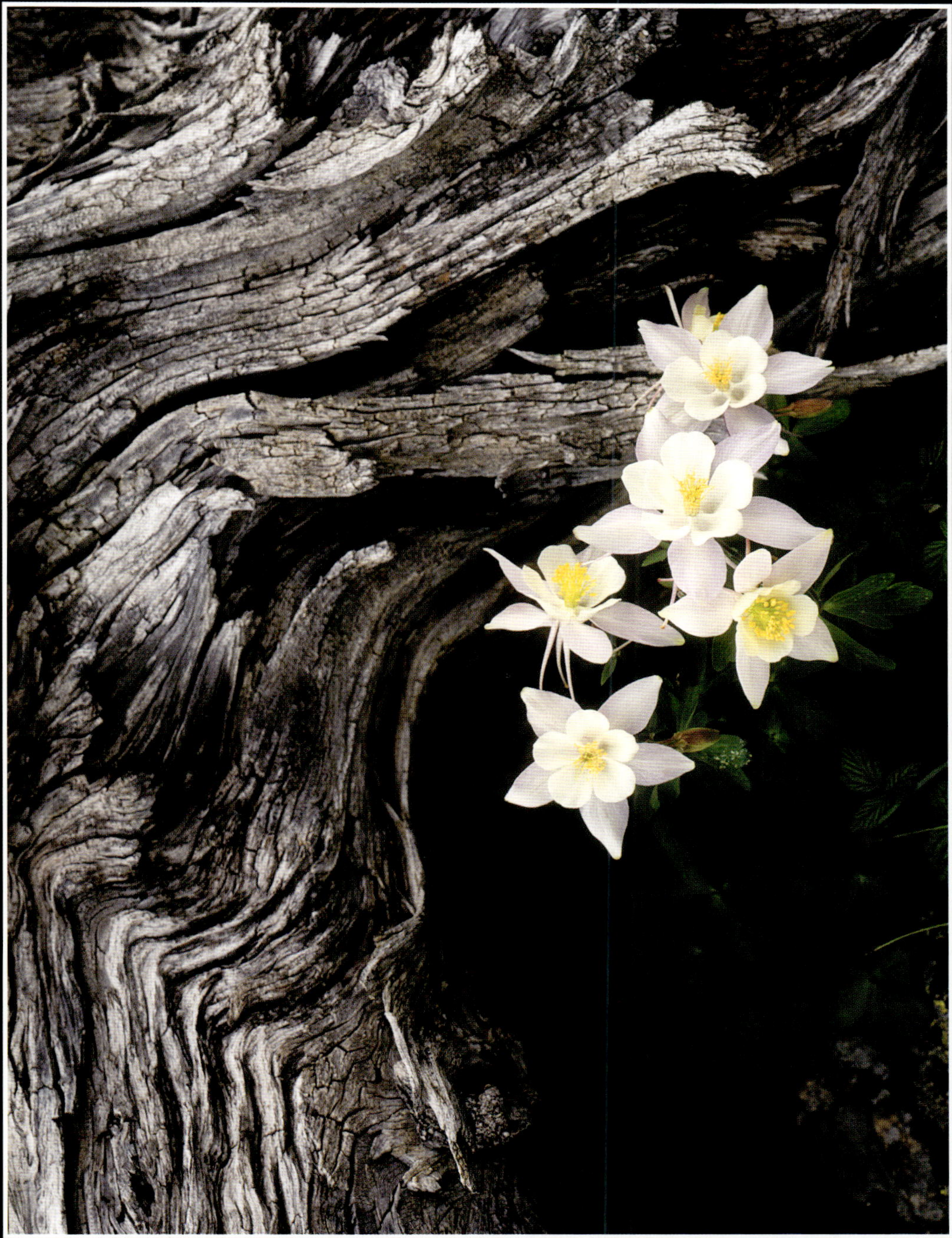

ABOVE: The columbine, shown here against a background of twisted, weathered wood, is Colorado's state flower.

LEFT: Climbing can be a family activity, as Trevor Mohlenkamp demonstrates when he tackles a near-vertical face in Boulder Canyon.

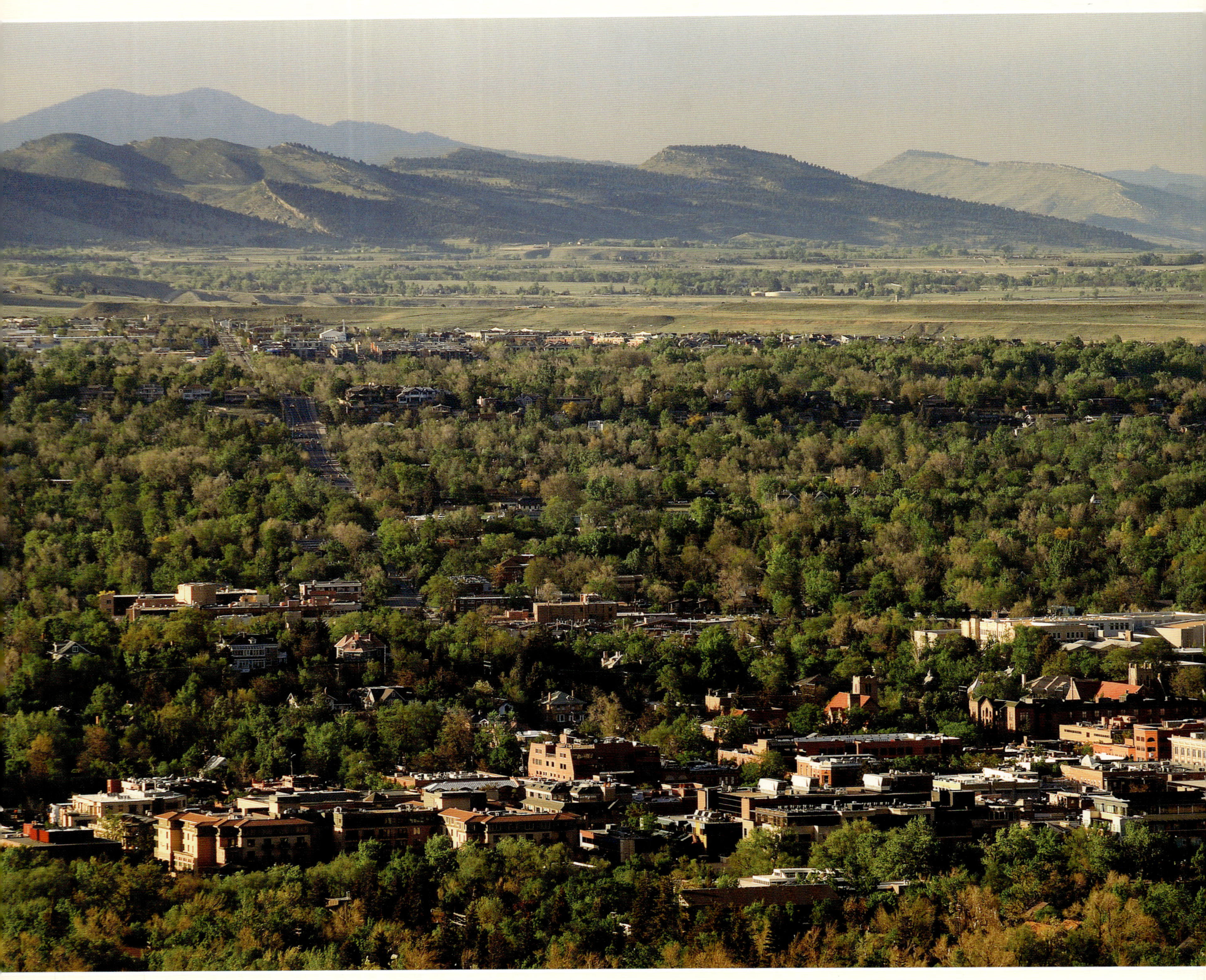

Boulder has approximately 26,000 street trees and 10,000 park trees under its urban forestry jurisdiction, earning the city a "Tree City USA" designation by the National Arbor Day Foundation. Nearly all of these trees have been planted, as the only trees native to the ecosystem of the plains are cottonwoods, willows, and box elders that grow along the waterways.

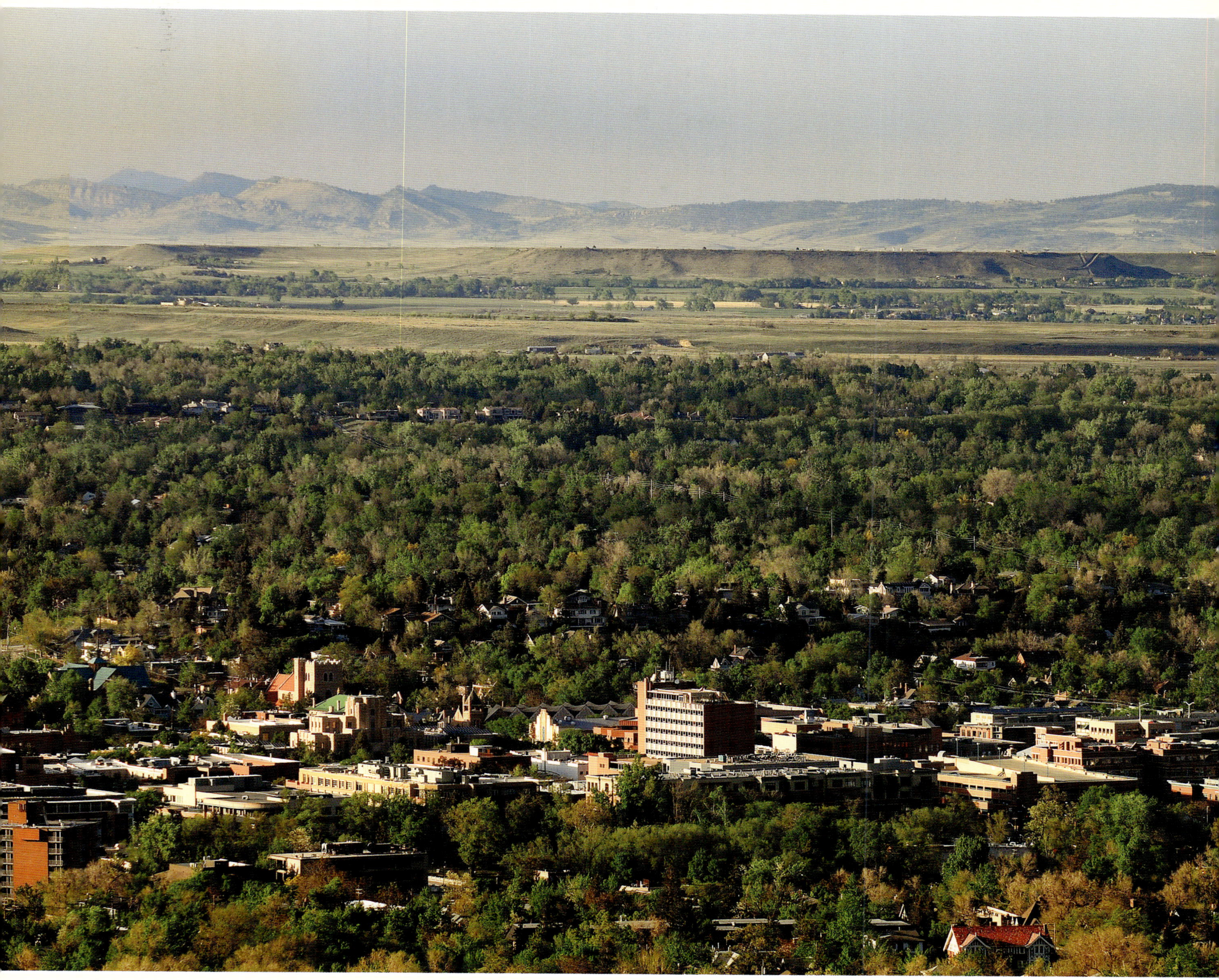

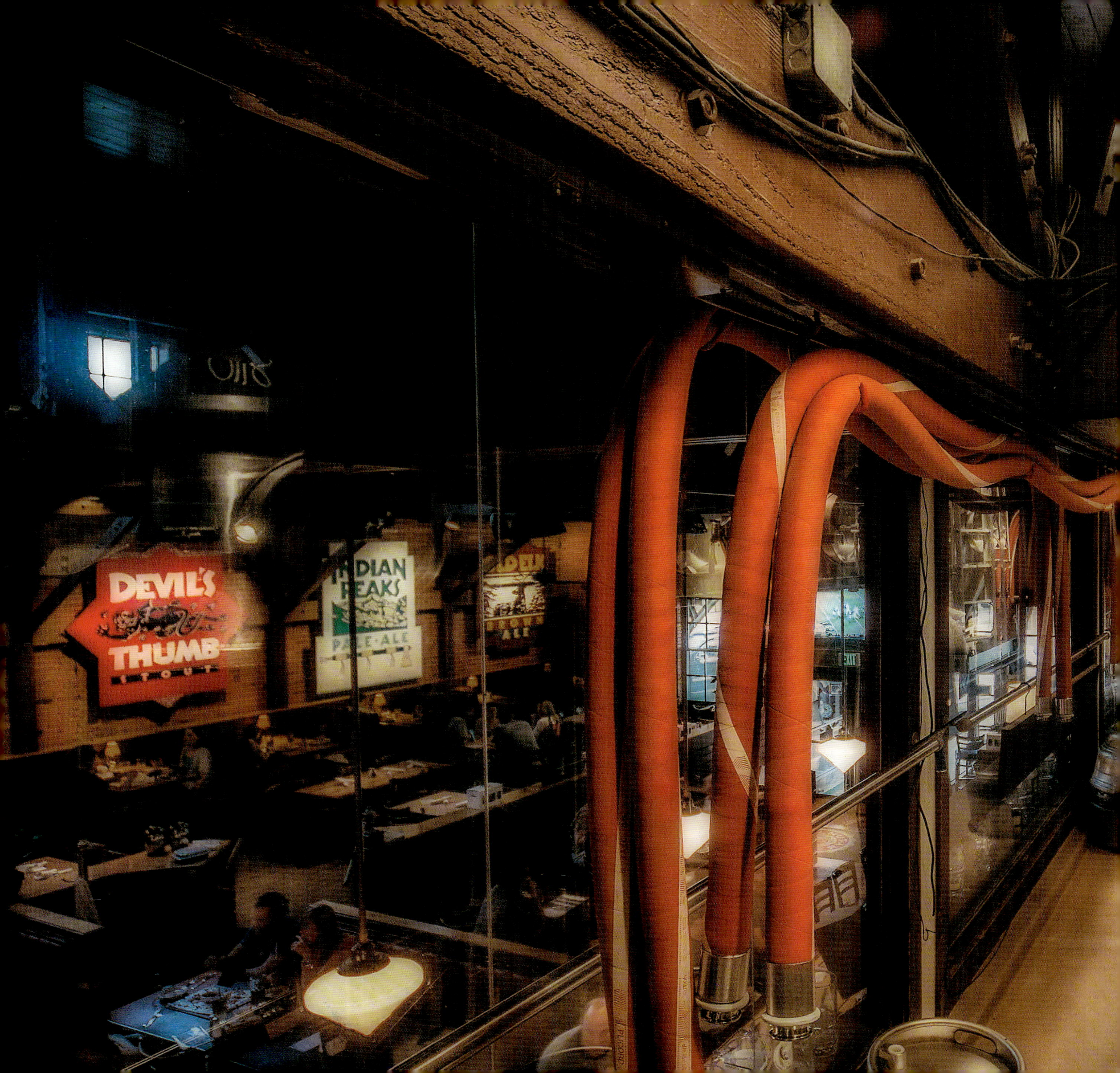
DEVIL'S
THUMB
STOUT
PALE·ALE
BROWN
ALE

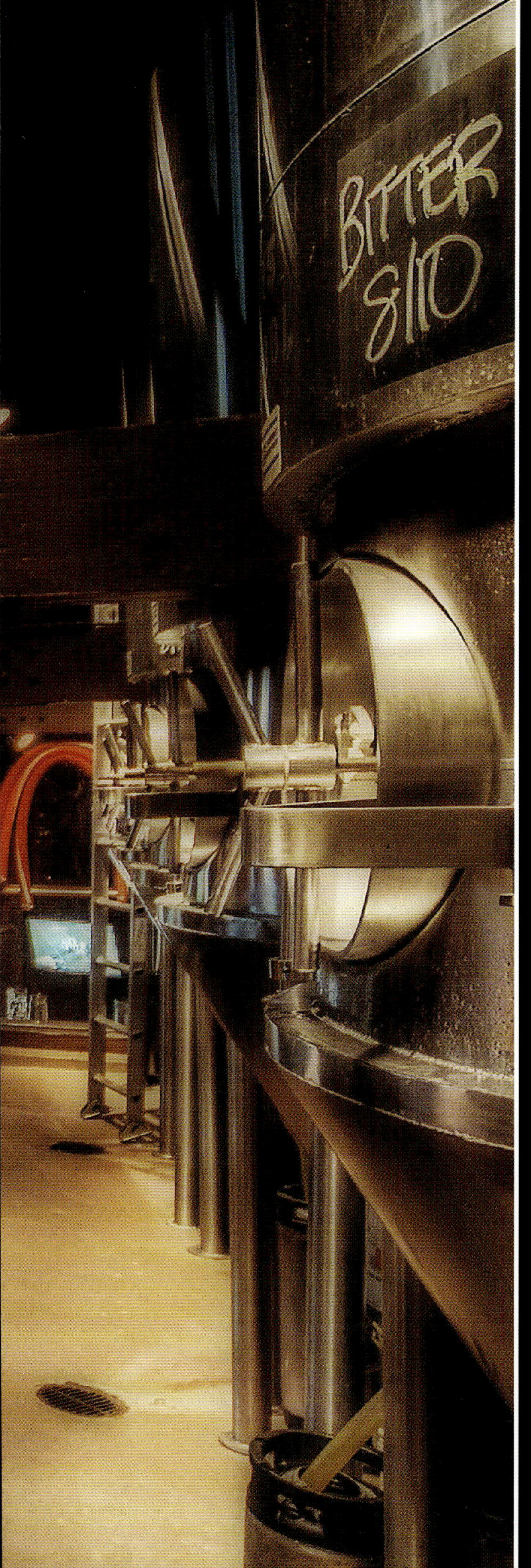

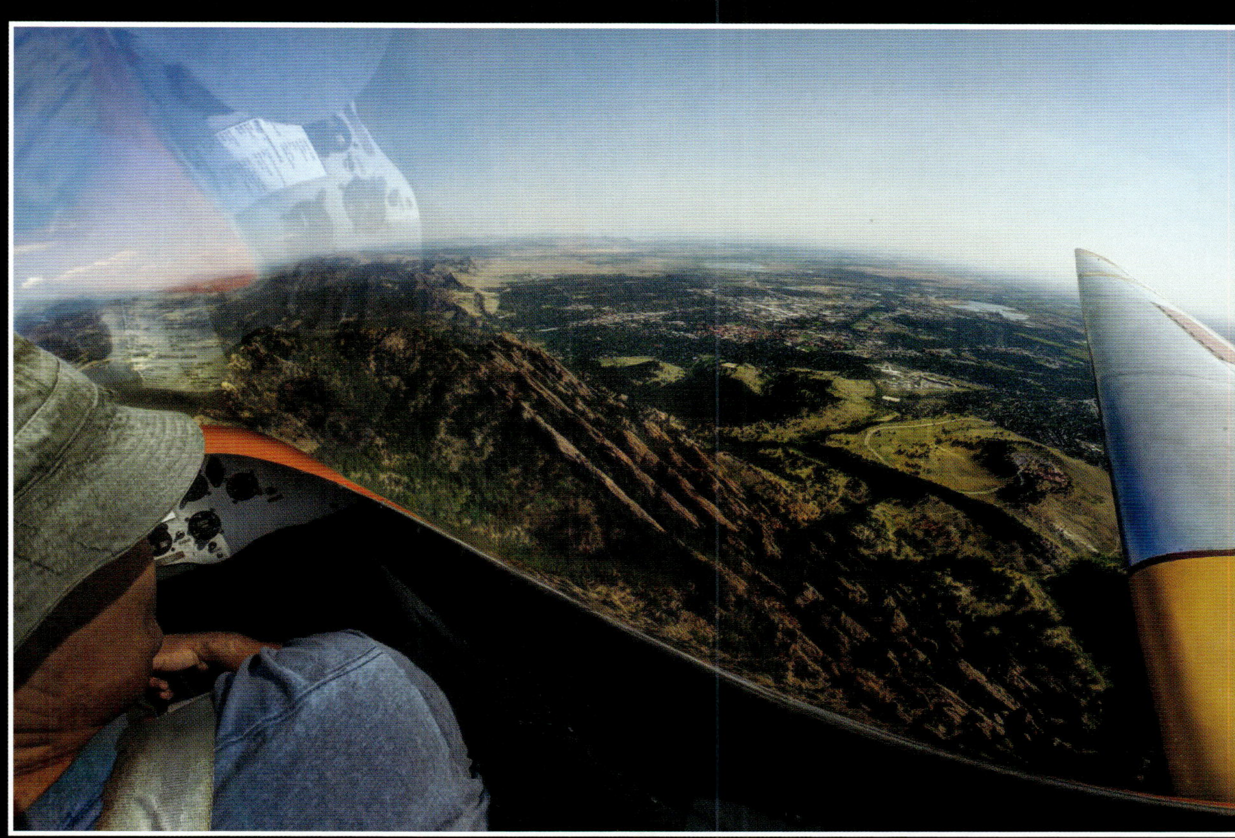

ABOVE: A vertical view of the Flatirons can be enjoyed while soaring through the sky on a glider ride provided by Mile High Gliding, Inc.

LEFT: Walnut Brewery is one of several downtown brewpubs that attract University of Colorado students, as well as Boulder residents.

RIGHT: For many years, this contortionist has been drawing crowds on the Pearl Street Mall.

FAR RIGHT: A unicyclist plays with fire on the Pearl Street Mall. In 1980, the commercial area of downtown Boulder was placed on the National Register of Historic Places, which was followed, in 1999, by the creation of a locally designated Downtown Historic District.

BELOW: Mall-goers enjoy a game of hacky sack.

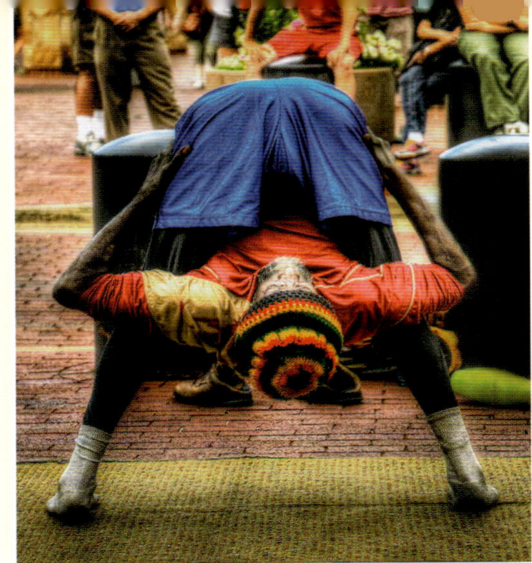

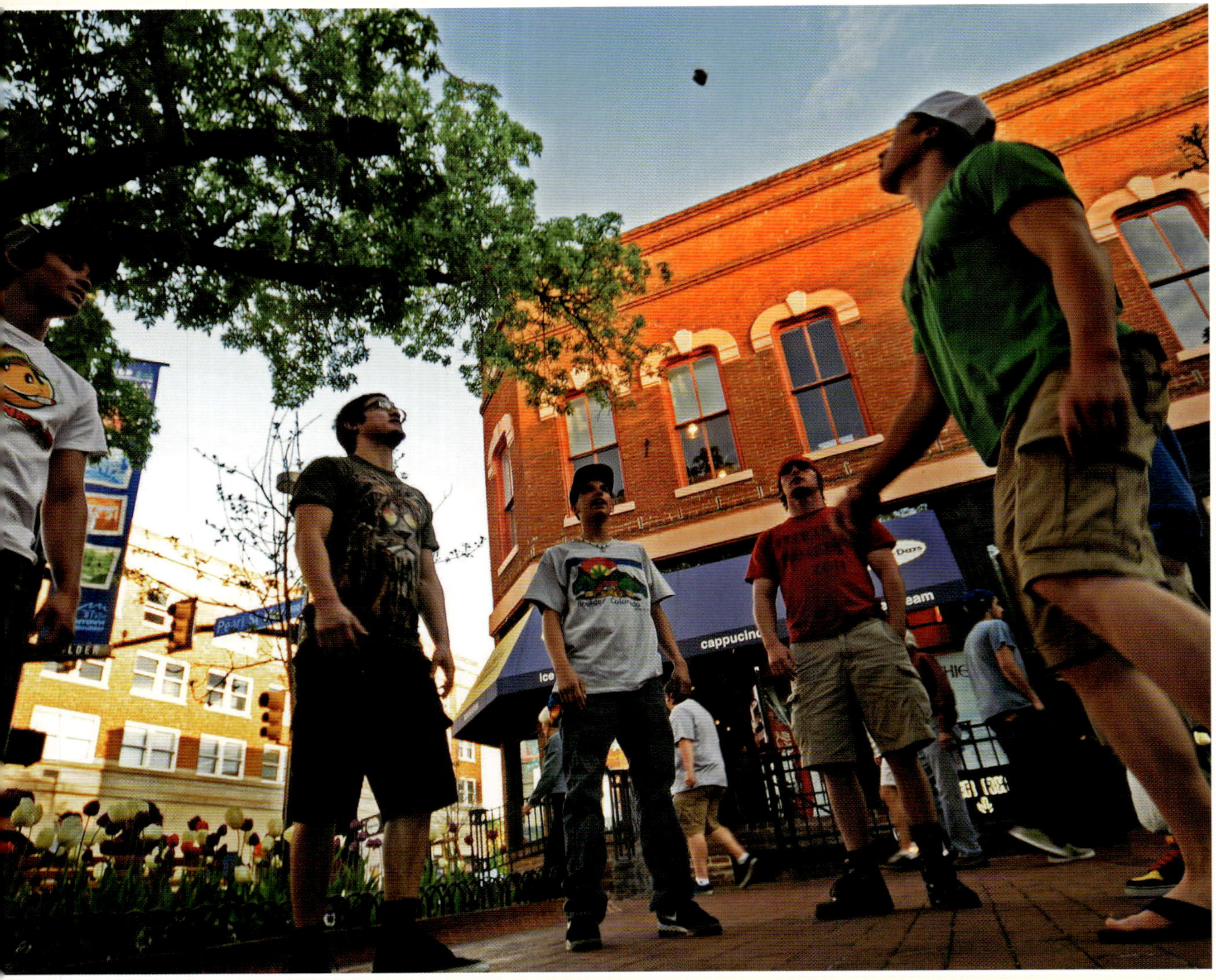

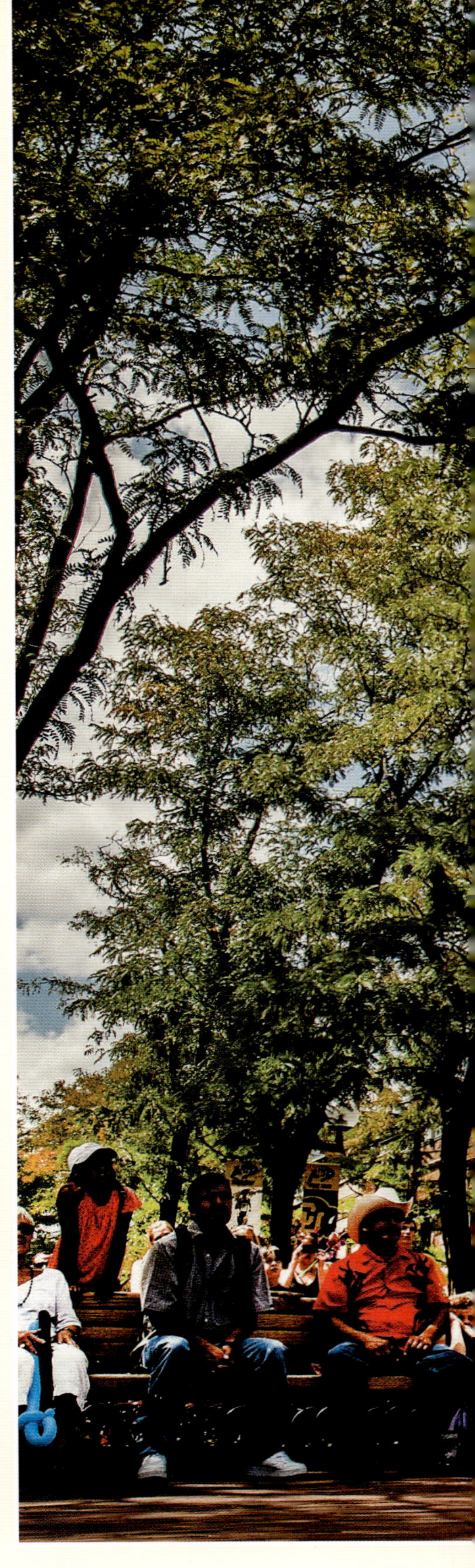

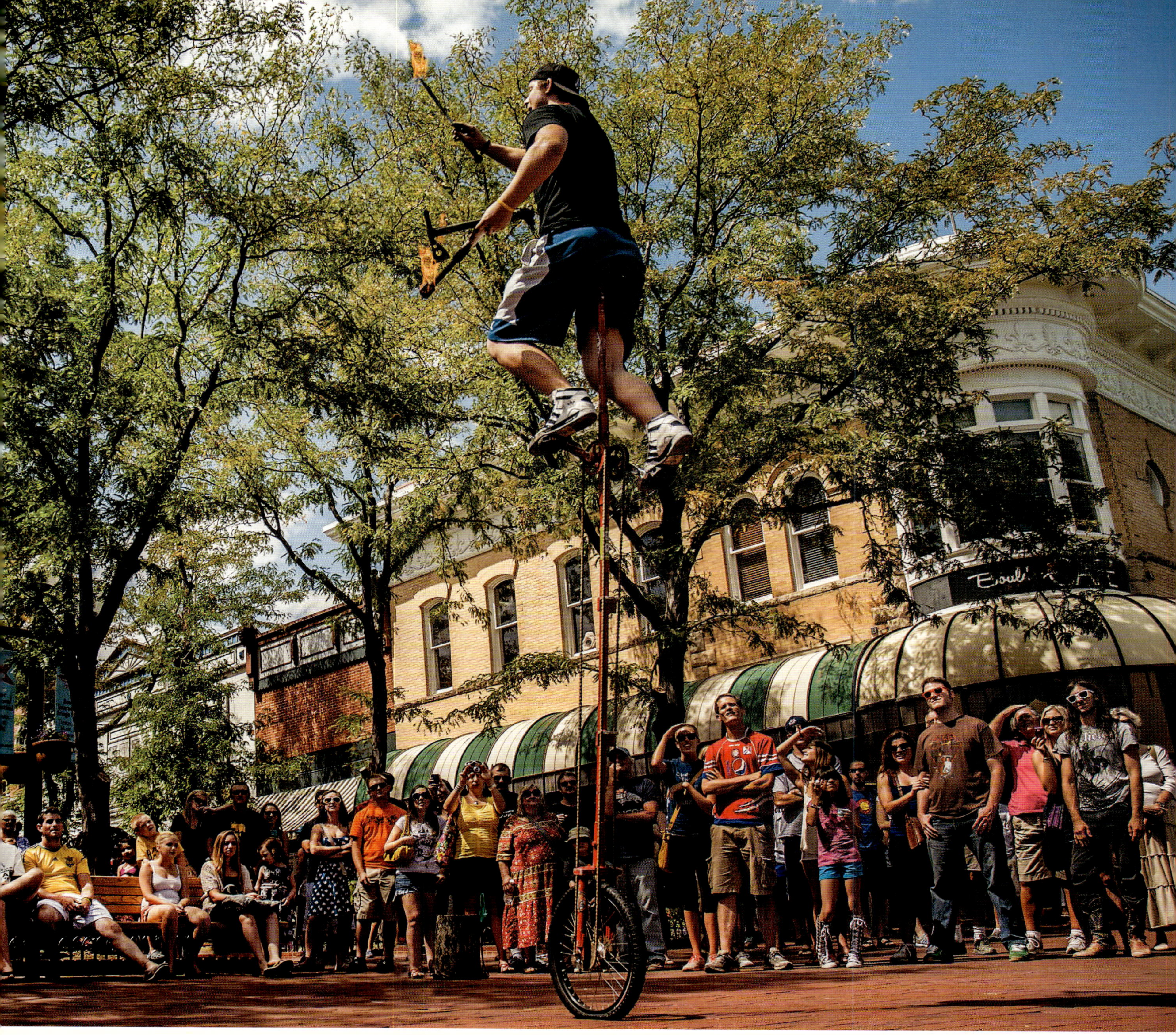

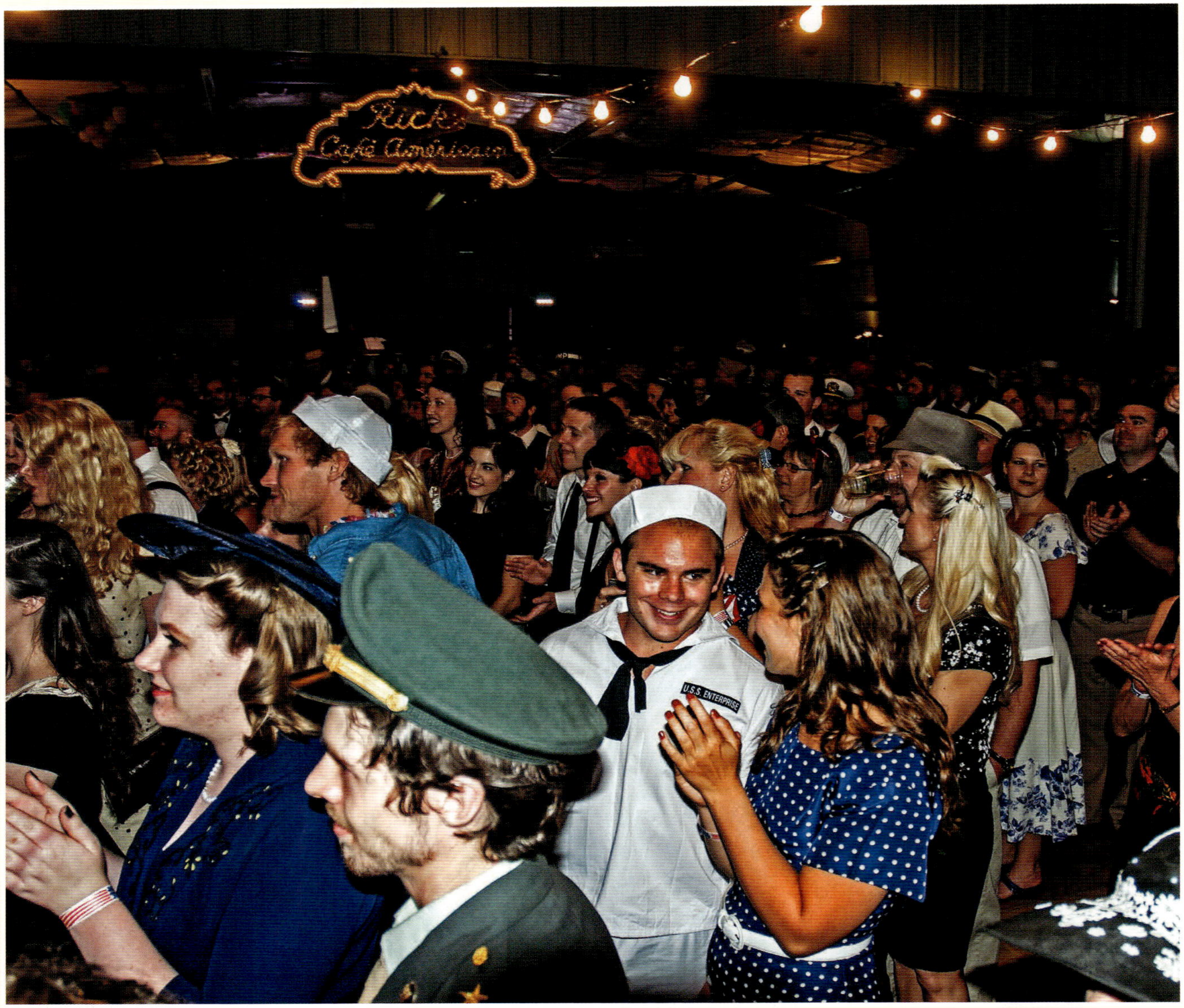

ABOVE: Reenacting a time long gone, both the Army and the Navy are represented at this 1940s costume ball in the Boulder Theater.

RIGHT: The Boulder Theater, opposite the Boulder County Courthouse in downtown Boulder, exemplifies another element of Art Deco architecture—neon lights. The building opened in 1936 on the site of the Curran Opera House.

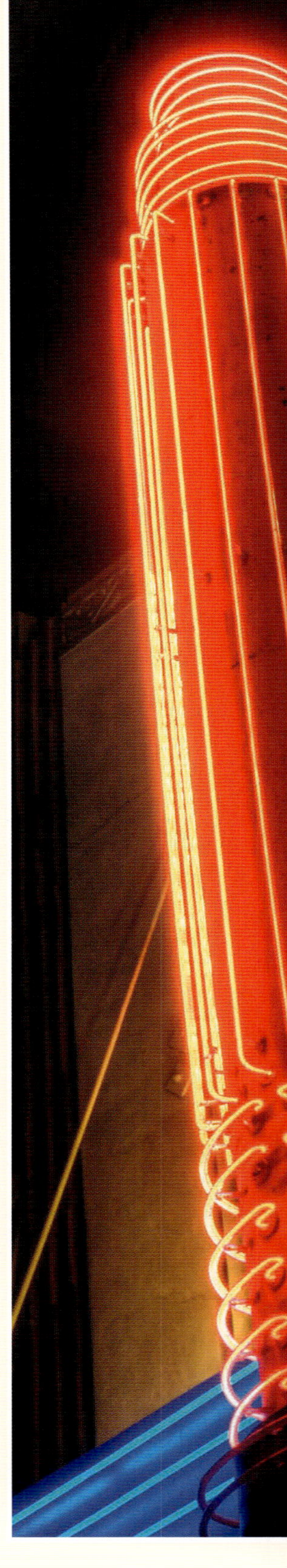

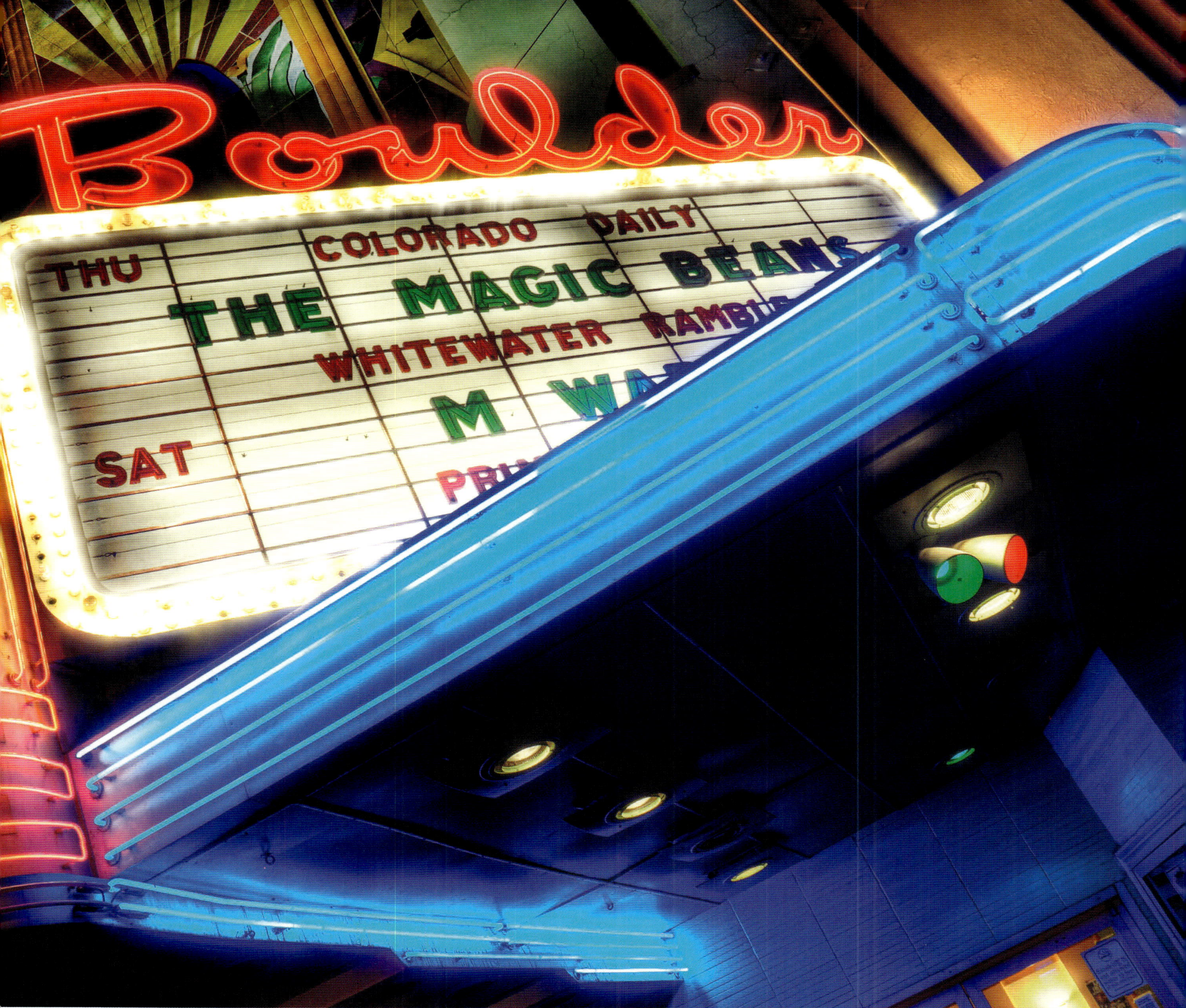
Boulder
THU
COLORADO DAILY
THE MAGIC BEANS
WHITEWATER
SAT

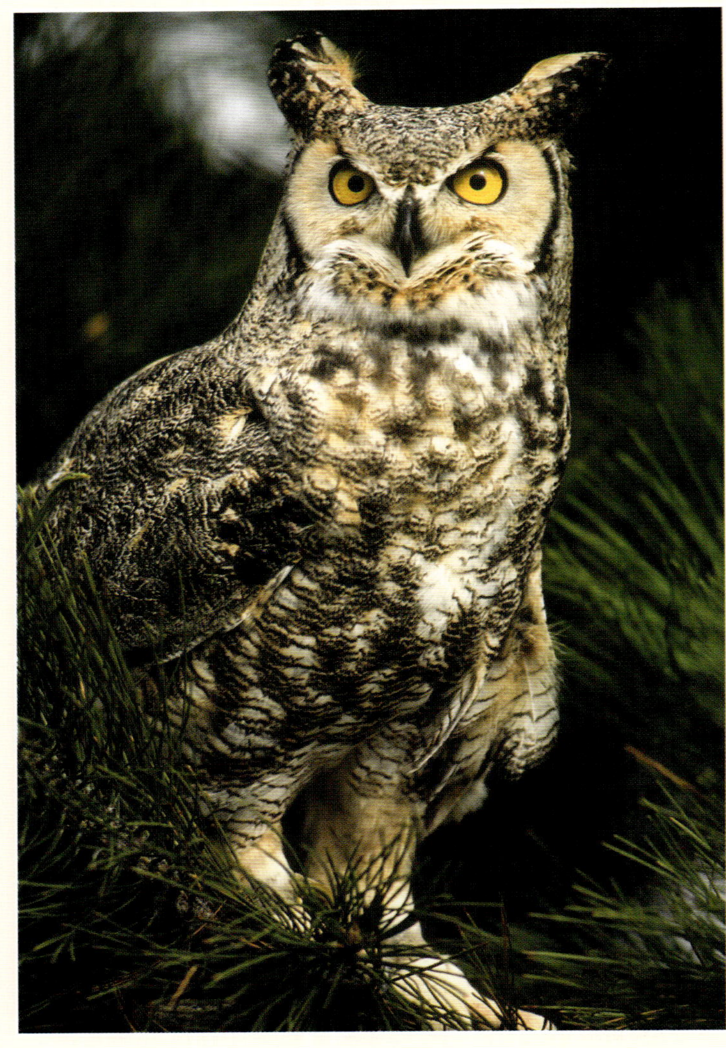

ABOVE: A great horned owl contemplates his next meal at the Twin Lakes Open Space, northeast of Boulder.

RIGHT: Rain and fog create an eerie scene in a bristlecone pine forest.

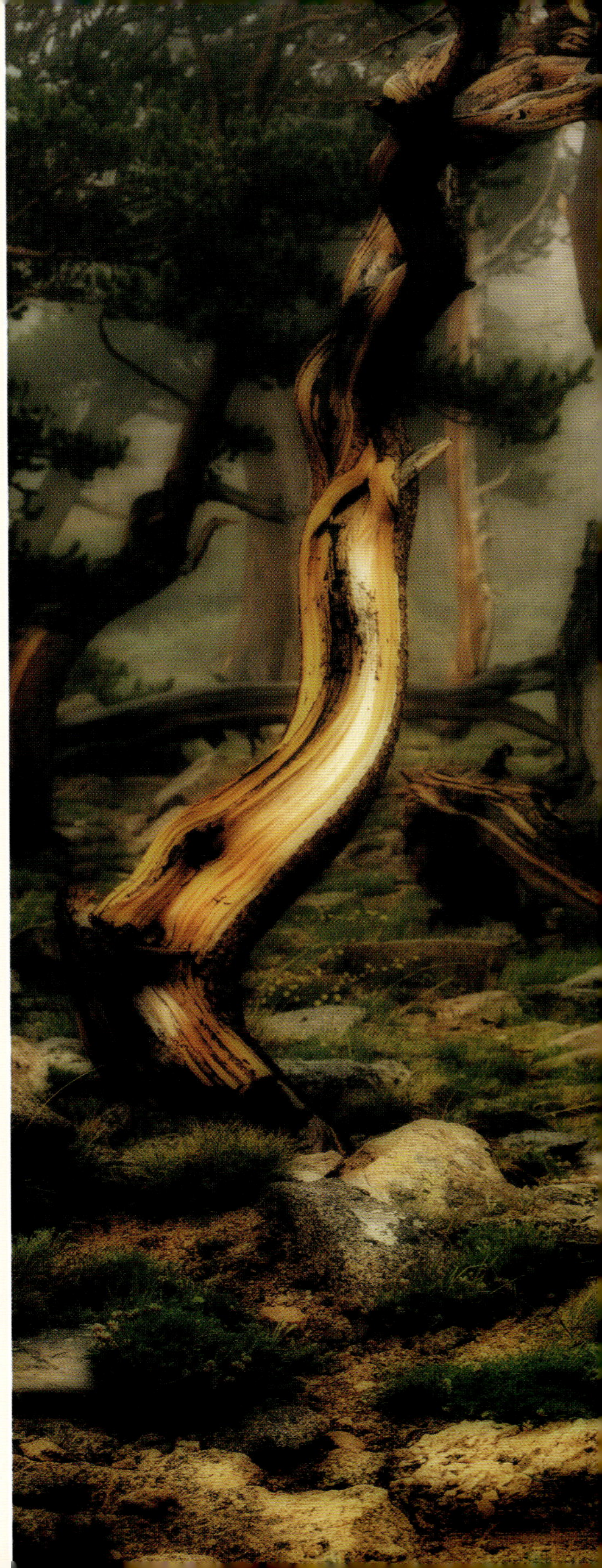

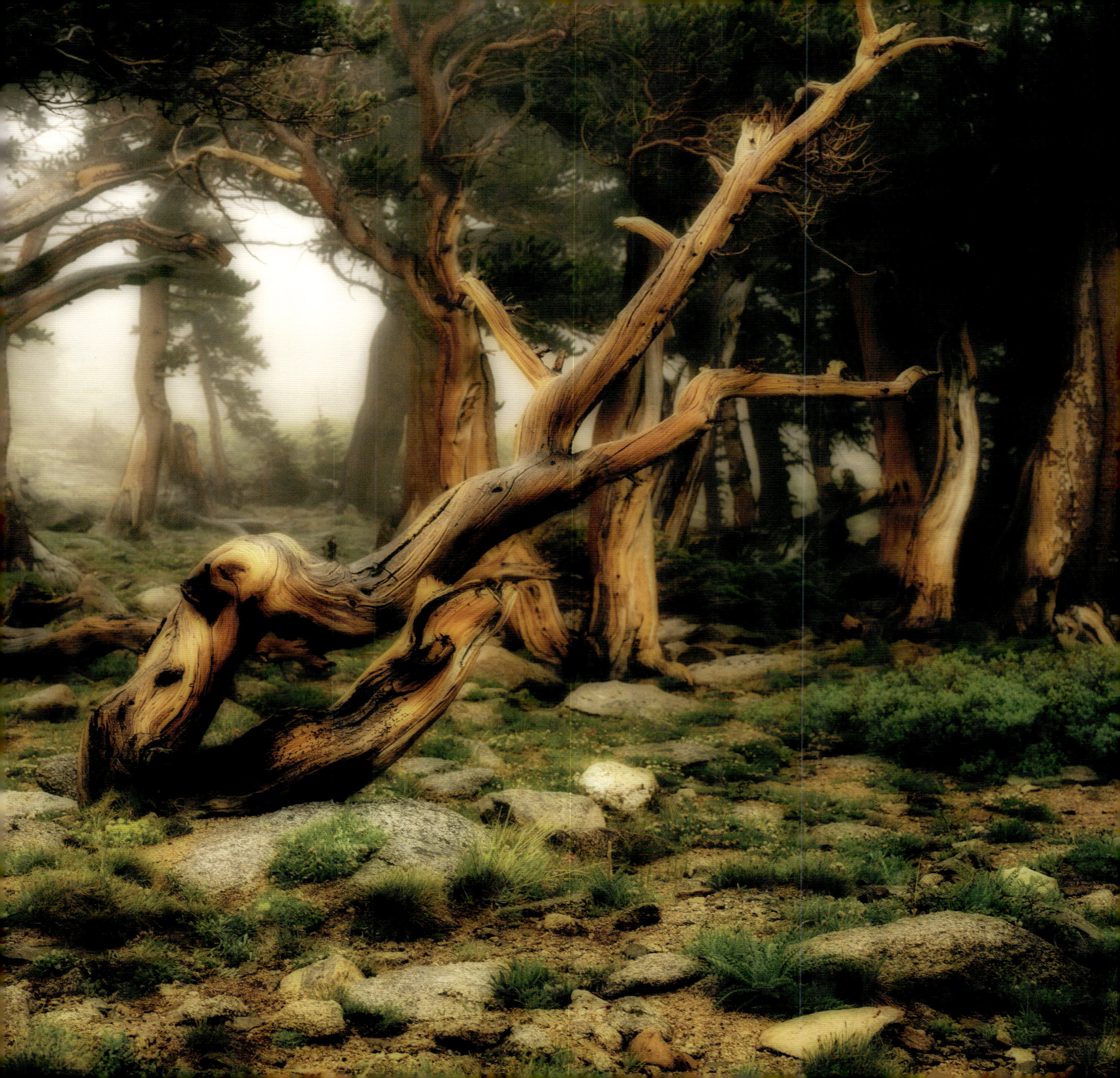

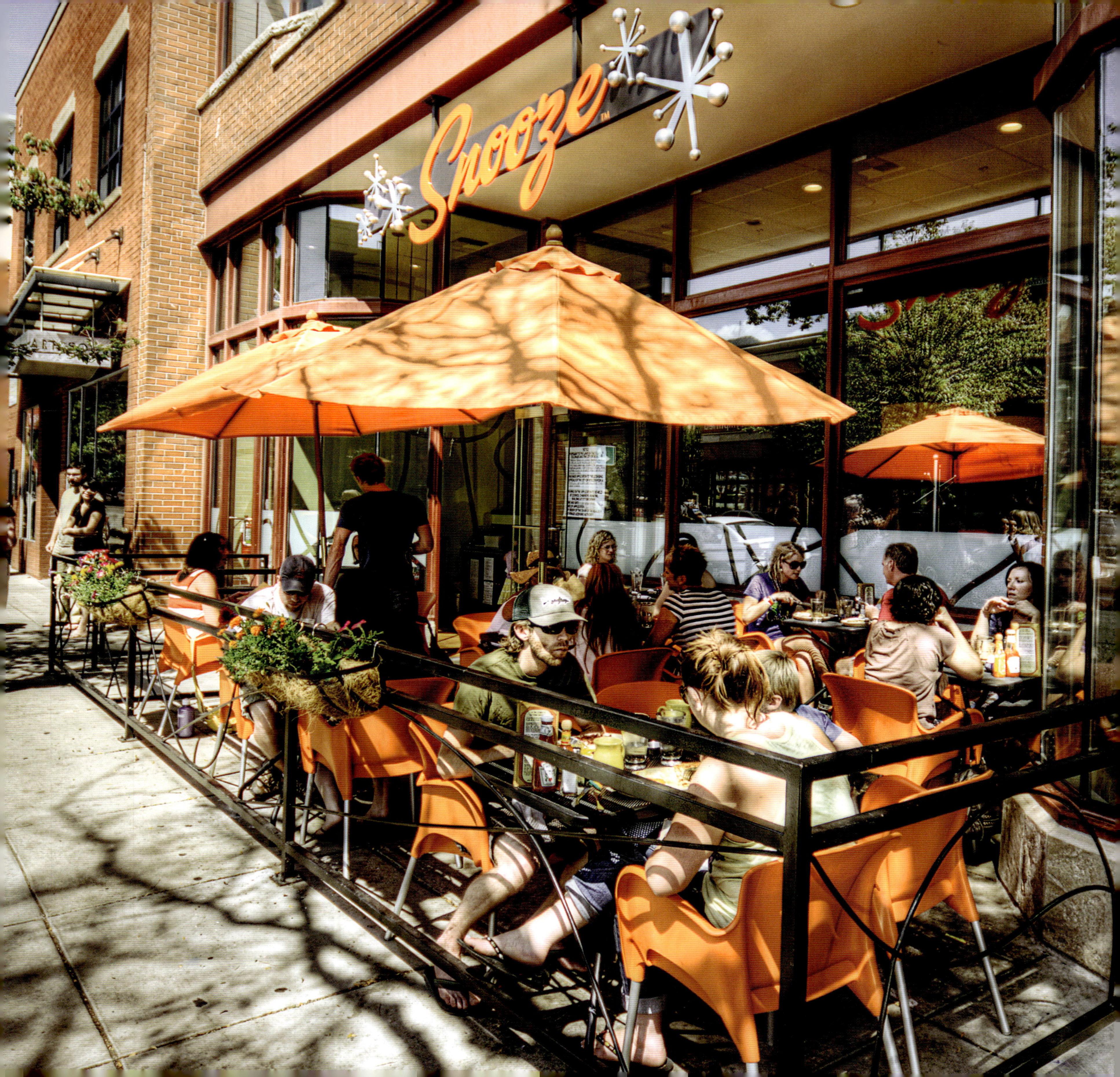
Snooze

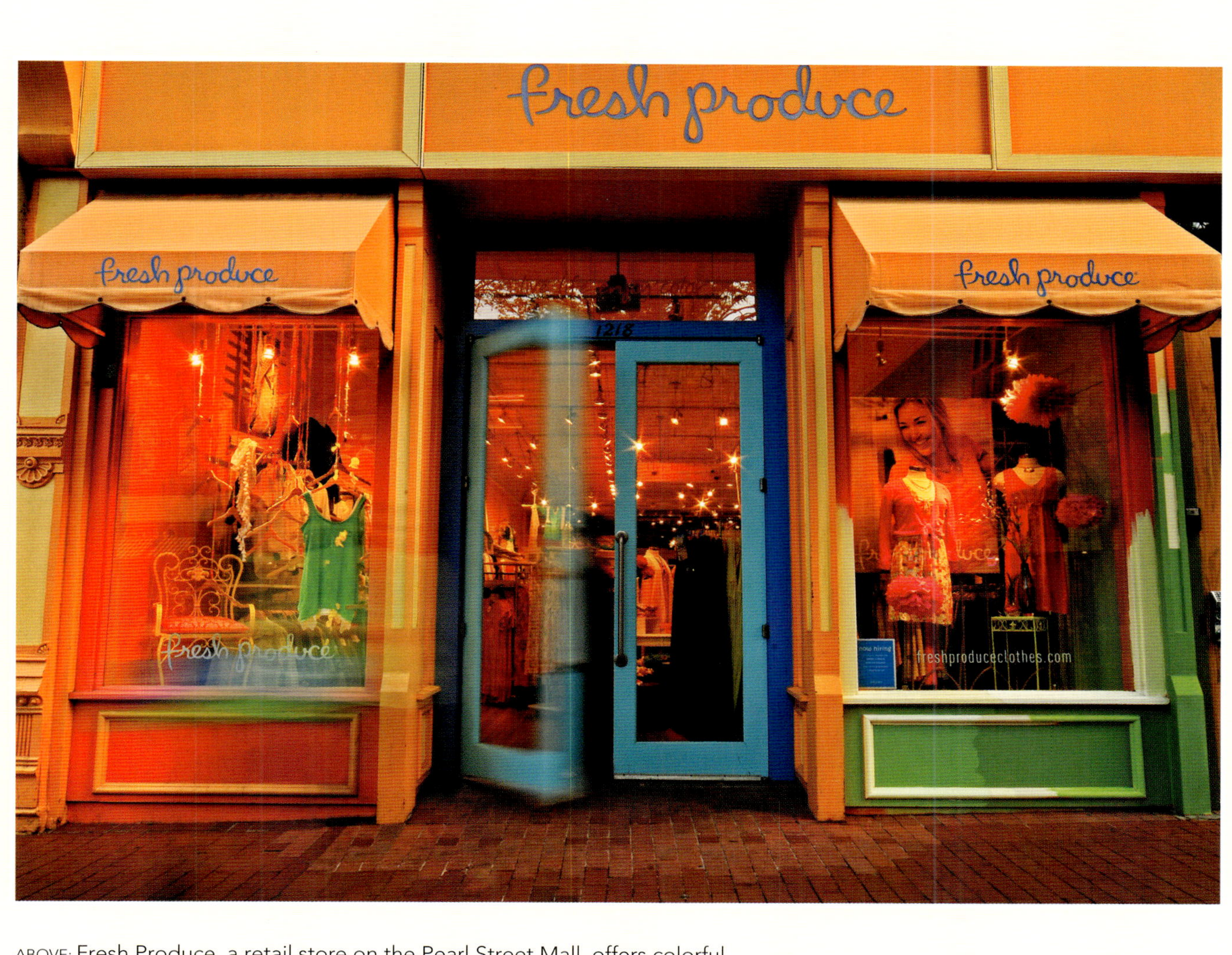

ABOVE: Fresh Produce, a retail store on the Pearl Street Mall, offers colorful, comfortable clothes for women and children.

LEFT: Boulder residents enjoy eating outside at Snooze, a breakfast and lunch restaurant located one and one-half blocks east of the Pearl Street Mall.

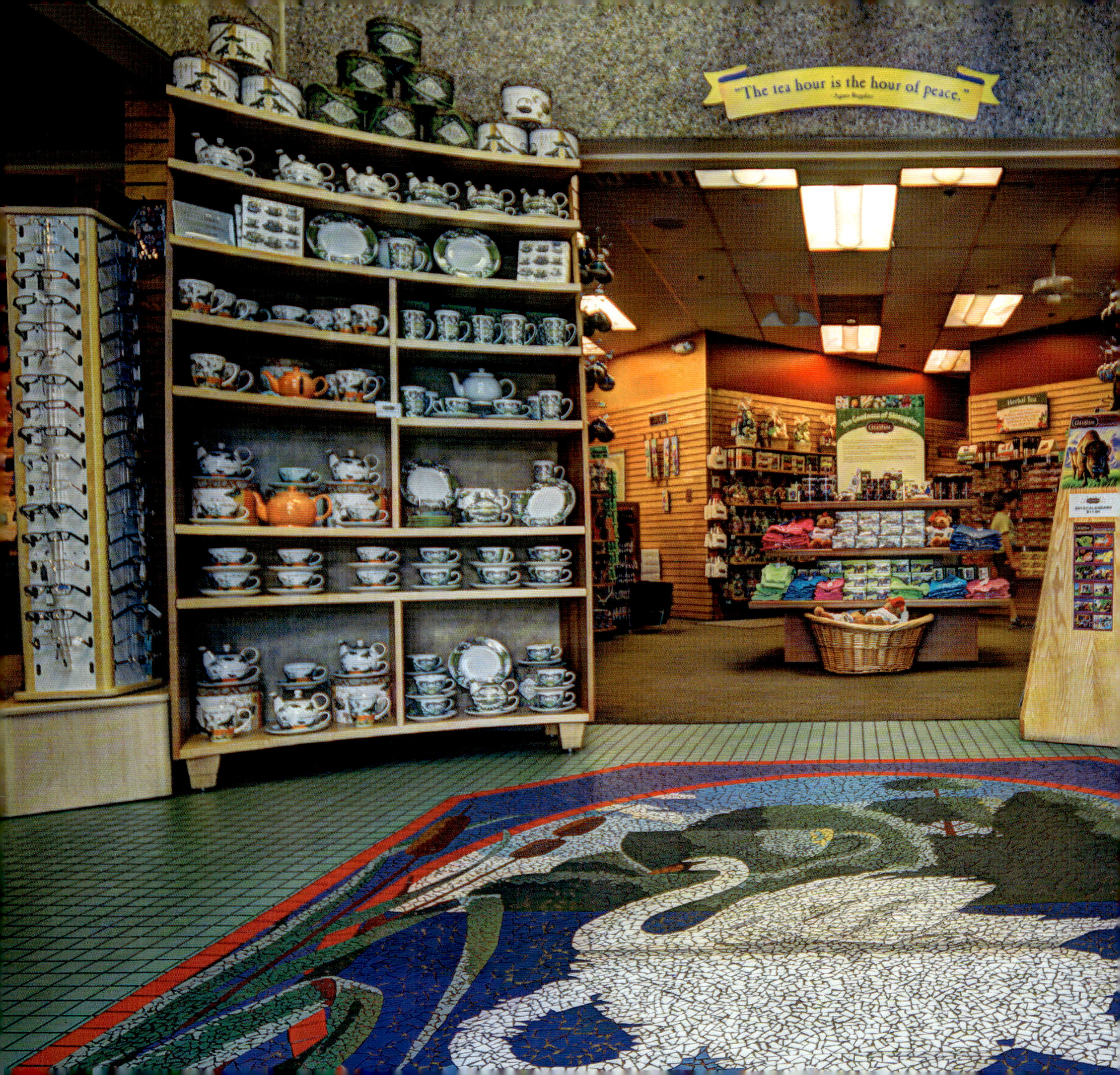
"The tea hour is the hour of peace."

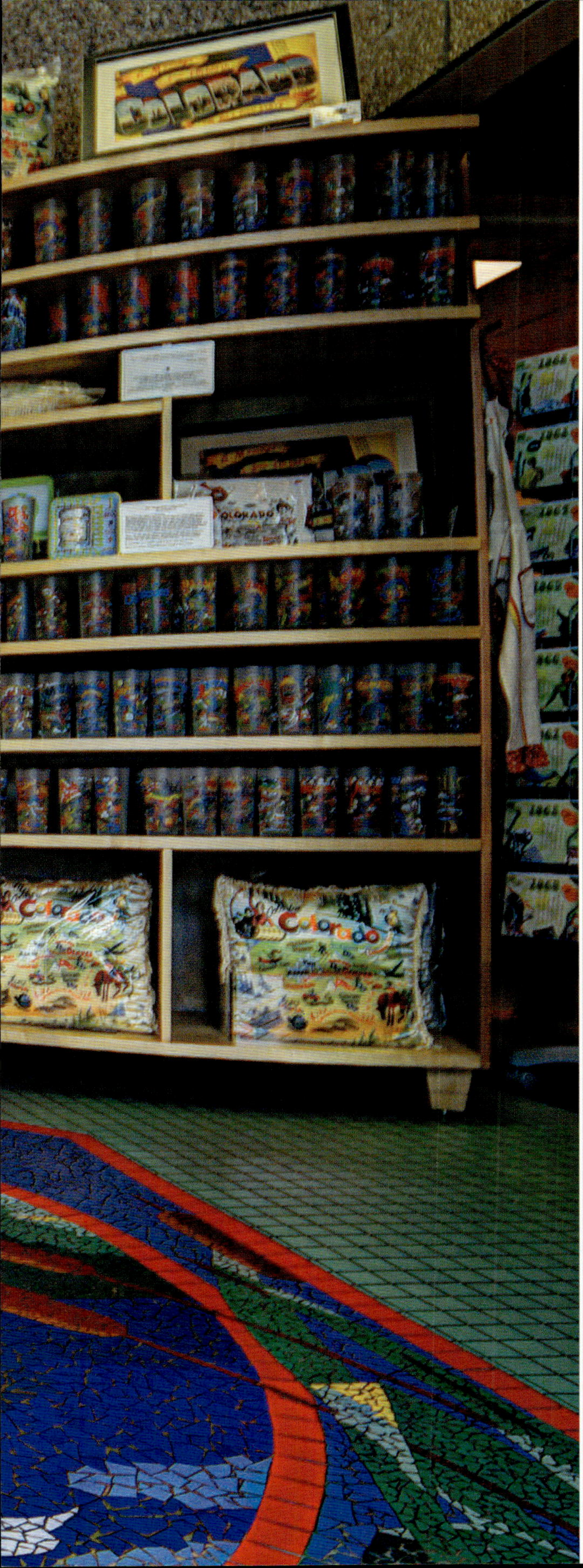

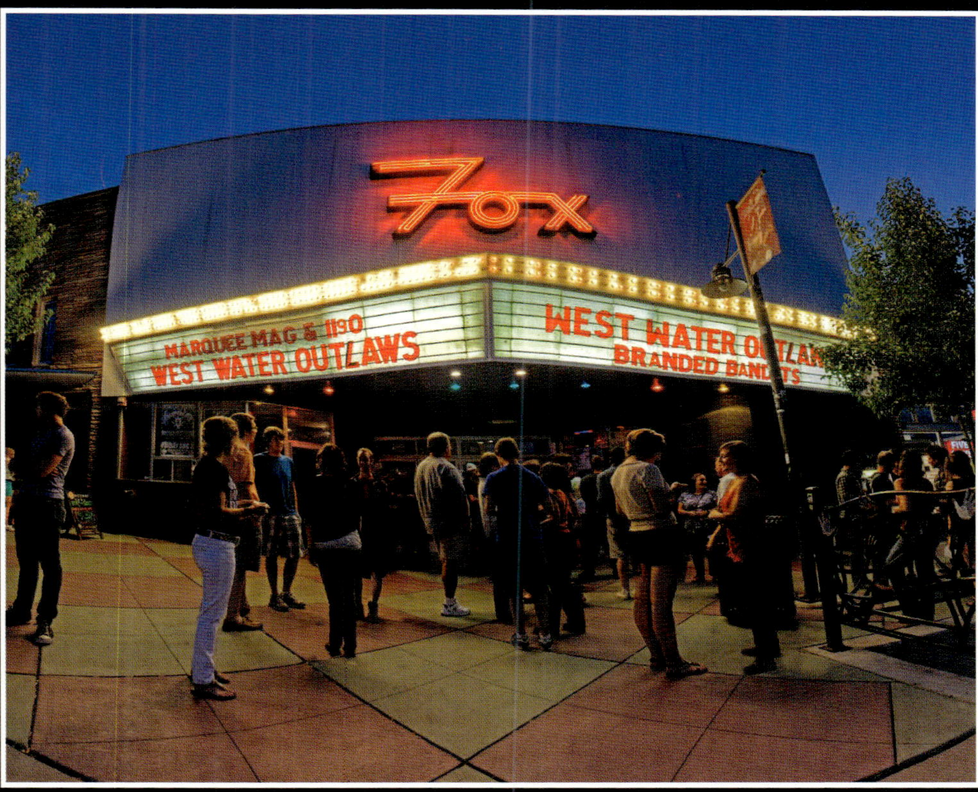

ABOVE: The Fox Theater has been part of the entertainment scene on University Hill since the 1940s. Now, instead of showing films, it is a popular music venue.

LEFT: The Celestial Seasonings Tea Shop is the place to stock up on natural teas after a free tour through the company's herbal tea production plant.

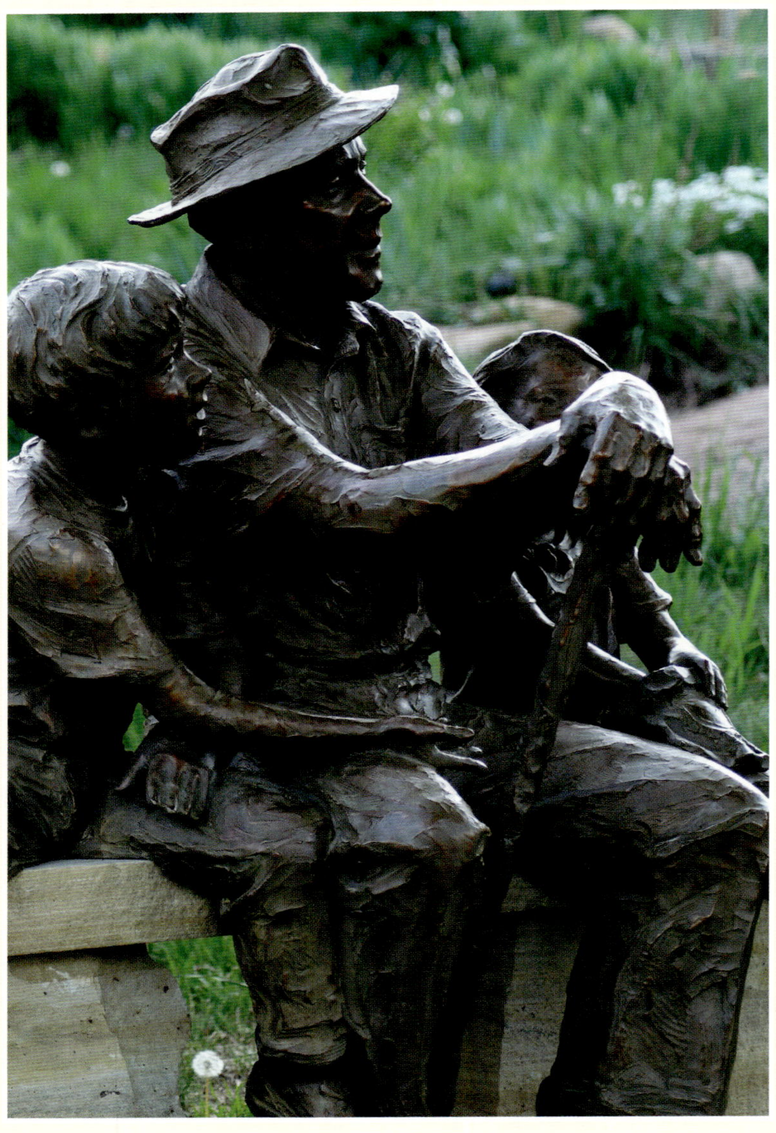

ABOVE: Frozen in time forever, these bronze "hikers" rest in Chautauqua Park, near the trail to Bluebell Canyon.

RIGHT: Indian paintbrush adds color to the banks of this tranquil mountain stream. The flowers resemble a ragged brush dipped in paint and come in various shades of red and yellow.

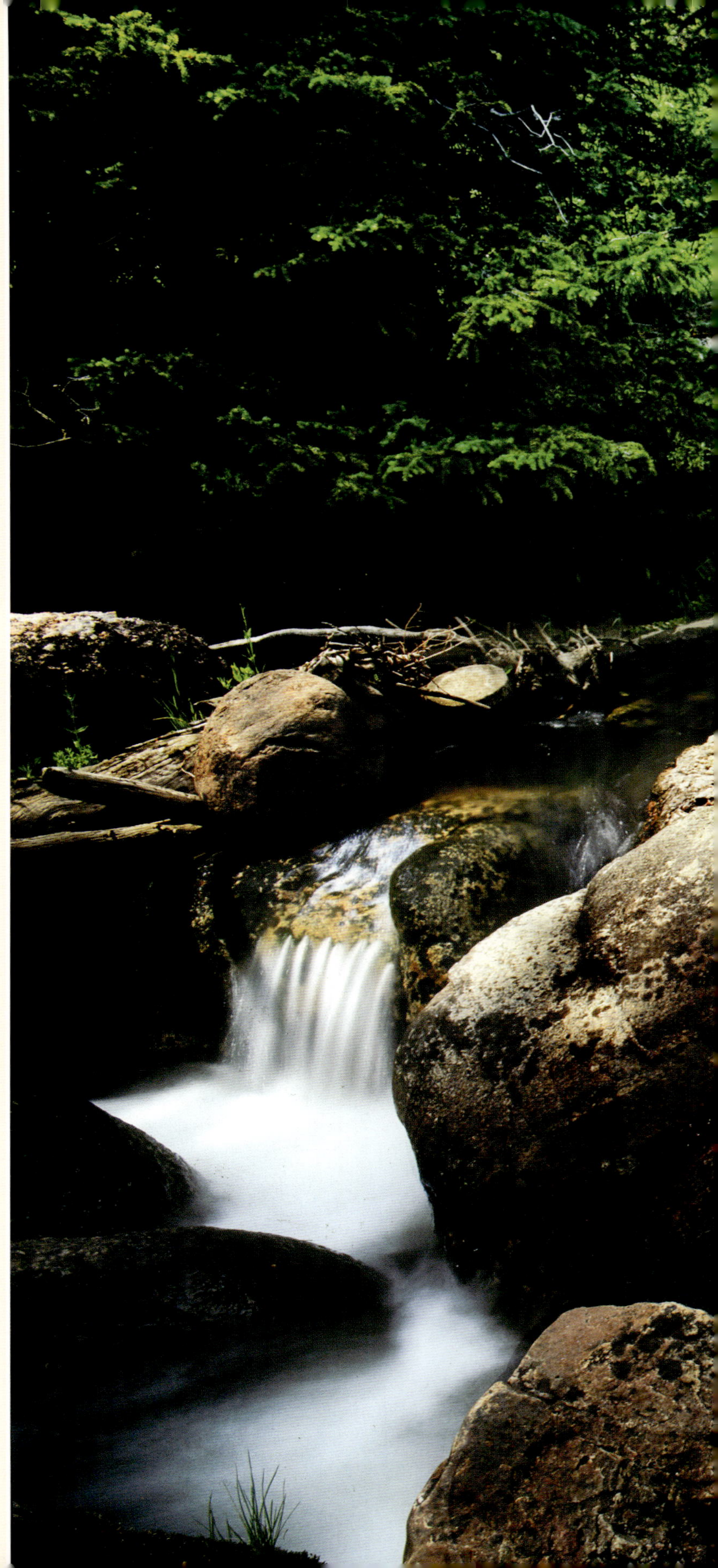

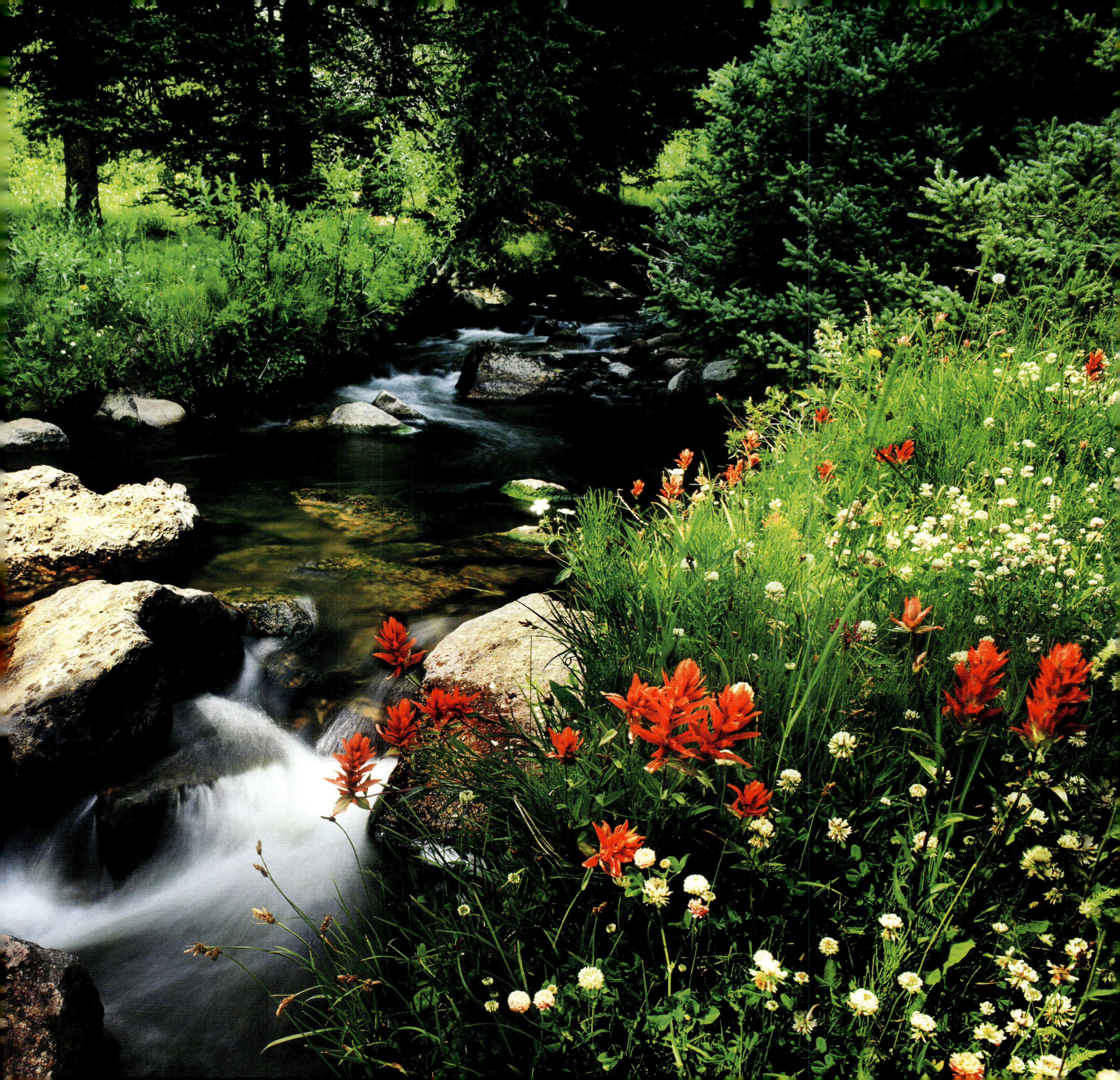

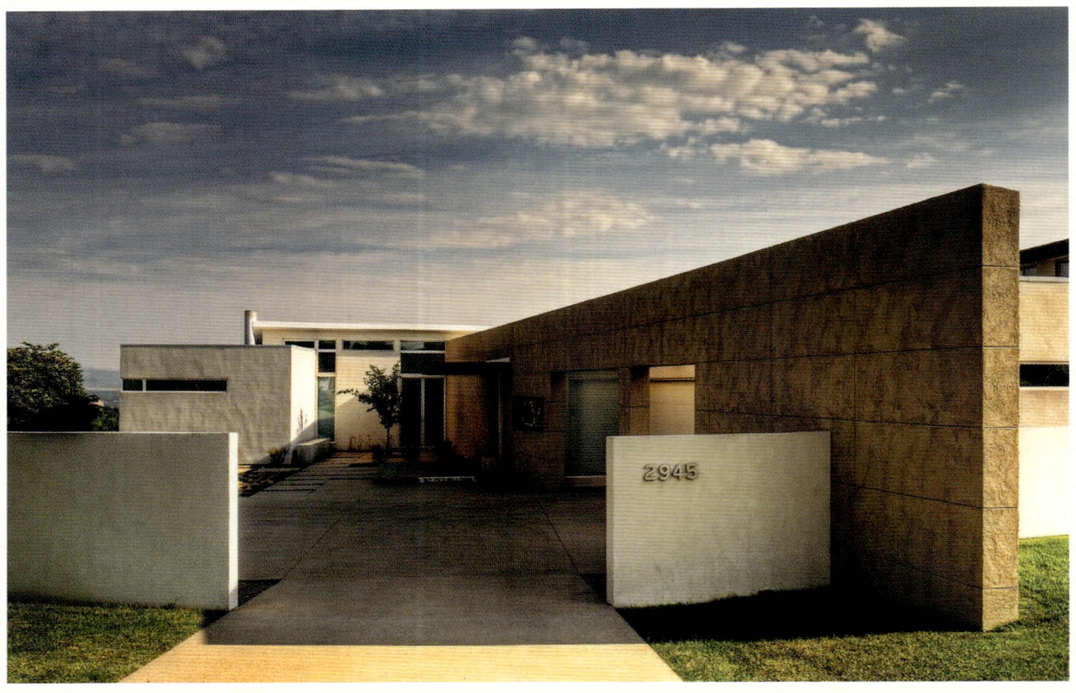

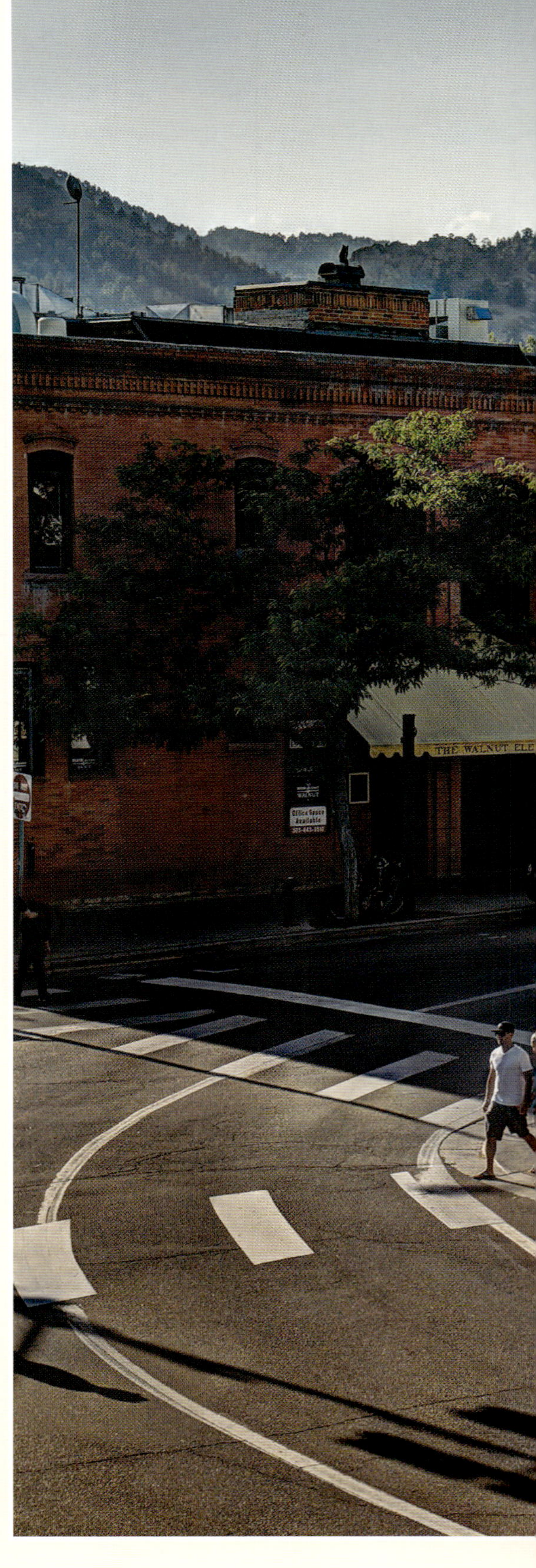

ABOVE: Architect Harvey Hine designed this 4,565-square-foot residence, built in Boulder in 2009.

RIGHT: The Rio Grande building is a good example of adapted reuse. Now a restaurant, the building was constructed in 1920 as an automobile garage and service station.

FOLLOWING PAGE: Bicycle racers find plenty of challenging curves in the foothills west of Boulder, including this curve on Lee Hill Road.

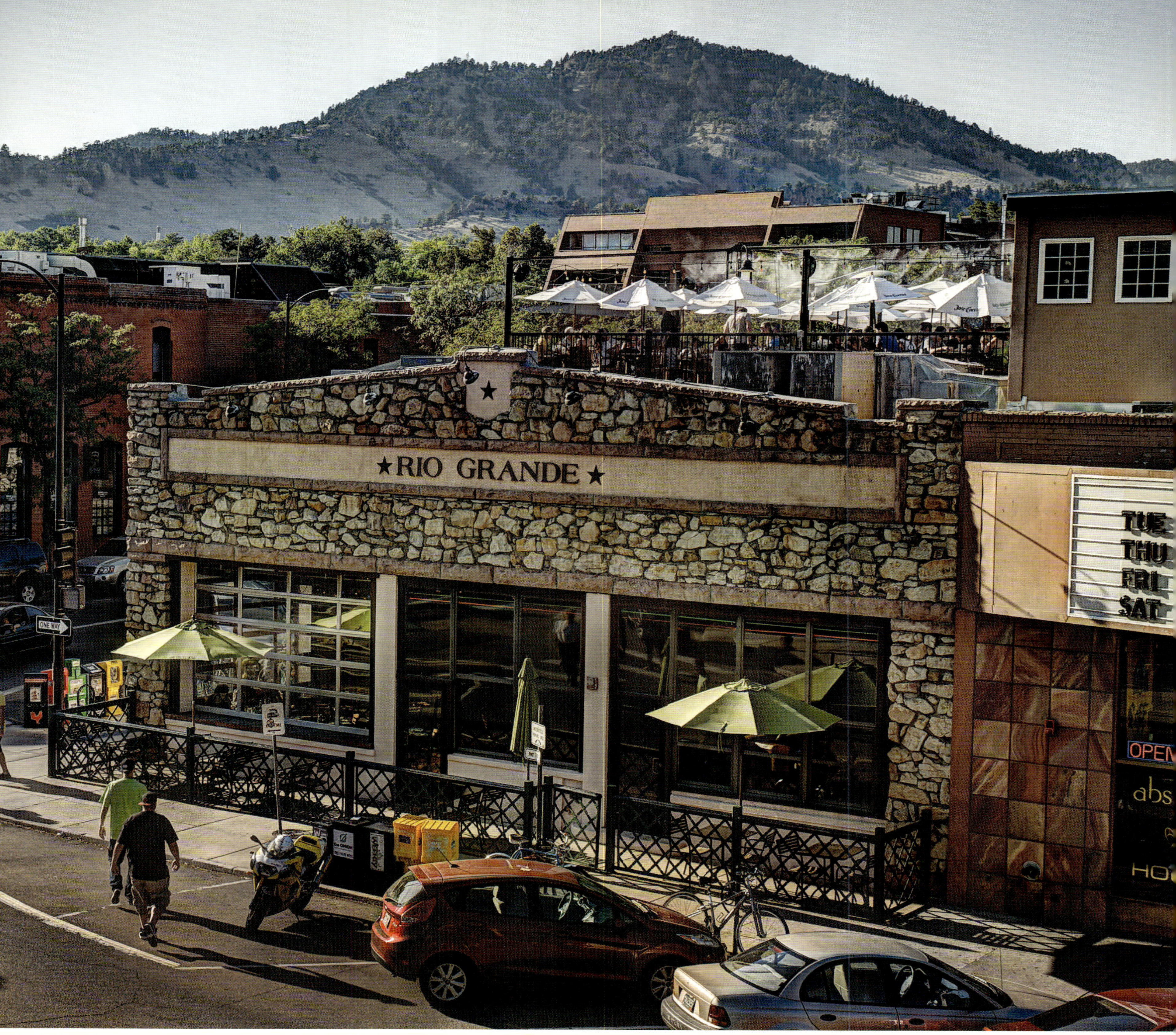
★RIO GRANDE★
TUE
THU
FRI
SAT
OPEN
abs
ONE WAY

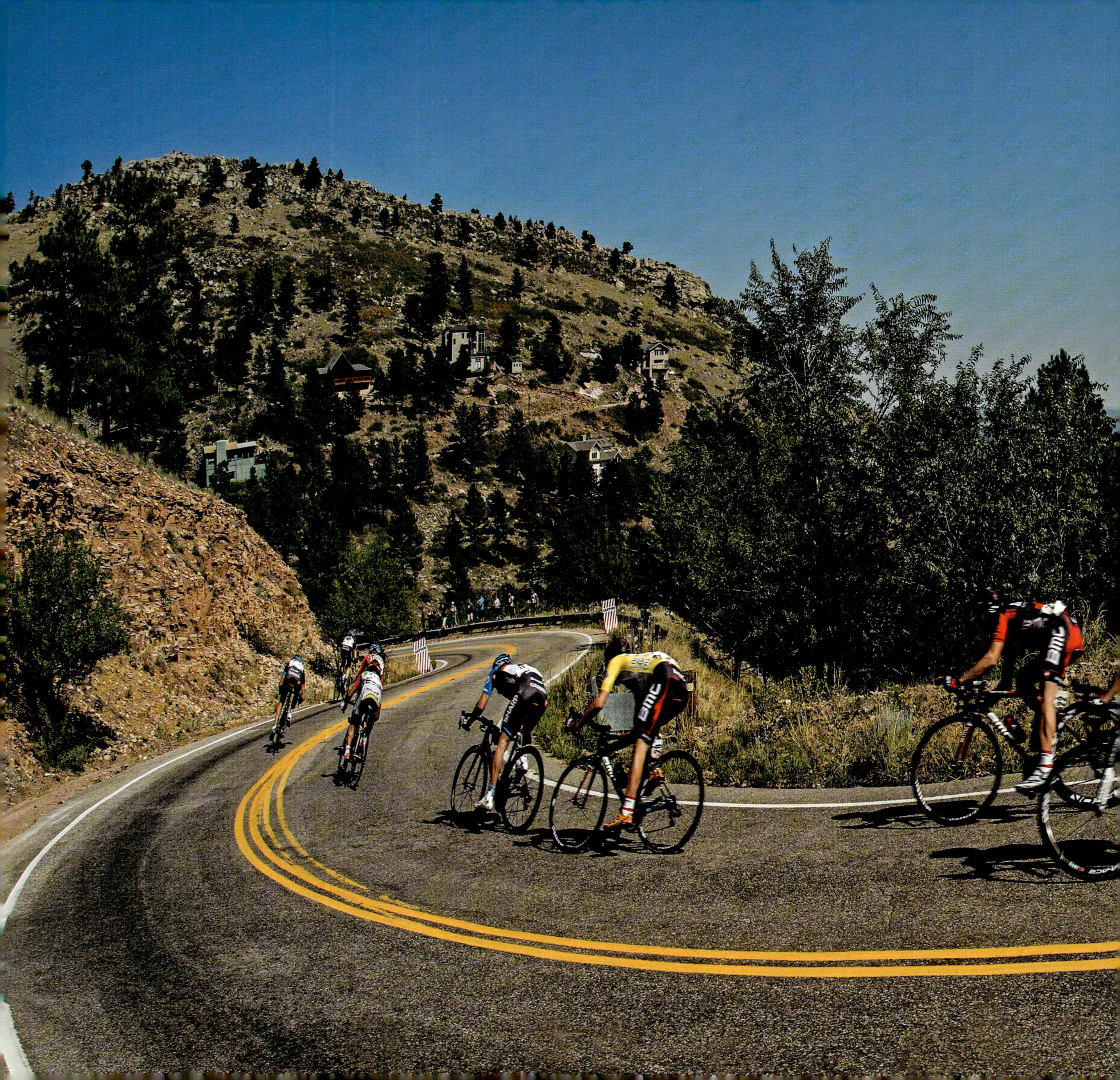
BMC

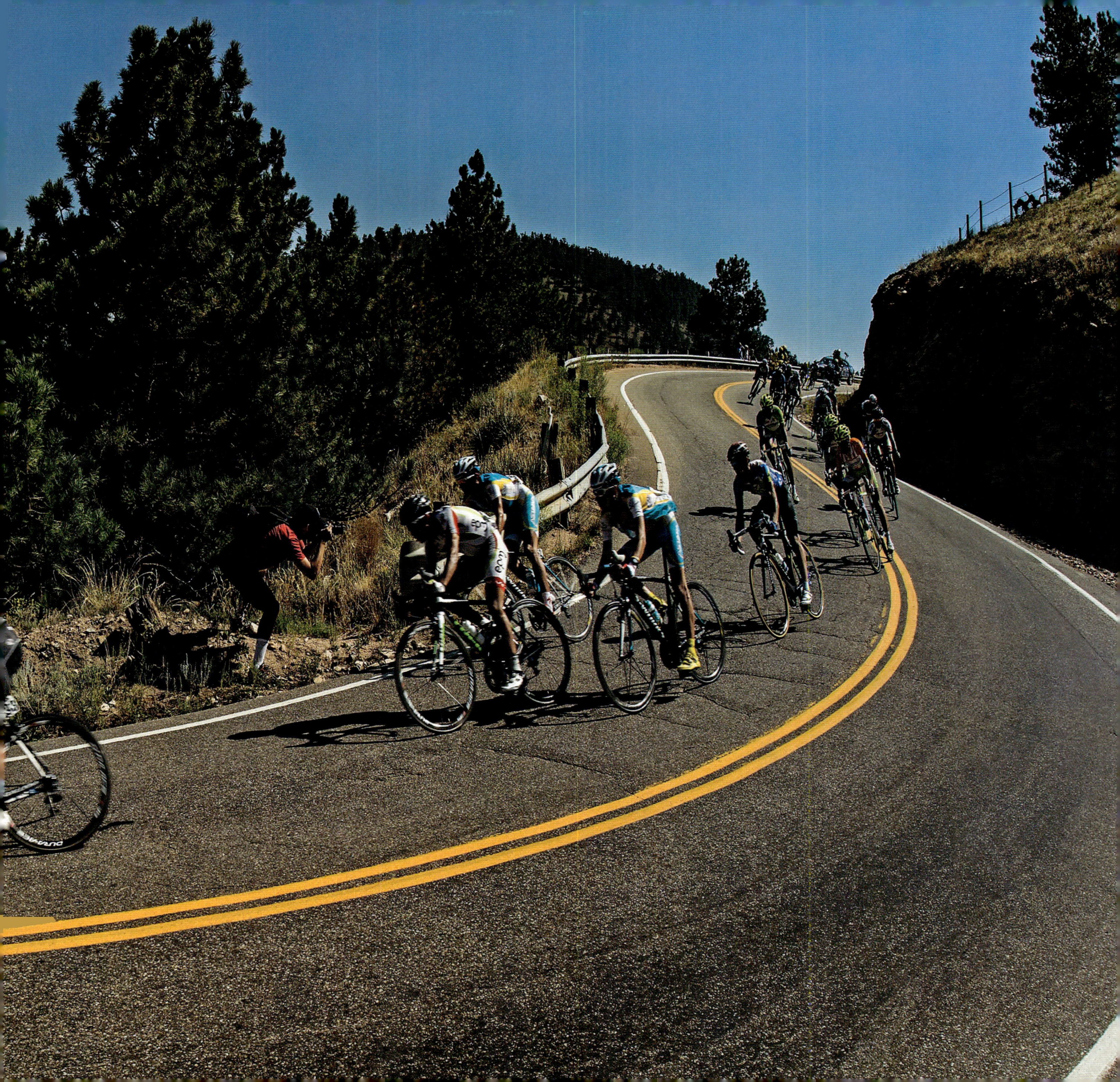

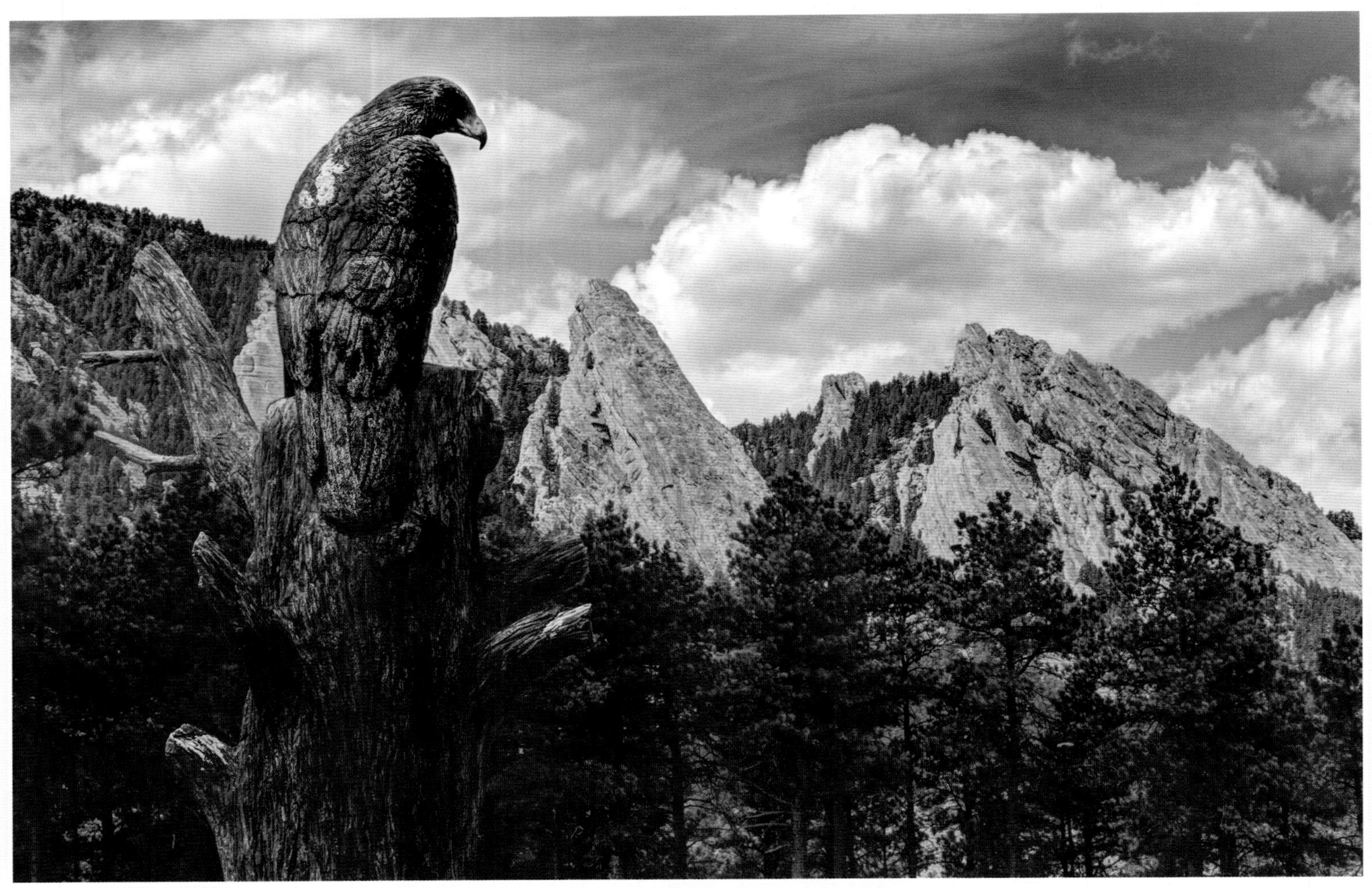

ABOVE: This lifelike golden eagle was crafted by Boulder County wood-carver Lueb Popoff and photographed against the city's iconic Flatirons at the National Center for Atmospheric Research (NCAR).

RIGHT: Reaching into the sky are Longs Peak (left) and Mount Meeker (right), dominating the town of Ward. The white Congregational Church survived a fire, in 1900, that destroyed most of the business district in this historic gold mining community.

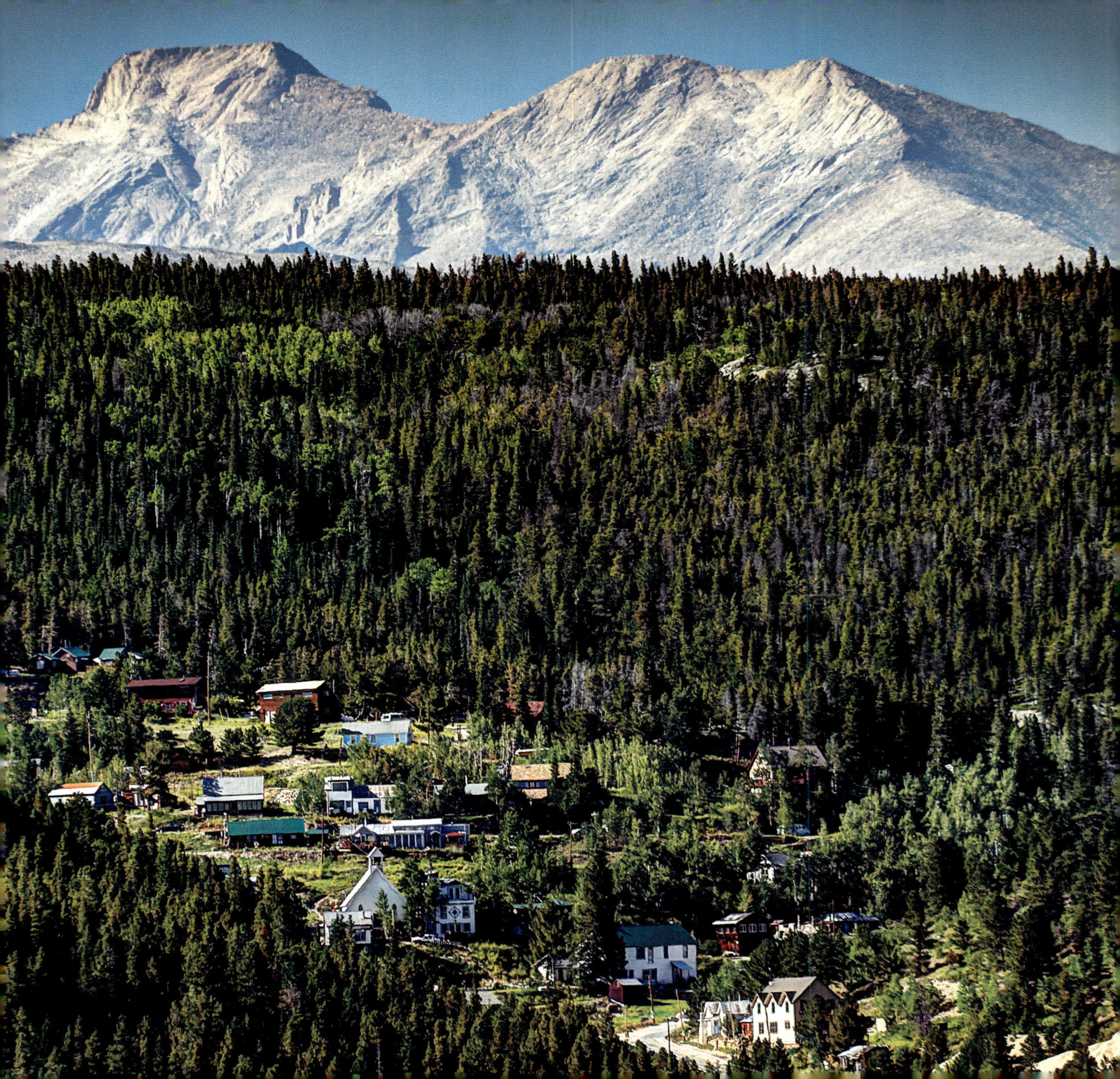

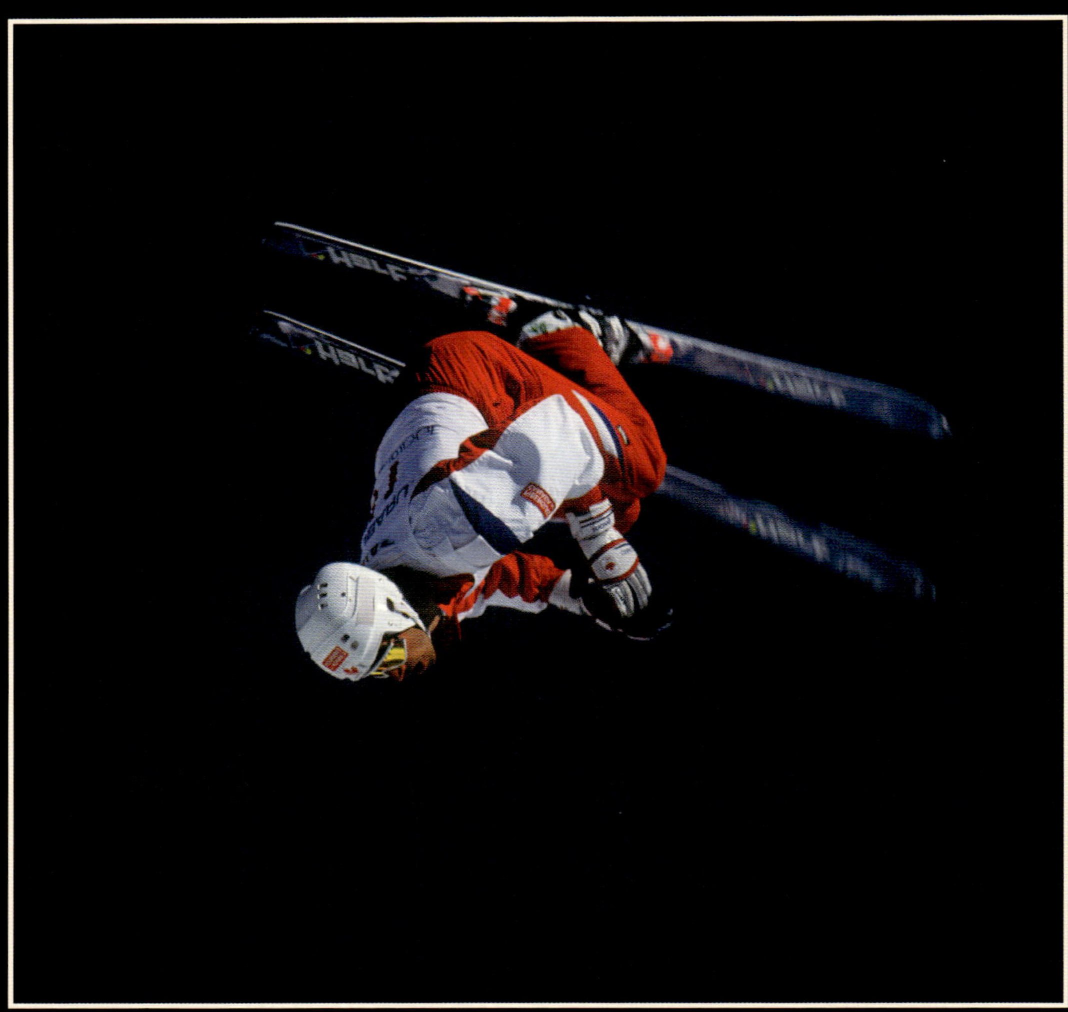

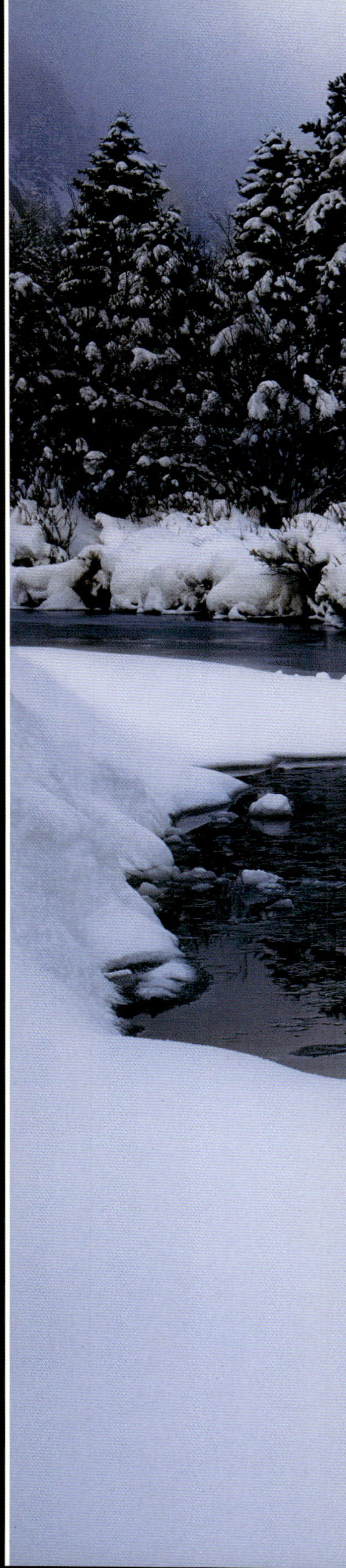

ABOVE: A skier twists in the air above the snow slopes at Eldora Mountain Resort—only a twenty-one-mile drive from downtown Boulder.

RIGHT: An early winter sunset is reflected in a mountain stream in Rocky Mountain National Park.

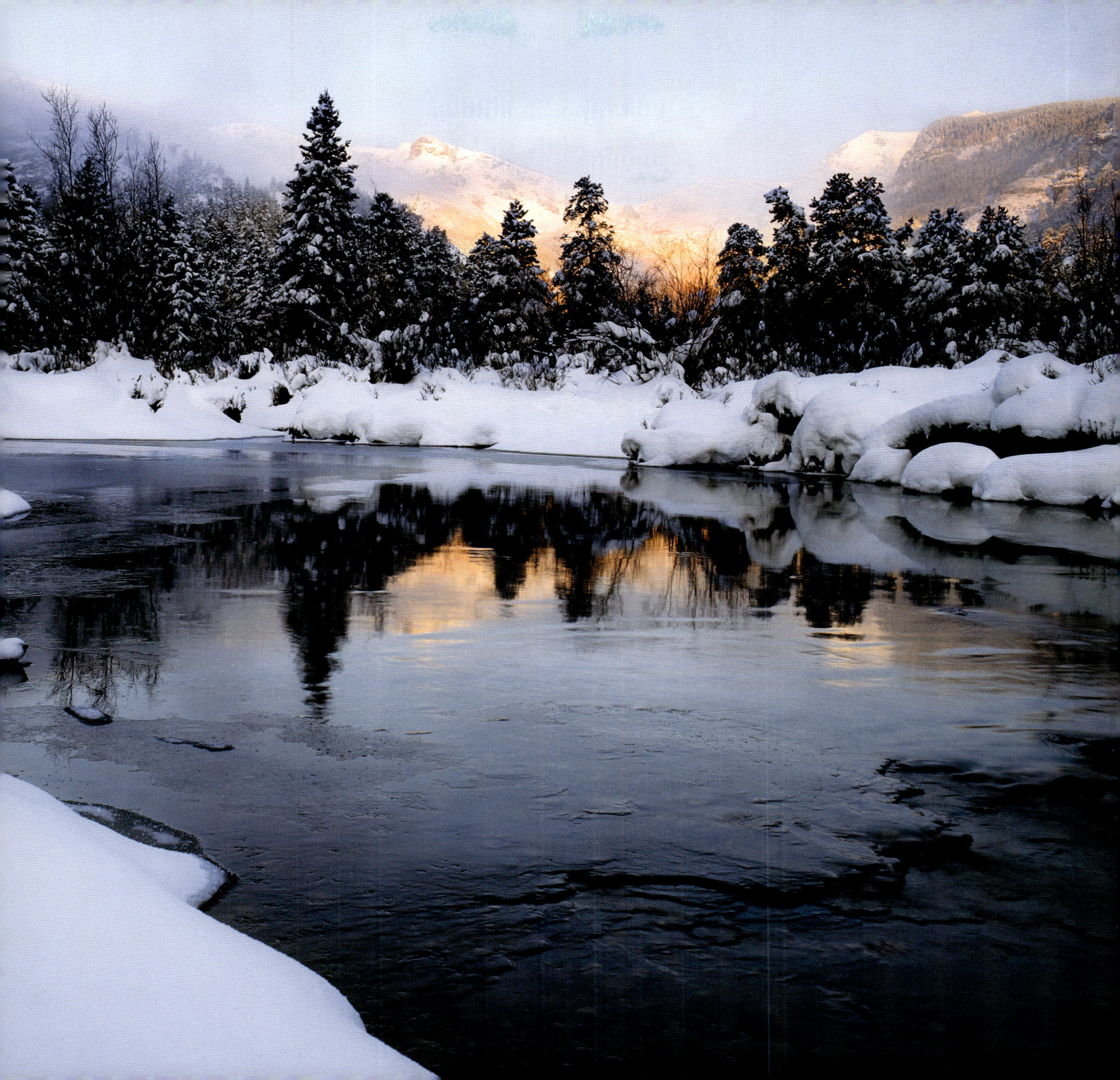

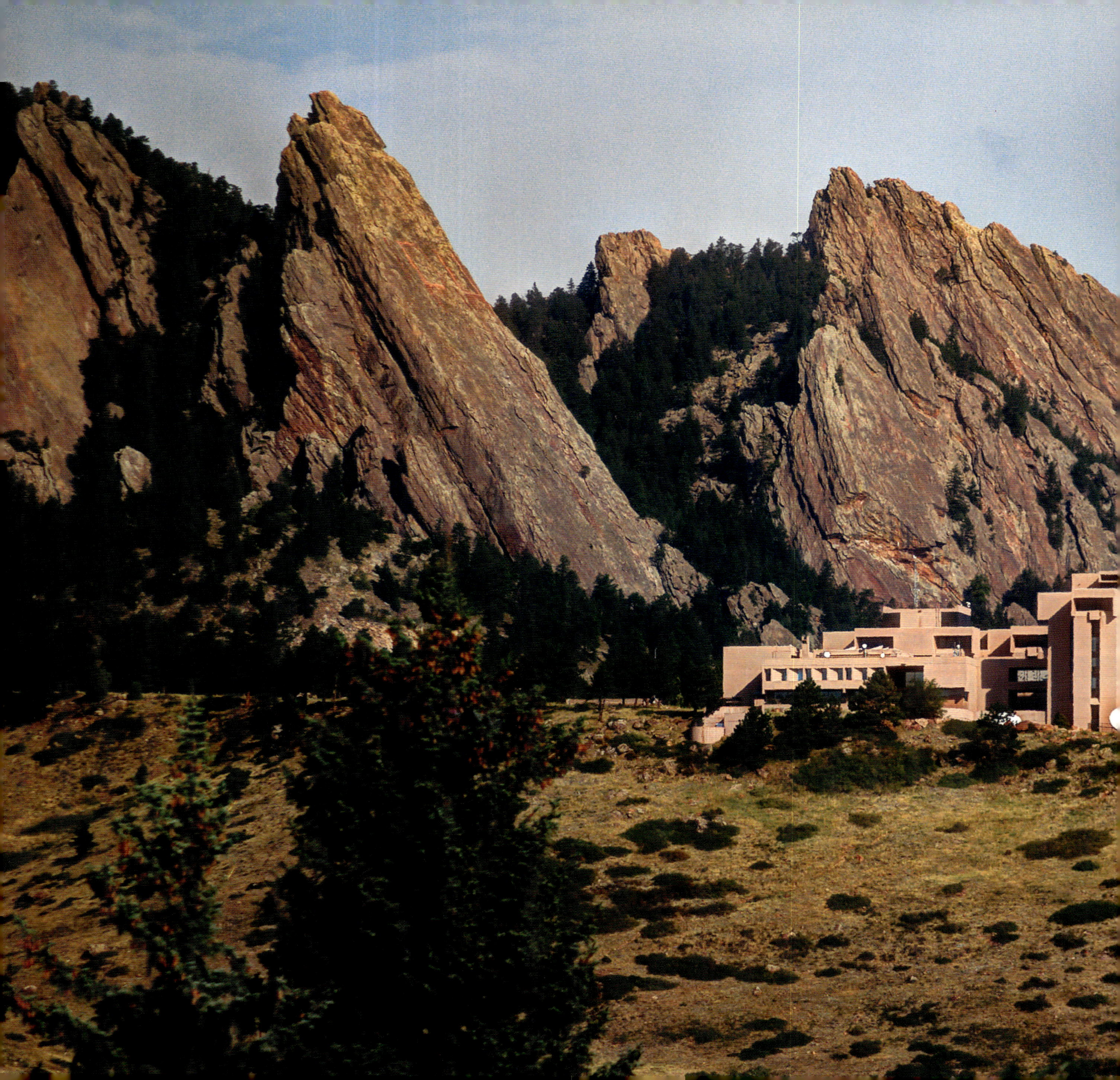

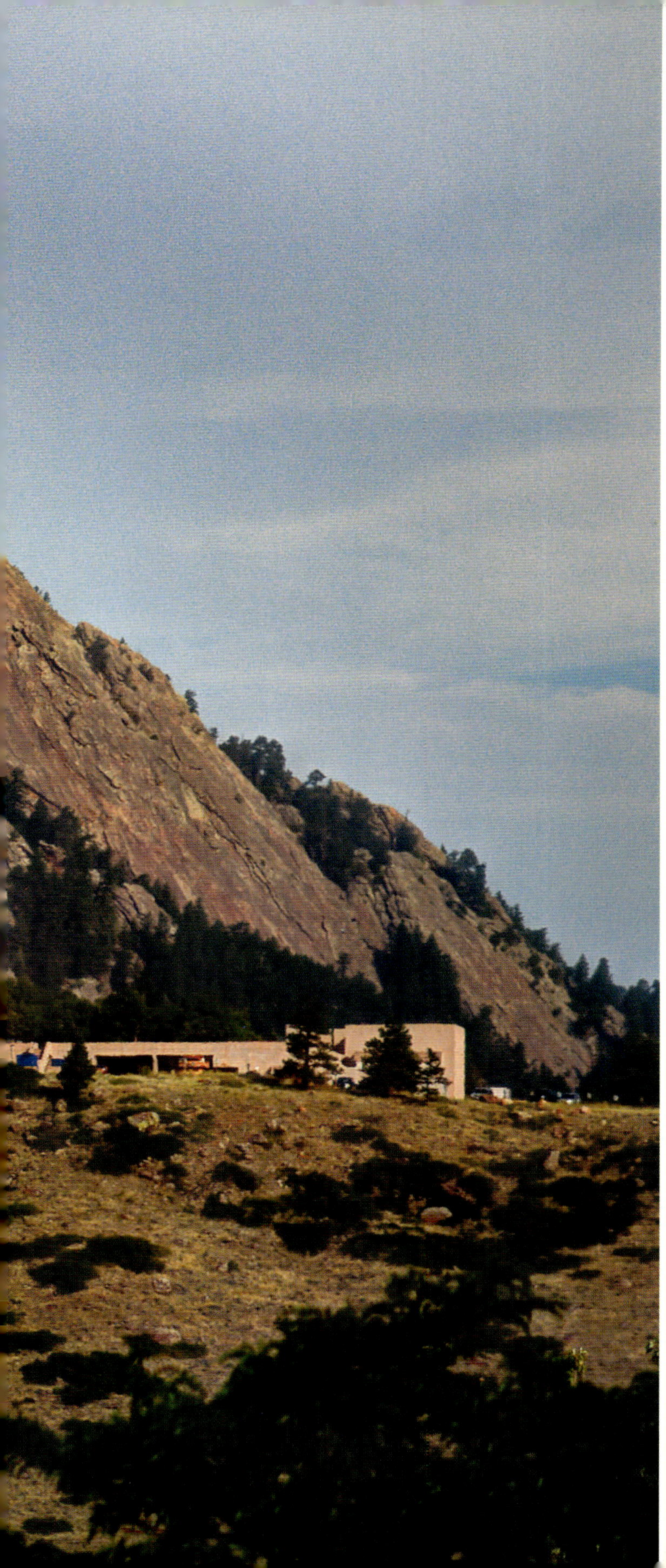

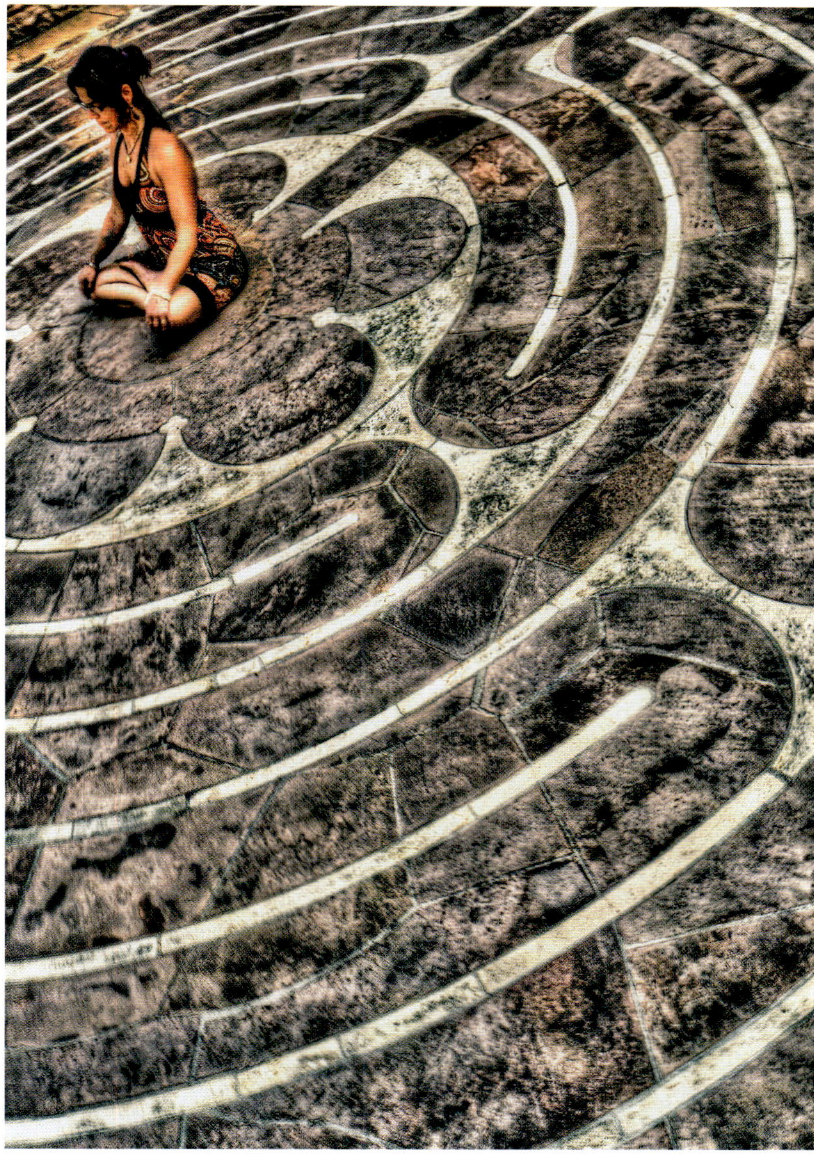

ABOVE: Boulder offers a wide array of open spaces and locations for those seeking a quiet reflection through yoga.

LEFT: The Mesa Laboratory of the National Center for Atmospheric Research (NCAR) opened in 1964. Designed by renowned Chinese-born architect I. M. Pei, the building is set against the Flatirons and overlooks the city of Boulder.

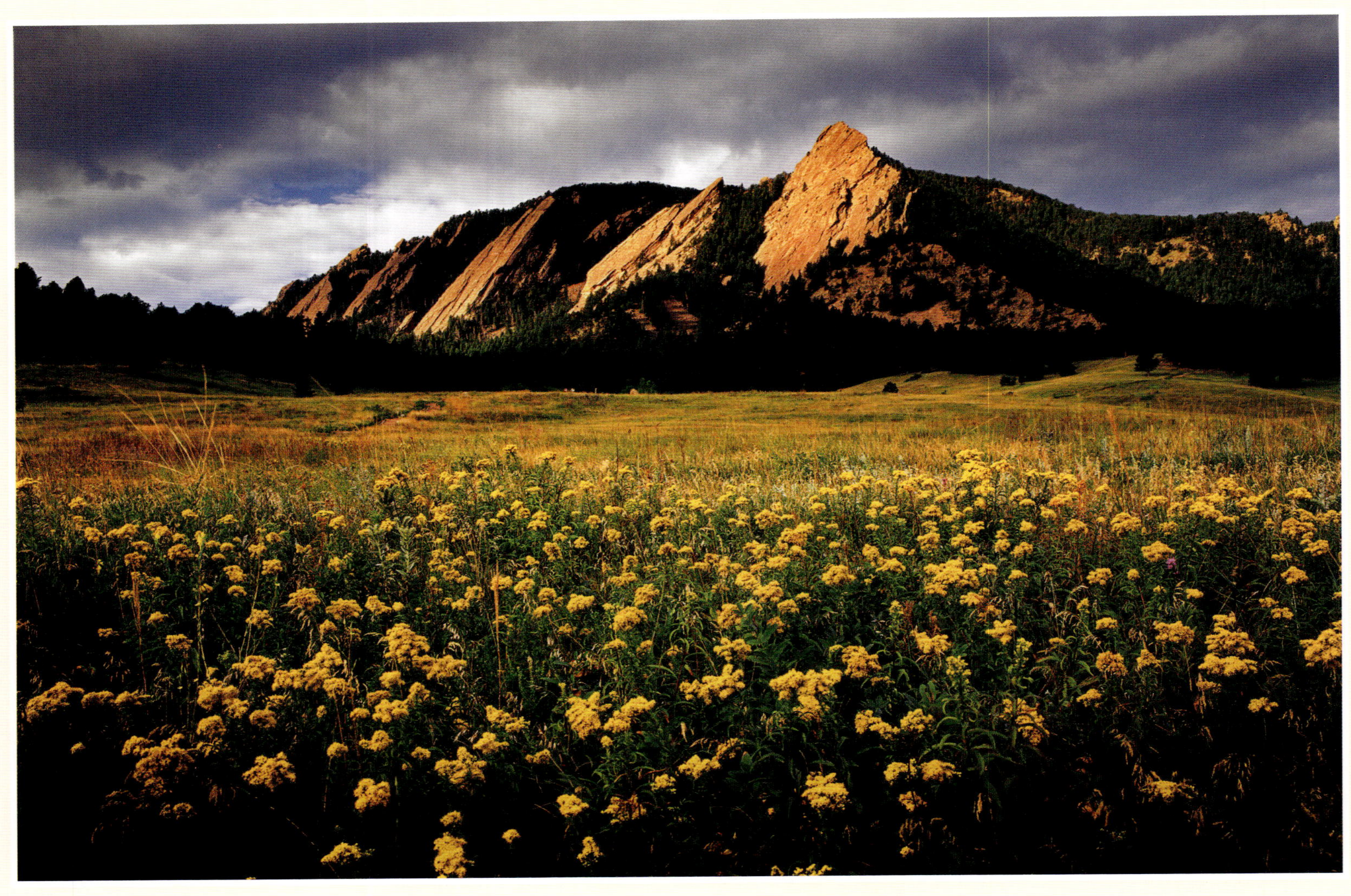

ABOVE: A sea of yellow invites nature lovers to hike, explore, and photograph in the City of Boulder's open space, east of the Flatirons—Boulder's iconic backdrop.

FACING PAGE: Granite buttresses tower over Boulder Falls, adding to the waterfall's ambience.

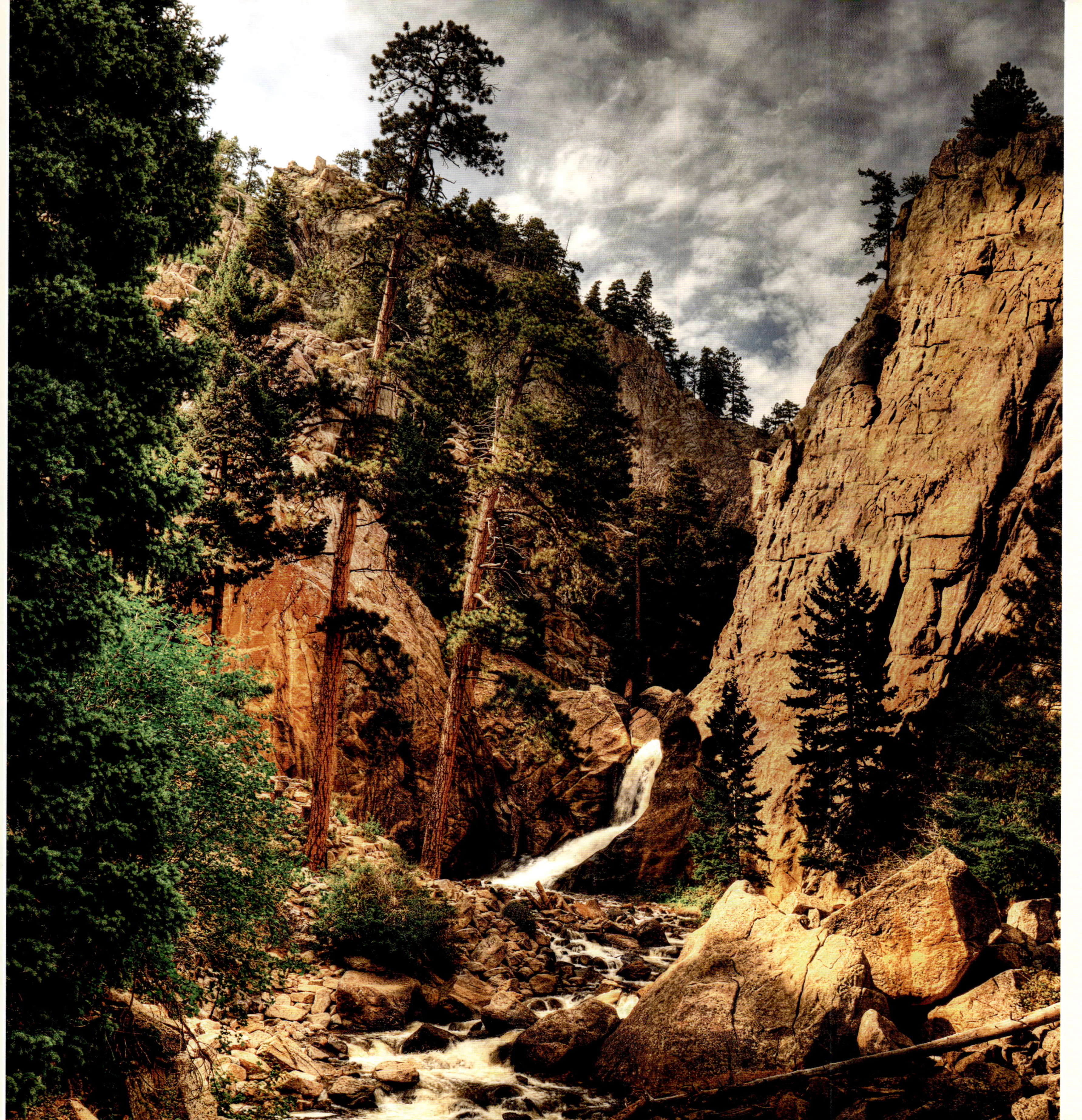

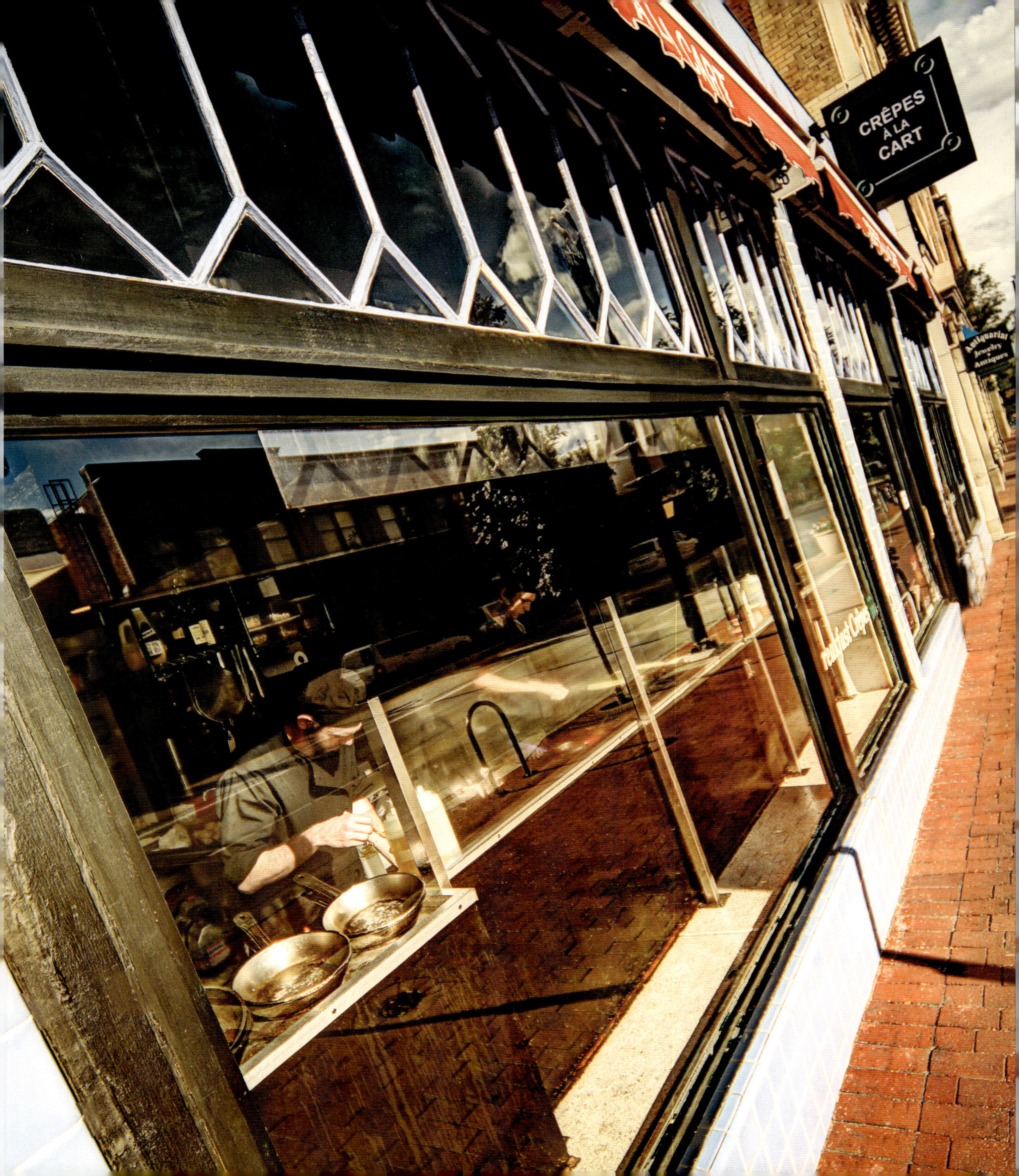
CRÊPES
À LA
CART
Jewelry
Antiques

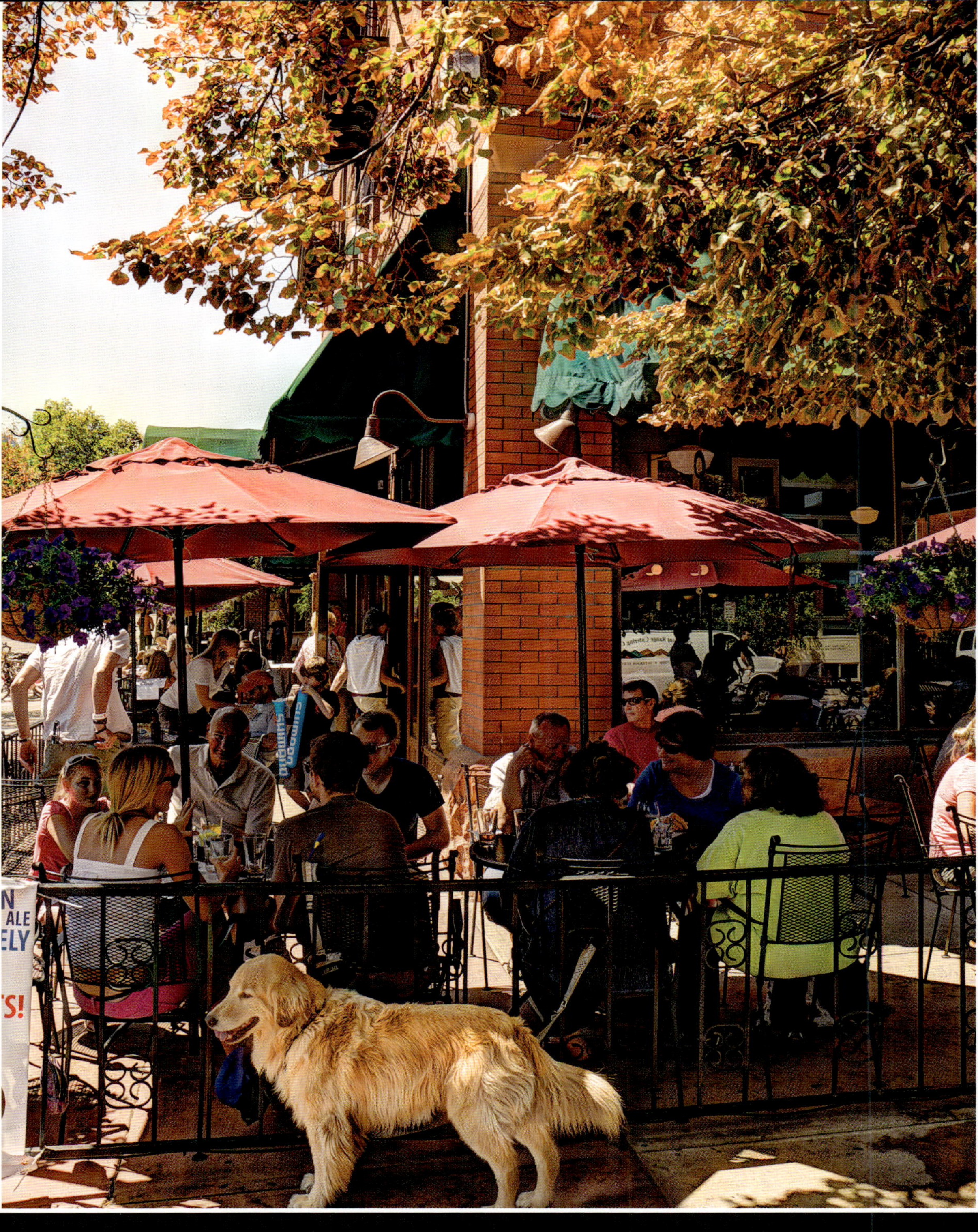

ABOVE: These diners at the Corner Bar (in the Hotel Boulderado) found a way to enjoy an afternoon drink without leaving their dog at home. Boulder is known as a dog-friendly town.

FACING PAGE: Boulder's restaurants are as diverse as the city itself. Crêpes Á la Cart is located on Broadway, one-half block south of the Pearl Street Mall.

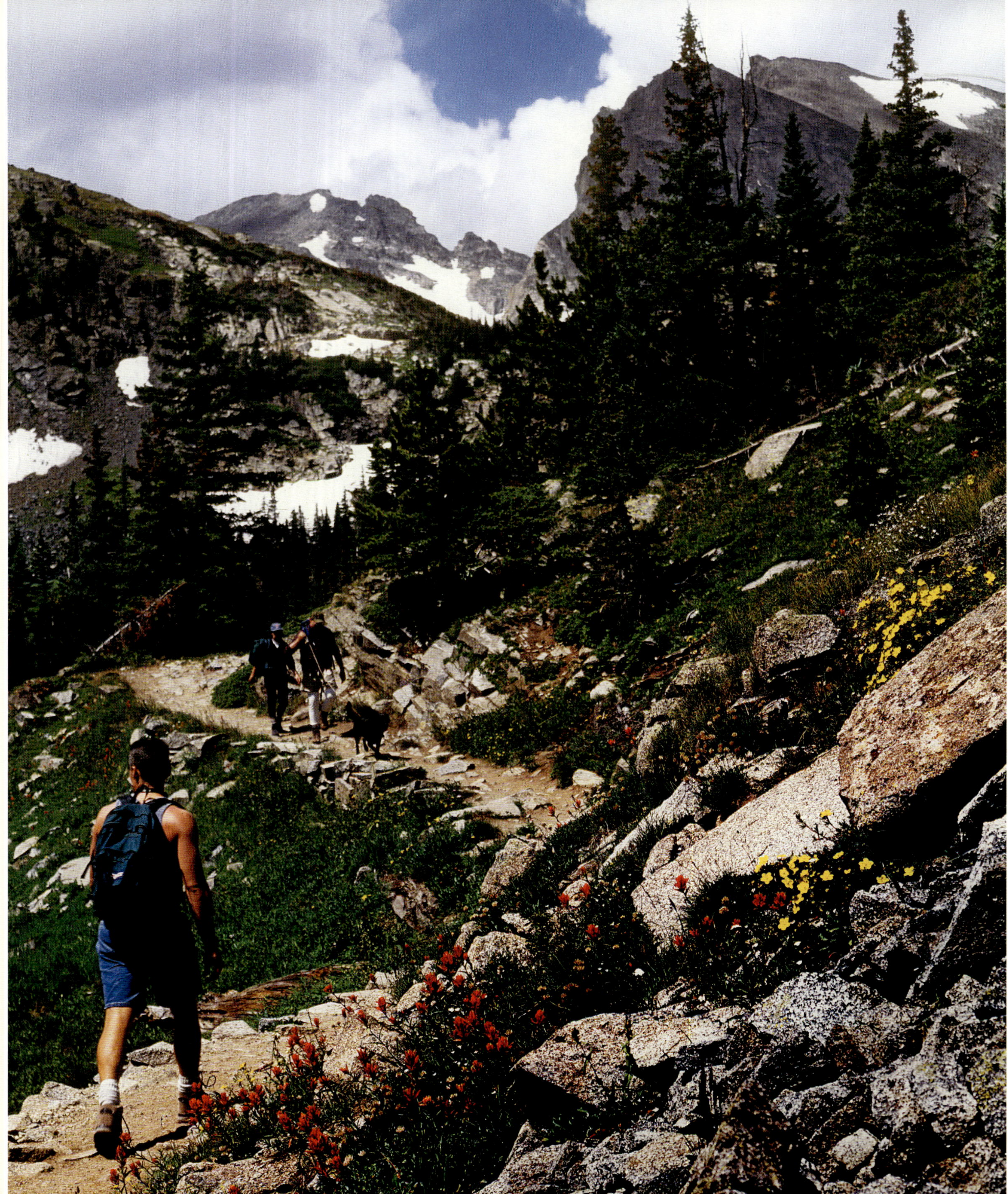

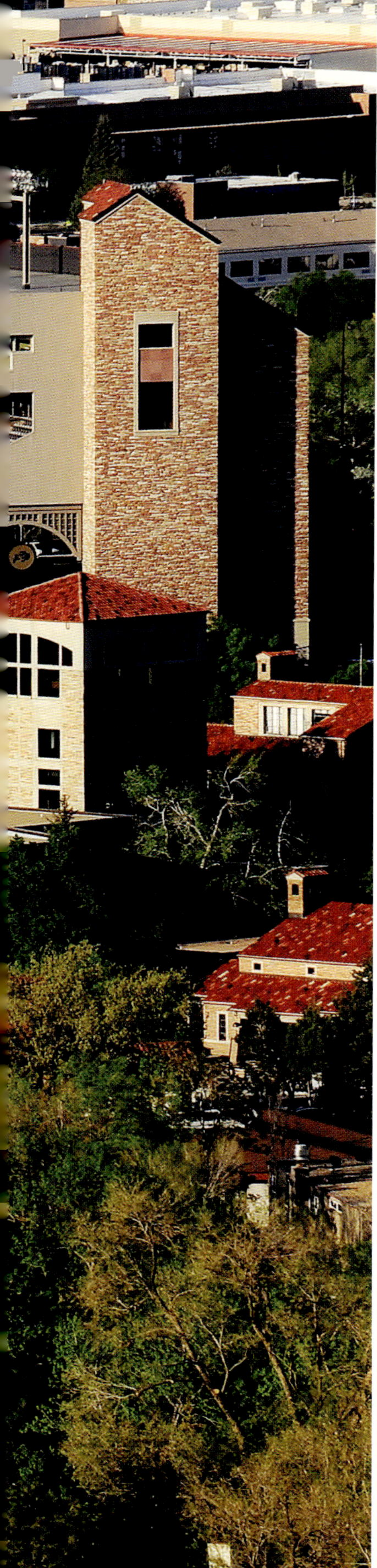

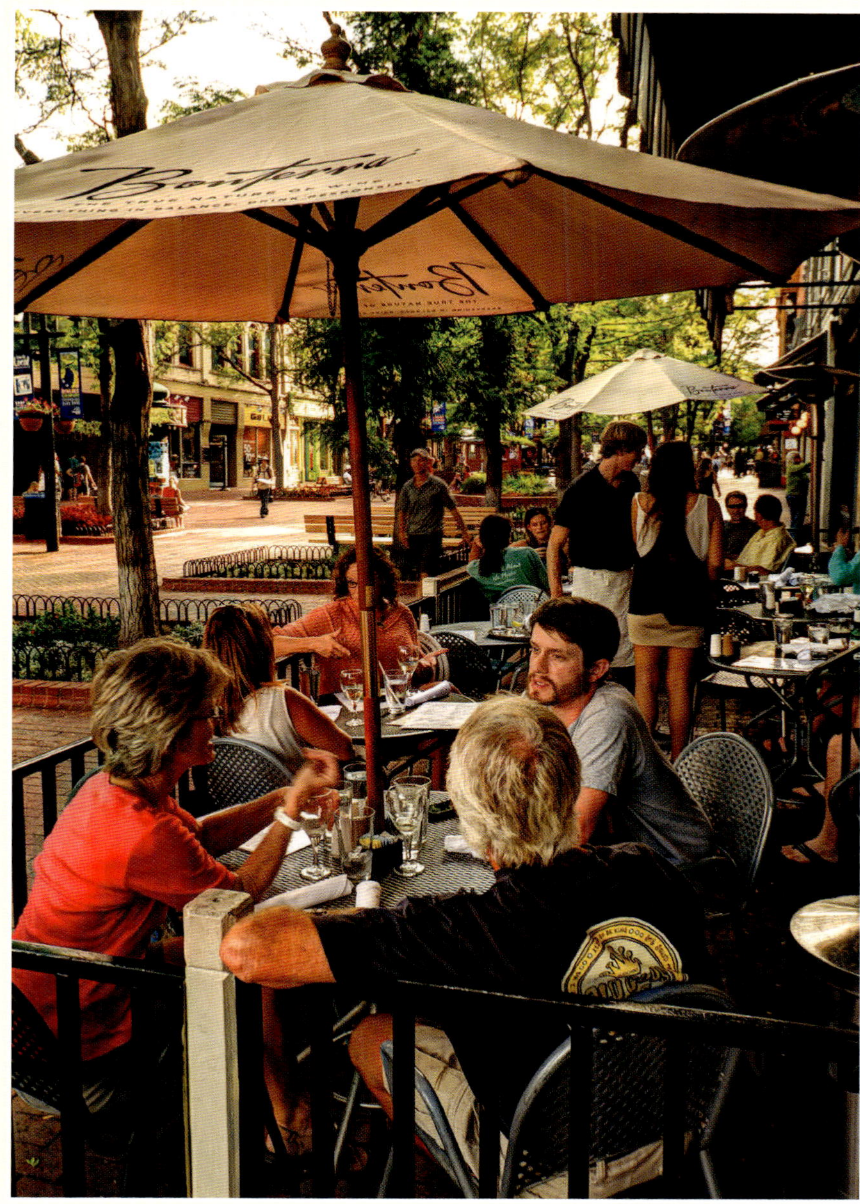

ABOVE: Outdoor dining at the Boulder Café, on the Pearl Street Mall, is convenient for enjoying Boulder's sunny weather, and for people-watching, too.

LEFT: The addition of suites and club seating, above the bleachers on the east side of Folsom Field, was completed in August 2003 and increased the stadium's capacity to 53,750.

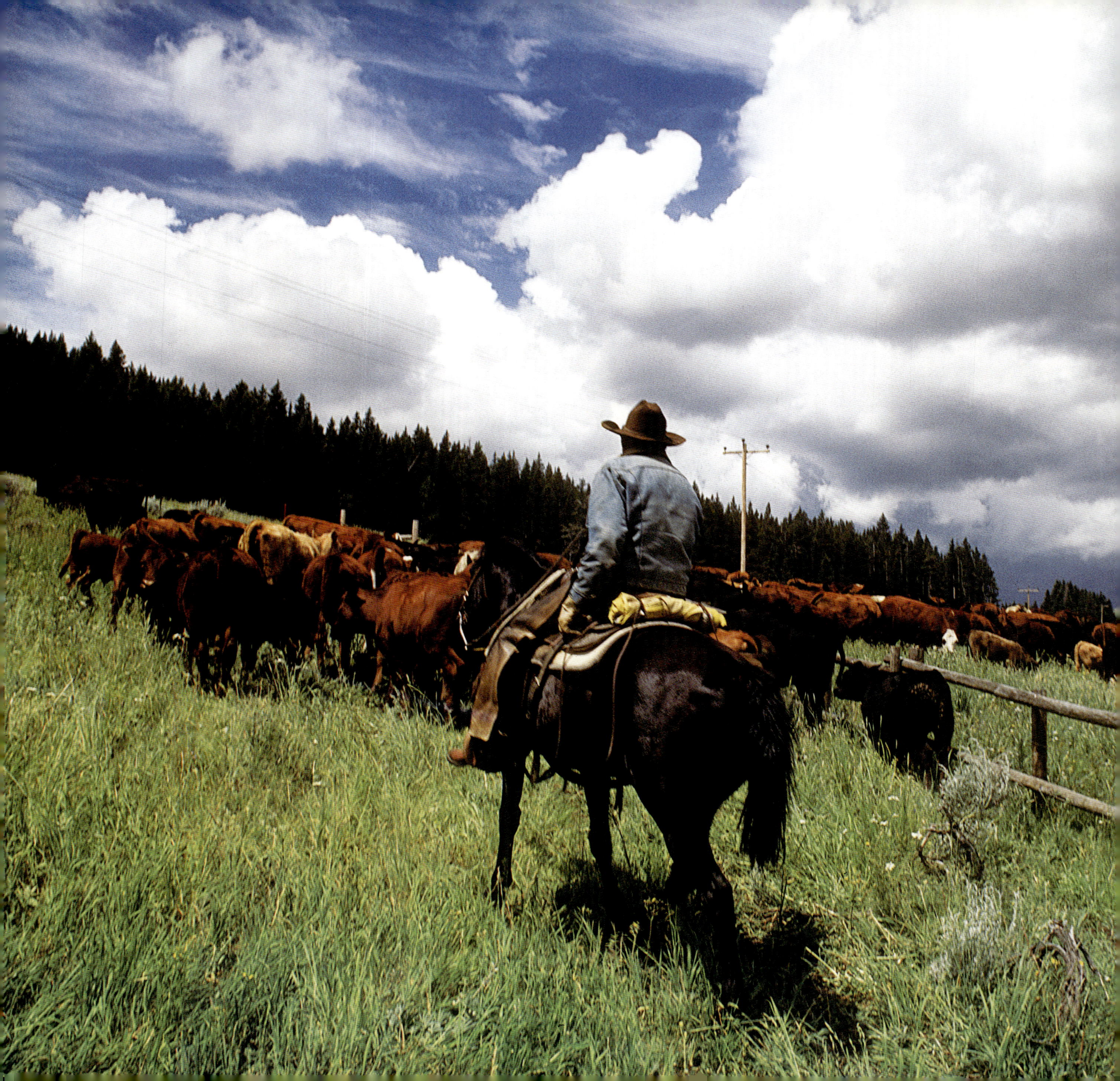

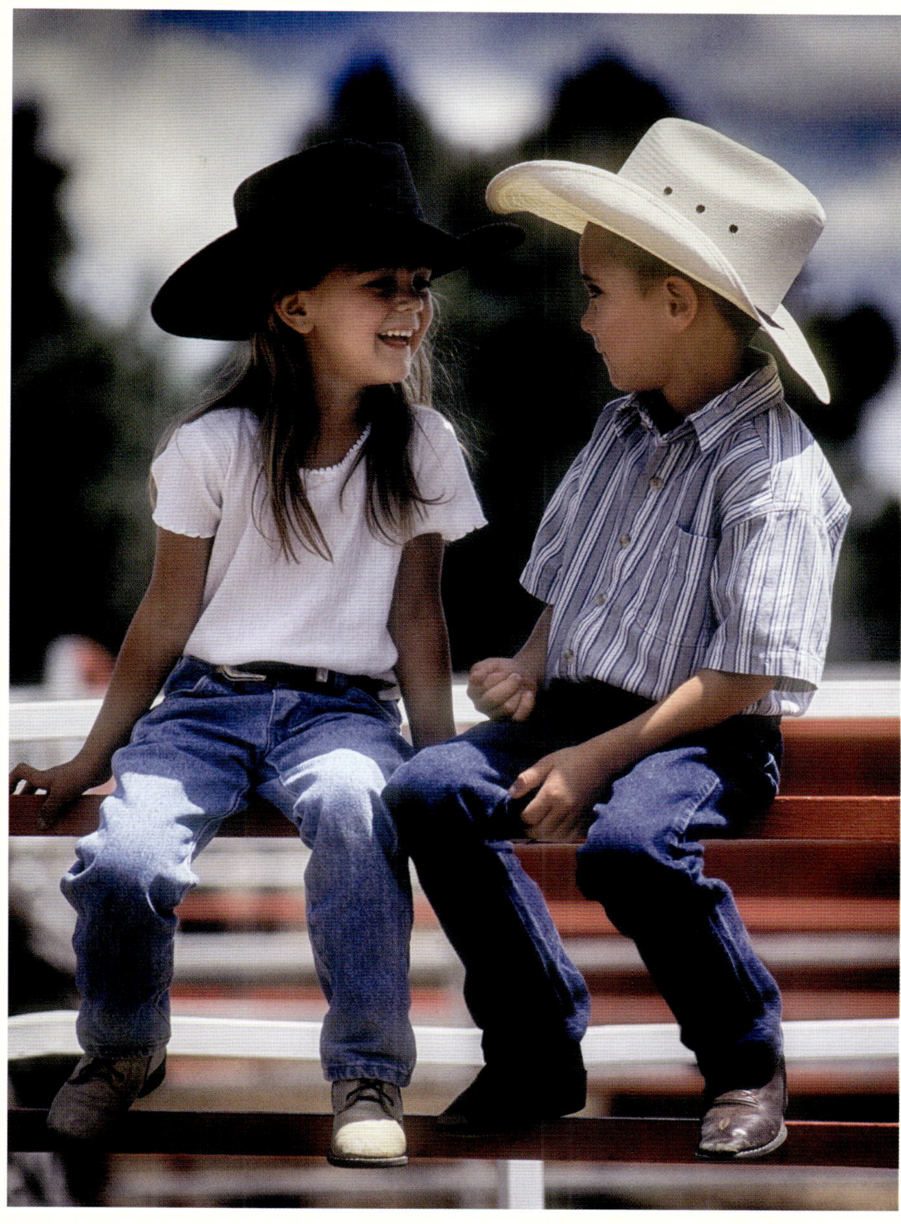

ABOVE: Boulder County still has cowboys and cowgirls, no matter how small, and will for generations to come.

LEFT: A rancher drives his cattle to new pasture, a Boulder County tradition that continues to this day.

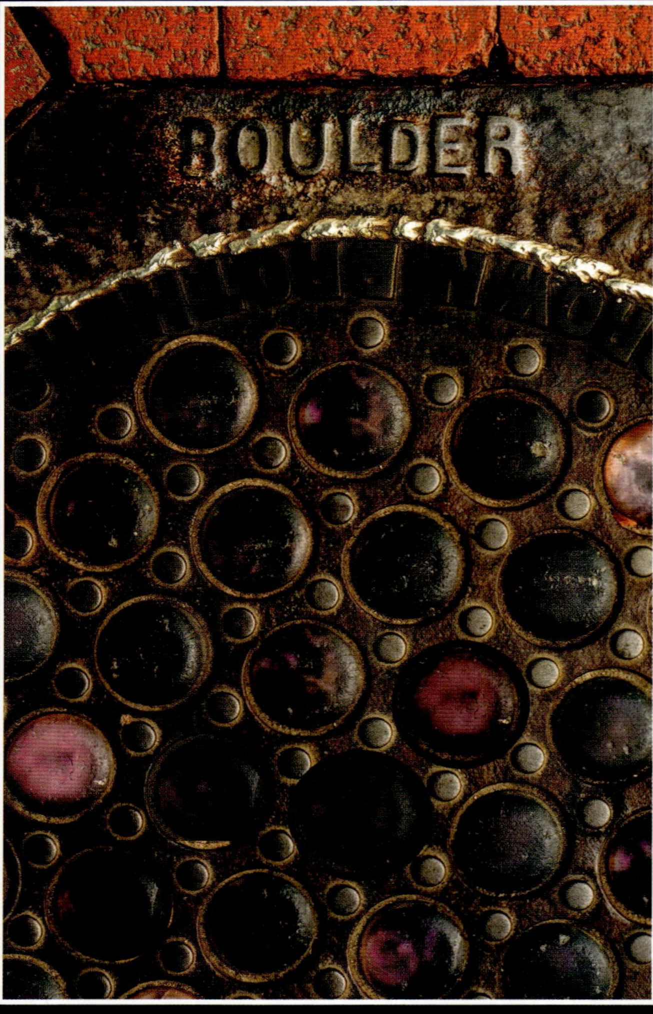

ABOVE: It's all about the details: this manhole cover adds unexpected color to a Boulder street.

RIGHT: The Hotel Boulderado has been a downtown landmark ever since it opened on New Year's Day 1909. It was named for the words "Boulder" and "Colorado," so guests would always remember where they stayed.

FOLLOWING PAGE: Boulder's city lights welcome diners to the Flagstaff House. The restaurant, surrounded by mountain parklands and open space, is only a five-minute drive from Boulder.

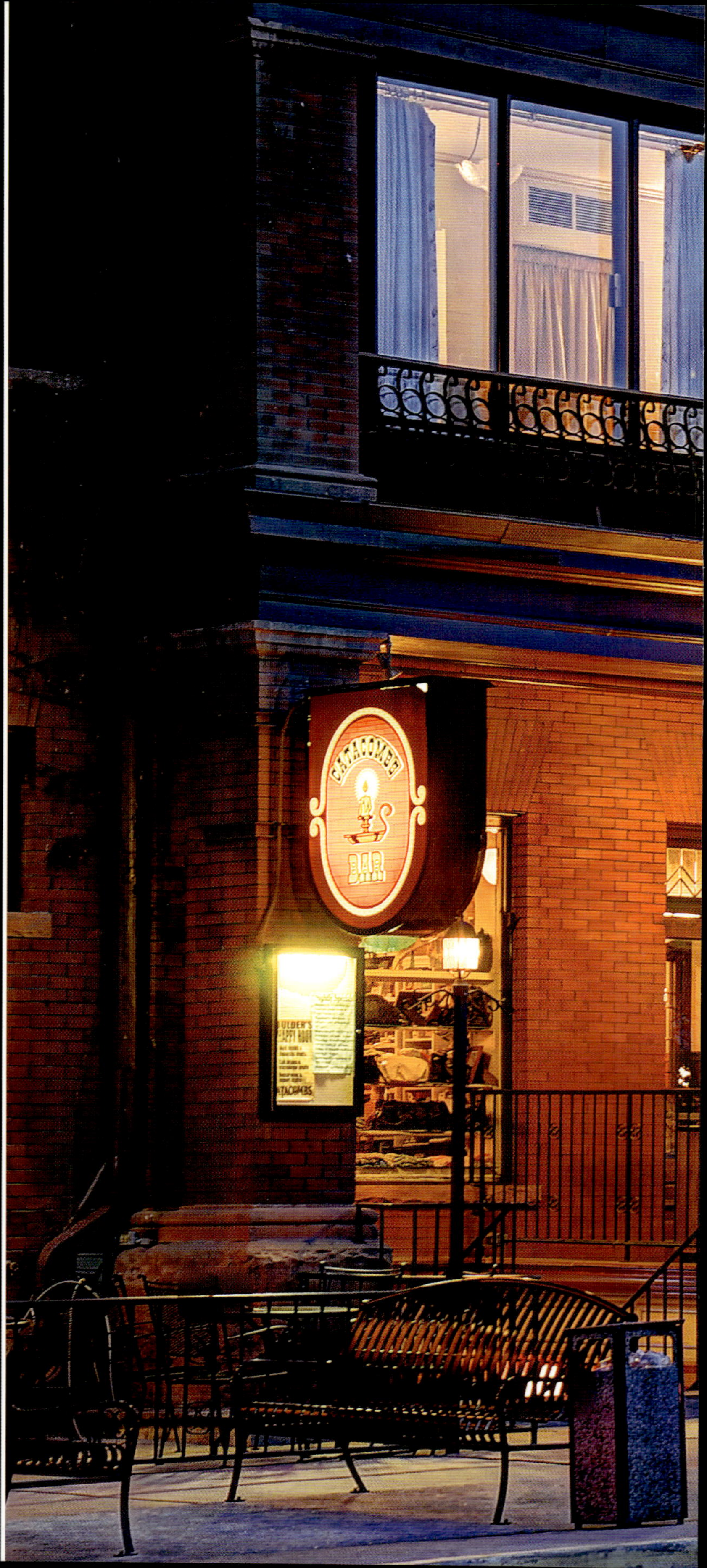

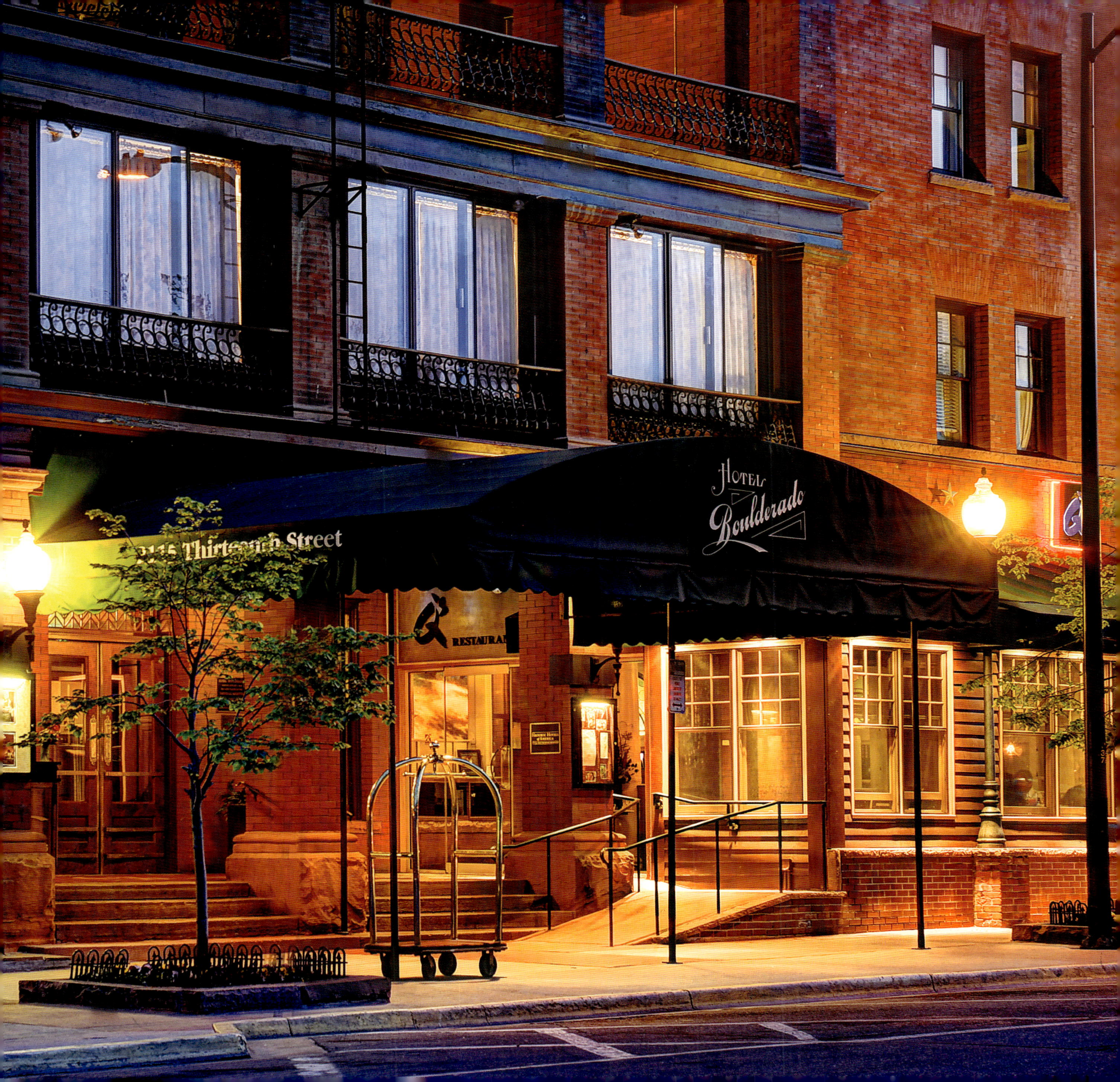
Hotel
Boulderado

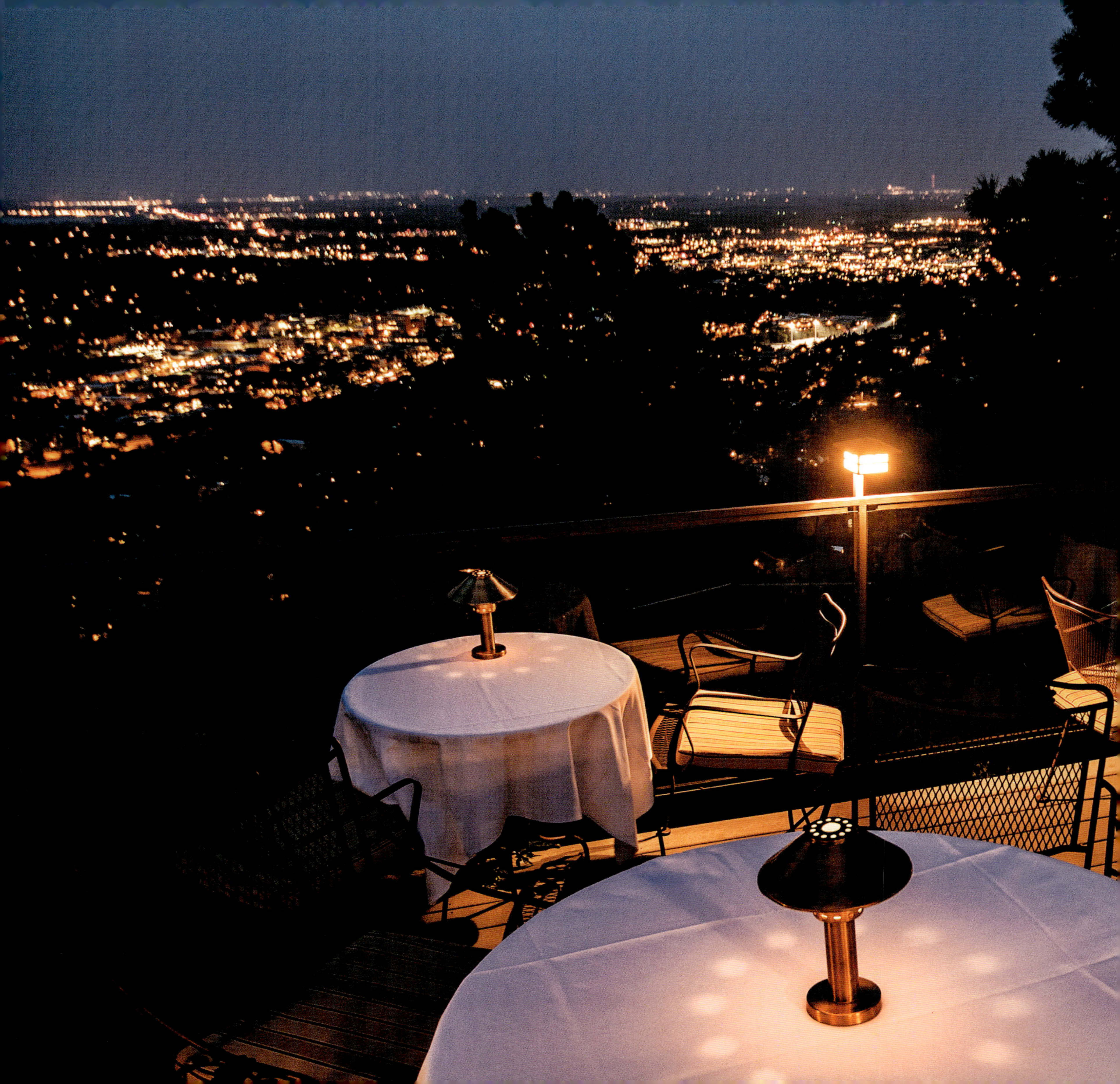